Vicious

ISBN: 978.1.84938.250.2
Order No: BOB 10208R

Exclusive Distributors
Music Sales Limited,
14/15 Berners Street,
London, W1T 3LJ.

Music Sales Corporation,
257 Park Avenue South,
New York, NY 10010, USA.

Macmillan Distribution Services,
56 Parkwest Drive
Derrimut, Vic 3030,
Australia.

Every effort has been made to trace the copyright holders of the
photographs in this book but one or two were unreachable. We would
be grateful if the photographers concerned would contact us.

Printed and bound in the UK by MPG Books Ltd, Bodmin, Uk.

A catalogue record for this book is available from the British Library.

Visit Omnibus Press on the web at **www.omnibuspress.com**

MARK PAYTRESS

THE ART OF DYING YOUNG

Vicious

**BOBCAT
BOOKS**

CONTENTS

'I'll probably die by the time I reach 25.
But I'll have lived the way I wanted to.'
Sid Vicious

'Sometimes I think we're all corpses.
Just rotting upright.'
Keep The Aspidistra Flying, *George Orwell*

Introduction: Threw a Glass Darkly

'Everyone has a beastly side to them, don't they?' – Sid Vicious, 1977

100 Club, London, Tuesday, 21 September 1976

SID did it.

Didn't he?

Dead or alive, the question 'Well, did he, or didn't he?' has been perpetually pinned to Sid's back, the answer – invariably affirmative – a foregone conclusion. We are, after all, talking about rock 'n' roll's ultimate Beastly Boy. Aren't we?

Sid wasn't always guilty. He wasn't unremittingly beastly either. In fact, if you believe what some of his old muckers say, the real Sid was a sensitive, Syd Barrett-admiring soul who would have his mates in stitches, leave women awestruck by his 'feminine side' and be the first to visit recovering friends in hospital. 'He only tried to be nasty,' says another early punk anti-hero Marco Pirroni.

All that 'Uh-oh, here comes trouble', they say, was the fault of inappropriate nomenclature. Vicious: it created an instant whiff of putrefaction about his person, and sent out a provocative message of invincibility to his fellow status seekers. That delighted the renegade loner schoolboy, the boy from Bash Street with the bored, rat-like countenance, who now was the lankiest looker on London's emerging punk scene. His Vicious epithet made him a marked man, and landed him into heaps of trouble, but that never bothered Sid. Attention, distraction, and damn the cost was all that mattered.

Tonight, though, on 21 September 1976, matters are going to get out of hand. We're in the 100 Club, a no-frills venue in London's Oxford Street more usually associated with foot-tapping jazz, robust R&B and boozy pub rock. It's the second and final night of the Punk Rock Festival. The crowd is young and wired. Some are delirious, others downright peculiar. Denim prevails, as is the norm, but tonight there's leather and lace too, the glint of a thousand studs and brooches and rings, weirdly disciplined hair, an excess of greasepaint, more risk, more invention. It's where *The Rocky Horror Show* meets a tough, urban rock crowd, where kitsch and kicks collide. Look closely and you'll notice a surprising number of faces holding a gormless grimace with studied calculation. Stupid, but somehow tinged with menace. There are intermittent outbursts of perpendicular pouncing, pogoing, The Pogo, as invented by Sid. Everything seems to be at an angle and out of sorts. Sid looks very comfortable indeed.

The Damned are four young Sex Pistols acolytes fresh out of the rehearsal room. Tonight, they're giving it a touch of the primeval with 'I Feel Alright', a deliciously disorderly take on The Stooges's '1970'. Only now, it's September 1976, and there's not a hint of nostalgia in the performance. In The Damned's impious hands, the song is reborn: joyous, cathartic, contemporary. 'Outta mah head on . . . *Tuesday* night.'

Sid towers above the crowd. He's well known on the punk scene, one of those faces that always seems to be there. He's well liked too, at least by those who've not felt the full force of his rusty old bike chain. Those who came last night probably recognise him as the bloke who bashed the hell out of the drums for those controversially under-rehearsed in-crowders, Siouxsie And The Banshees.

Sid adores The Stooges. He adores them because their records are loud and nasty. Because they gave their songs titles like 'Search And Destroy', 'Gimme Danger', 'Dirt', 'Death Trip'. Because Bowie loves them. And because singer Iggy Pop never ever gives a toss. One minute, he's baring his skinny arse on stage. The next, he'll be exorcising his dark, disturbed soul in an outrageous display of blood-letting and crowd-taunting.

Sid is pissed up on cheap booze, buzzing on cut-price sulphate, and the sound of speed-freak rock 'n' roll is choking up his earholes. The Damned play even faster than The Sex Pistols. They're more like The Ramones, and that's the band Sid likes best of all.

But Sid hates The Damned. He hates all the new London punk bands unless they're The Sex Pistols. Oh, maybe he has a soft spot for Subway Sect, have-a-go heroes from the previous night. They care even less about competence than Sid does, as Sect frontman Vic Godard remembers only too well. 'To us, The Sex Pistols were the equivalent of a band like Yes,' he says today.

The Damned are the enemy. They're getting good, there's a record company buzz about them, and that's troubling Sid. And when Sid feels troubled he starts to wobble and when Sid starts to wobble that's when something usually happens.

Sid is deep in the crowd, not too far from the bar, and at an angle to the stage. With him is a clutch of *nouvelle vague* notables. There is cackling Vivienne Westwood, bottle-blonde matriarch of punk epicentre SEX – basically an ideologically-charged clothes shop – and seamstress to the new rising anti-stars. Steven 'Two-Tone Spunker' Severin and Siouxsie Sioux stick close by too. Like Sid, they're two of The Sex Pistols' most celebrated, visible followers. Unlike him, they're middle class and come from the suburbs. Caroline Coon, *Melody Maker*'s resident punk enthusiast, recently described them as 'The Bromley Contingent', and now they're already legends at punk hangouts such as SEX and Louise's.

Twenty-four hours earlier, these Bromley bizarros had blasphemed all over the 100 Club stage, twisting and shouting with untrained irreverence over a gloriously moronic beat bashed relentlessly by fellow debutante Sid Vicious.

Tonight, though, Sid's in the shadows. There are no borrowed drumsticks in his hands. Instead, he nurses a pint of beer. In a glass.

'Me and Siouxsie were going, 'The fucking Damned are rubbish', and stood there moaning,' remembers Steven Severin.

And Sid?

'Sid didn't say anything. He blithely finished his pint and threw the glass towards the stage.'

Sid's poorly aimed message to The Damned hits one of two concrete pillars positioned awkwardly near the front of the stage. It smashes, and sends shards of glass raining down on the crowd.

'It was meant for us but Sid slung it badly,' shrugs The Damned's bassist Captain Sensible.

There's a commotion. The din of punk rock, the sound of London awakening from a decade-long slumber, grinds to a pathetic halt. Singer Dave Vanian's graveyard bellow is replaced by grave and desperate cries for help. Vanian switches off the horror shtick and leaps into the crowd. One of his friends is among the injured. Some are simply numb with shock. Others who are more obviously distressed and in pain are helped to the back of the club. The Damned play out with 'So Messed Up'.

An ambulance arrives and the wounded are quickly wheeled away. Vanian's pal is one of several who end up in hospital. She's one of the lucky ones. One girl is rushed into emergency, a splinter of glass embedded in one of her eyes. She's 17 years old, and her eyesight has just been permanently ruined.

Ron Watts, the 100 Club's burly manager, is furious. 'If there are any more glasses thrown, you'll all have to go home!' he barks through the PA system. The barman refuses to serve any more drinks. After tonight, there will be no more punk rock at the 100 Club for some considerable time.

Headliners The Vibrators restore some sense of normality to the evening. Too much so, perhaps, for they knock out a set of greasy, revivalist favourites – 'Great Balls Of Fire', 'Jumpin' Jack Flash', even guitarist Chris Spedding's recent novelty hit, 'Motor Bikin''. The group's name throbs with naughtiness, but The Vibrators are clearly out of place here. No one throws a glass in protest. That's probably because the original culprit – though everyone's keeping shtoom about his culpability – has been bundled away by a quartet of London coppers.

'The police came automatically in those days once an ambulance had been called,' says Jonh Ingham, an early new wave champion at *Sounds* magazine.

'There was a bit of talk as they stood by the door, then they walked over to Sid, and frogmarched him out without saying a word to him.'

Twenty-four hours earlier, Sid Vicious was a punk rock anti-hero on the 100 Club stage. Tonight, he's even more the centre of attention, putting up a desperate struggle as the coppers manhandle him out of the venue and towards the police van parked outside. A phalanx of friends, including Ingham and Clash guitarist Mick Jones, follows behind. The Pied Piper is Caroline Coon.

'The police had come storming into the club, mob handed, and I see Sid being dragged out. At that point, I went into Release mode,' Coon recalls, referring to the organisation she founded in 1967 to give support for those arrested on drug charges. 'Next thing, I see Sid being bundled into a cop car.'

COON: 'What are you doing? Where are you taking him?'

COP: 'None of your business.'

COON: 'Actually it is my business.'

COP: 'Go away.'

COON: 'I'm not fucking go away.'

COP: 'Alright, lady, we're arresting you too.'

The punk and his protector are driven away. They are not alone. Also wedged in the back is a copper all decked out in rock punter apparel.

'Sending plain-clothes guys down to the 100 Club! That was when you began to realise that the cops were taking all this talk of anarchy and chaos very seriously,' says Jonh Ingham.

Driven down to West End Central, in Tottenham Court Road, the pair are taken off to adjacent cells for questioning. Coon wears tight black trousers, high-heeled boots and a T-shirt held together with 200 safety pins. Sid is in his regulation tight jeans, ripped and torn, with a condom dangling from the belt, a distressed T-shirt and outsized jelly shoes. They don't much look like your typical London villains.

Coon strains to hear what's happening behind the wall that separates her from Sid. The cops bark questions at him. The voices become louder. There's a stroppy 'Fuck you!' then a smothered thud. That's Sid's head on the table. The process starts all over again. More profanities. More headbanging. An occasional yelp. Then Coon hears no more. She's been bailed out, and is on her way back to the 100 Club. Sid is kept in overnight. The thuds and the 'Fuck you!'s continue.

'When he appeared in court the next morning, his face was just one big mass of bruises,' Jonh Ingham recalls. 'All the skin above his cheekbones was swollen and his eyes were puffy. He looked a real mess.'

The bruises were still visible the following week after Sid was released from the Ashford Remand Centre. They would heal – eventually – but the entire episode, from the moment he raised his glass to those last lonely nights in captivity, had transformed him:

Before: Sid Vicious – Sex Pistols Superfan
After: Sid Vicious – Punk Psycho

His mother, Anne Beverley, always insisted that Sid's spell in Ashford marked a pivotal moment in her son's life. This was unlikely to have been because of any deep psychological scarring – that had come to Sid rather earlier in life. But the experience certainly intensified the anger, the sense of alienation, that already festered inside him.

'One of the things I believe in since being slung in here is total personal freedom,' he scrawled emphatically at the end of one letter. This wasn't some utopian hippie homily. This was a cry for freedom in its widest sense. And to Sid, who hurt and hated in roughly equal measures, that meant the freedom to disintegrate, to wrap himself in a martyr's shroud, to take punkish imperfection to its absolute limit.

While at Ashford, Sid found succour in a book brought to him by Vivienne Westwood. *Helter Skelter* was a vividly detailed account of the Manson murders – 'the event that killed off the '60s' according to every cultural historian of the era. No one blamed society for the world's ills more than Charles Manson, a charismatic jailbird turned hippie terrorist. No one exacted such spectacular revenge either, culminating in the extraordinary, slogans-daubed-in-blood Tate-LaBianca murders in August 1969 – ironically at the moment half a million idealistic young Americans were making their way to the Woodstock Festival.

Manson's nuggets of nihilistic wisdom – 'Nothing is anything, anything is nothing', 'No sense makes sense' – were lapped up by Sid, his apprentice in apocalypse studies. 'I am finding it quite fascinating,' Sid wrote in one letter. He rarely bothered with books, but Vivienne Westwood had the measure of him. 'Sid didn't know bad from good,' she told Malcolm McLaren's biographer Craig Bromberg. 'He didn't know right from wrong most of the time, that boy.' But even Sid was aware that the spectre of Manson and his stab-happy disciples hung heavy over '70s rock culture, that Manson's resentment of and alienation from society wasn't much different to his own. The revenge exacted by the mad-eyed cult leader was, even for horror-loving Sid, perhaps a little too extreme. But he admired Manson's despotic mind, and how this man from nowhere managed to apply his unswerving belief in personal freedom to himself, but not necessarily to the world around him.

But Sid hadn't spent years in jail, like Manson had done, with both eyes firmly fixed on personal growth and, above all, survival. In Ashford, and without his north London wrecking crew to look out for him, Sid's nerve had wobbled. 'He could barely look us in the eye,' remembers Steven Severin, who visited him with Siouxsie Sioux soon after the 100 Club incident. 'He was a bit bruised and battered. Worse still, Sid looked lost and scared, as if he'd woken up in the cell and thought, 'Fuck, what have I done?' '

He tried to exorcise the pain, the guilt and the loneliness by writing a few letters. 'He said that the violence in Ashford was very real,' his mother told *Sid's Way* author Alan Parker. Anne was moved to tears by the desperation she felt in his words: 'I get so agitated in here that I can't sleep at all,' he complained in one letter. 'When I do, I get the most awful nightmares.' But Anne was under strict instructions not to visit him. Sid Vicious was no 'mummy's boy'.

Sid didn't know who he was. His life was gripped by a sense of impermanence. To the outside world he was Vicious, but in Ashford, surrounded by serial hard-nuts who'd spent years in and out of juvenile institutions, he didn't brag about it too much. That changed as soon as he stepped outside the doors and felt freedom again. Ashford was the moment that 'marked the death of Simon and the birth of Sid', insisted Anne Beverley. It was the birth of Sid the legend. Sid Vicious.

After his release, Sid returned to London's punk rock dungeons, where he was now a *cause célèbre*. Not everyone was pleased to see him. 'The 100 Club incident left a bad taste in the mouth,' says Mark Perry, whose *Sniffin' Glue* fanzine had emerged earlier that summer as the mouthpiece of the new wave. 'The incident was a one-off, but it was a one-off that actually meant a lot. It made us all think about what we were doing.' A lot of early adherents to the punk cause felt things were going awry that autumn.

Vicious by name, vicious by reputation, Sid next became Vicious the new punk mouthpiece and star turn of Jonh Ingham's 'Welcome To The (?) Rock Special' feature in the 9 October issue of *Sounds*. 'I missed the Summer Of Love – and I don't care. The New York Dolls ain't bad at all. Sex and sexuality? Who needs it?' The thoughts of Chairman Vicious had become headline news. With the court case arising from the 100 Club incident several months away, it seemed as if Sid's moment of madness – hardly his first but thus far certainly the most significant – hadn't done him much damage at all.

Anne Beverley had stopped crying. Sid's nightmares never left his Ashford pillow. But one young woman's life was never quite the same again and neither, in truth, was Sid's.

And, yes: Sid did it. Again, and again, and again.

Punk

'I've met the man in the street and he's a cunt.'
Sid Vicious

1. WHAT'S MY NAME?

HIS BIRTH certificate, issued on 13 May 1957, names him Simon John Ritchie.

After his mother remarries in February 1965, Simon Ritchie becomes Simon Beverley.

During 1972–73, at the height of Bowiemania, Simon reverts back to being John, though he sticks with Beverley.

By late 1974 and for the next year or so, some of his acquaintances start calling him Spikey John.

Some time during the winter of 1975, his best mate John Lydon decides to rename him Sid. The rest of the world still knows him as John, except for those who call him Spikey John and his mother who, as always, prefers a simple 'Sime'.

Early in 1976, most likely as an answer to John Lydon's new 'Rotten' epithet, he becomes Sid Vicious.

By January 1978, with The Sex Pistols preparing to split up in a hotel room in San Francisco, Sid Vicious is dropped in favour of the apparently more apt 'Useless'.

According to his death certificate, issued on 9 February 1979, he was John Simon Ritchie. A box marked 'Other names by which the deceased was known' is left blank.

THE GLASS-throwing incident at the September 1976 Punk Rock Festival had wider repercussions for 19-year-old John Beverley. Vicious for several months, and Sid for a little while longer, he'd already been implicated in a handful of scrapes, including a nasty, unprovoked attack on debonair rock writer Nick Kent, again at the beleaguered 100 Club. Caroline Coon was protectively coy in her cover story report on the festival for *Melody Maker*, though Sid's arrest was picked up elsewhere. In some reports, he was portrayed as 'the fifth Sex Pistol', the beastliest brat in the beastliest rock cult yet. The hate-filled hyperbole had all grown a little out of hand.

'Sid just wasn't a tough guy,' says Jah Wobble, and he should know. As teenage tearaway John Wardle, one of the handful of Johns that hung around John Lydon (alias Sex Pistol frontman Johnny Rotten), he was one of the punk era's genuine tough guys. Don Letts, Roxy Club DJ and manager of ACME Attractions, SEX's chief rival along the King's Road, concurs. He remembers Sid as 'a loveable oaf' who had an unfortunate habit of getting picked on.

Loveable?

Well, there must be something in it because Letts wasn't the only one who thought so. 'He was a loveable bloke, really,' says Banshees bassist Steven Severin. 'Being around John [Lydon] meant that he became associated with that intimidating crew of characters he had around him. With Wobble you knew the menace was real, but with Sid it was almost like he was playing around. He deliberately dumbed down in order to appear hard.'

Perhaps all the fights were made up by a vindictive media gunning for a punk victim. Didn't *anyone* witness any punch-ups involving Mr Vish? 'Yeah,' admits Alan Jones, part of the furniture at SEX throughout 1975 and '76. 'But it was all done with a certain amount of jest and irony. Sid wasn't violent at all.'

John Lydon is the man who ought to know. He was Sid's best mate in the mid-'70s, found a place for him in The Sex Pistols early in 1977, and famously owned the hamster with the vicious temperament that was responsible for the name. Lydon has insisted on a thousand different occasions that Sid was the 'least vicious' person he'd met in his life. But, then, John Lydon does specialise in contrary thinking.

Chrissie Hynde found him 'very sweet and very honest'. 'A gentle soul,' cooed Tessa from The Slits. Even Siouxsie Sioux, rarely one to suffer a fool gladly, 'got on well' with Sid – at least until he started bragging about his cat-killing exploits. Caroline Coon knows quite a bit about Sid's hideous mistreatment of animals, but she's more concerned by his callowness. 'How old was he when he died?' she asks. 'Twenty-one? I'd forgive him anything . . .'

One suspects a full portrait of the man may not be quite so sparing. As Sid instinctively knew, it's easy to kick a man when he's down. It's easier still when he's been dead for 25 years, so it's important to resist the temptation. It would be a travesty to rebrand Sid as someone with the layers of complexity of, say, Bolan and Bowie, two perennial identity paraders (and a huge influence on the teenage John Beverley). But knotty contradictions in his psyche have emerged, which at least add an element of chiaroscuro to that one-dimensional line-drawing handed down by history.

Still, Sid is loveable. He is also sensitive to women. No doubt he's a comic genius, too . . .

'I loved Sid,' says Marco Pirroni, the fourth inaugural Banshee, and later guitarist and musical brains behind Adam And The Ants. 'I thought Sid was hilarious. One of the funniest people I'd ever met. Everything was a huge joke to him.' But what if something wasn't funny at all? 'Well, then he'd make it funny.'

An early SEX regular and an eager people-watcher, Pirroni was aware of Sid long before infamy whipped him off the streets and dumped him on a stage. He liked him, and admired his instinct for style, but he has no illusions about Sid's darker side. 'He was quite violent,' Pirroni says. 'He was like a big psychotic baby.'

Marco inhabits a pink and zebra-patterned film set of a lair tastefully adorned with pop culture relics, a vintage jukebox and die-cut doors straight out of a zany comic strip. It's not difficult to imagine that, had things turned out differently, Sid could have ended up in a place like this. Marco has an inkling why Sid never made it this far. 'You always felt he was trying to live up to his name: *Sid Vicious*.'

Guevara's hop from Ernesto to Ché, Garbo's alluring leap from Gustafsson, Ali's proud departure from Cassius Clay, and of course David Jones's major blast-off into Bowie: never underestimate the energising effect of a name change on the psyche. 'If it had been Sid The Loon, I wouldn't have worried,' said Anne Beverley, years after her son's death. 'But Vicious was totally unlike what he really was.'

John Beverley delighted in being 'Vicious'. 'I'm Sid Vicious,' he'd say, his emphasis a tacit acknowledgement of the inherent comedy in his comic book designate. But he hated 'Sid'. 'It's a right poxy name,' he'd sniff, 'really vile.'

Though not someone who would activate his personal rewind facility voluntarily – thoughts of tomorrow or yesterday rarely troubled him – Sid would become uncharacteristically animated when recounting his futile attempts to shrug off the evil of unwarranted nomenclature. 'I stayed in for about two weeks because everyone kept calling me Sid,' he complained in 1977, 'but they just wouldn't stop. Rotten started [it] . . . He's 'orrible like that, always picking on me . . .'

A Biblically derived triumvirate of David, Mark and John prevailed in the mid-'70s teenage wasteland. Sid was old and corny, a name only to be whined sing-song style ('Oh, Sii-ii-iid!') by Diana Coupland, while hectoring crap husband Sid James in the ITV sitcom *Bless This House*, or else grunted Stone Age style by monosyllabic *Carry On* buffoon Bernard Bresslaw. Any mention of 'Sid' was invariably accompanied by laughter.

Another Sid existed on the periphery of The Johns – Beverley and Lydon – world, an altogether cooler, cultier namesake. He was Syd Barrett, the flowered up genius who fronted the original Pink Floyd, and gorged on the psychedelic experience so thoroughly that it's said he has never truly left it. (Christened Roger Keith Barrett, he too was no natural-born Syd.) The Barrett legend had been upgraded during the mid-'70s, prompted by reissues of his work, and an extensive reappraisal of his madcap magnificence by Nick Kent in *New Musical Express*. The cult of the fallen rock 'n' roll anti-hero – Brian Wilson, Iggy Pop, Lou Reed, Marianne Faithfull, 'Ziggy Stardust' – was a prescient signature of pre-punk times.

Student Mike Baess has vivid memories of The Johns at Kingsway College: aloof Lydon, chilly Beverley, 'tasty' Wardle. He also recalls John Beverley's passion for Syd Barrett. Together, they'd listen to *The Madcap Laughs*, Barrett's 1970 solo album, a raw and haunting portrait of an artist in the grip of personal disintegration, that rare place where the boundaries between life and art, madness and sanity are dissolved. 'Sid loved that album,' says Baess, 'especially one song, 'If It's In You', which keeps breaking down. We'd be in hysterics listening to that.'

It was hysterical – 'He's bloody mad!' – but even thrill-seeking teenagers could recognise the desperation in Barrett's work. When Syd sang, 'I'm wondering who could be writing this song', you knew he wasn't joking. 'If It's In You' shocked and amused because it disturbed the myth of pop perfection. To teenagers searching for cracks in the respectable, stage-managed monolith that mid-'70s rock culture had become, the frail humanity evident in Barrett's work was a masterclass. Bugger the long-winded concept album: the art of falling apart was the highest art of all, the ultimate refusal, the most exquisite protest.

The Syd mythology emerged out of the backdrop of pop disintegration – 'STONE DROWNS', 'JIMI DIES', 'MANSON: GUILTY', 'BEATLES SPLIT', 'DREAM: OVER'. The flowers worn by the Love Generation were in the dustbin: disappointment, decay, even death was as integral to pop as fun, fucking and freaking out. In the mind of loner miscreant John Beverley, to whom contrariness came naturally, the early '70s were strewn with Lorelei-like sirens, calling out from behind treacherous rocks, tempting him to dally with danger.

None proved more seductive than David Bowie. By 1972, mutability – or at least testing the limits of personal identity – had become the key motif in Bowie's work. His space-age rock 'n' roll suicide epic, *The Rise And Fall Of Ziggy Stardust And The Spiders From Mars*, aestheticised the strange, the destructive, the very out of sortsness that made rock such an appealing battleground for drives that are often buried in everyday life. Bowie was a cultural provocateur, his *raison d'être* more personal than obviously political, his ironic, theatrical detachment a discourteous gesture in the direction of (adult-orientated) rock's new politeness.

Bowie was God in the eyes of John Beverley. At least that's what John Lydon says – over and again – in his autobiography, *Rotten: No Irish, No Blacks, No Dogs*. His style-obsessed mate was 'mortally in love with the whole Bowie thing', a poseur and a 'Dave' Bowie 'copyist'. Bowie on the turntable.

Bowie on the walls. Bowie on the brain. Bowie was a riot of thrilling contradiction – Ziggy/David, masculine/feminine, sound/vision, Rise/Fall. It's little wonder that Bowie's loud, glitzy articulation of cultural insecurities were seized upon by lost, lonely, identity-seeking 15-year-olds. Including John Beverley, high up in a tower block in Hackney, wondering what it's all about.

When he came down from his concrete cloud, and found some of the answers lurking in the subterranean haunts of the London punk scene, Sid no longer felt so alone. He was still saddled with that 'poxy name' of dubious provenance, but in giving him something extra to moan about, even that started to feel good.

So did the explanation: 'I got it from Rotten's hamster.' What could be more banal? But Mike Baess, who knew John Beverley as 'Spikey John' both in and out of Kingsway College, still harbours his Syd Barrett suspicions. 'If there was a hamster, I'm sure that would have been named after Barrett too,' he says. But that doesn't explain the ferret . . .

Many years earlier, way before he cracked up to Syd Barrett songs or cracked open the heads of pets unlucky enough to have crossed his path, there had been a ferret. 'Everyone else had dogs and cats, tortoises and goldfish,' remembers classmate Jeremy Colebrooke. Not the pre-teen, Tunbridge Wells-dwelling Simon, the schoolboy scion of an errant military man and a dotty bohemian. His first genuine expression of desire to be different came via the company he kept, and he seemed to prefer his pet ferret, which he'd smuggle into school, to his classmates. His ferret Sid.

So the genealogy of 'Sid' may be more complicated than received wisdom suggests. John Lydon, who remembers his friend's strange predicament over his identity ('Even he wasn't sure which [name to use]'), nevertheless has his hamster story and he's sticking with it.

'I called him after my pet, the softest, furriest, weediest thing on earth,' Lydon states in his autobiography, reiterating a tale he's been recounting for the best part of 30 years. It is also possible that Sid, the 'soppy' white hamster that lived in a cage in the Lydon's front room, may also be responsible for that 'Vicious' epithet too, though that particular tale has changed down the years. Back in 1977, it was John Beverley's finger that felt the full force of the hamster's molars. 'Your Sid is vicious!', he said, unknowingly uttering the words that became his passport to fame, infamy and an early grave. Years later, though, it was claimed that John Lydon Sr. was the recipient of the vicious rodent's fury.

The most plausible – and fitting – explanation, and one that Lydon too has acknowledged, is that 'Vicious' came loud and direct from Lou Reed's *Transformer*. The ex-Velvet Underground man's 1972 comeback album, *Transformer*, was co-produced by David Bowie and issued in the full glare of Ziggymania. 'Vicious', with its ironic line, 'Vicious/You hit me with a flower', was one of its key songs.

Whether prompted by a depraved hamster, or a coy song inspired by Reed's mentor Andy Warhol, the 'Vicious' designate was a more than worthy companion to Lydon's recently acquired 'Rotten' back in winter 1975–76. Vicious? Of course not! Ah-ha-ha. Ever get the feeling the joke was going to backfire on punk rock's big, psychotic baby?

2. HE BANGS THE DRUM

100 Club, London, Monday, 20 September 1976

FIRST NIGHT at the Punk Rock Festival and the place is packed. The ones onstage wear expressions like 12-year-old war babies wielding their first AK-47s. No one has seen crowds like this at a Sex Pistols gig before. A 600-strong queue, surprisingly orderly, winds round into a side street. 'Indisputable evidence', notes a Zeitgeist-seizing Caroline Coon for her report in *Melody Maker*, 'that a new decade in rock is about to begin'.

British punk rock – as opposed to the more richly flavoured New York variety – revolves almost entirely around The Sex Pistols, the inner city firebrands who have been subject to much debate in the music press since the spring. They claim they've come to destroy rock, though now they're on the cusp of signing a deal with EMI, the world's most prestigious record label. Several months ago, the Pistols too were regarded as have-a-go herberts. They won their reputation by rattling out a robust mix of unfashionable '60s B-sides and their own brutalist anthems of teenage alienation with a nonchalance hitherto unthinkable in the limp mid-'70s. Now they're getting really good, fashionable too, and everyone wants to sound like them.

The Pistols' gleeful, mocking iconoclasm has been a long time coming. For years, there have been mutterings in the music weeklies that rock 'n' roll – once so offensive that Frank Sinatra (of all people!) dismissed it as 'a rancid smelling aphrodisiac' – had lost its potency. Bowie has been a key dissenter, championing Iggy Pop, The Velvet Underground, and that band's deadpan poet of the street Lou Reed. The New York Dolls injected some serious trash into glam rock. American rock critic (and lately Patti Smith guitarist) Lenny Kaye chipped in by compiling *Nuggets*, a two-disc archaeological dig into the hitherto overlooked world of psyched-up garage punk misfits from the mid-'60s. More recently, London's pub rock scene has reverberated to the sound of R&B and rock 'n' roll revivalists, united in their opposition to the caped crusaders of progressive rock.

All this pales in comparison to recent happenings in downtown New York. In Lower East Side clubs such as Max's Kansas City and CBGB's, a new wave of musicians, high on rebellion, higher still on dope, decadence and a reconfigured 'punk' aesthetic, are hellbent on reclaiming rock 'n' roll's original inheritance. Their street-snappy names – Patti Smith, Television, Blondie, Talking Heads, The Heartbreakers and four cartoon mopheads called The Ramones – reflect their intent.

Johnny Rotten hates it when people draw transatlantic parallels ('cheese and chalk,' he snarls in the Pistols' put-down, 'New York'), but there's little doubt that the thriving New York scene – widely covered in the desperately-seeking-anything British music press – provides plenty of inspiration in London. Why else were all the major players on the nascent punk scene at the Roundhouse back in May and June sweating profusely to the magnificently unruly sounds of Patti Smith and The Ramones?

The desire to break with the contemporary malaise is infectious. Wherever The Sex Pistols rattle their sabres, very soon an unruly mob begins to follow. London; the suburbs; Manchester. Most of the neophytes are here tonight, the biggest showcase yet for the growing punk rock scene. The Pistols headline. Some of their biggest fans – best mates included – have formed bands and are using the two-day festival to seize the moment.

It's mid-evening and Sid is on the stage. He's one of those fans who's formed a band. Of sorts. Four head-turners who, less than 72 hours ago, had been virtually cattle-prodded into playing by Malcolm McLaren's sidekick Nils Stevenson. They are Sioux and Severin from Bromley, Marco Pirroni from Harrow and, from his squat in Hampstead, Sid Vicious.

'Sid already had a group called Flowers Of Romance but he hadn't unveiled it yet,' Severin remembers. 'He said he wanted to drum for us and that he had absolutely no ability as a drummer. That sounded absolutely brilliant to us, so we got him in.'

Twenty-four hours before the performance, the hastily convened quartet met at The Clash's rehearsal studio in Camden Lock. Only Marco had any idea how to play his instrument.

'We banged around for about ten minutes,' Severin says, 'then Sid said, "That's enough". That was the rehearsal. It was more about learning how to plug everything in.'

'I plugged in my guitar, turned this bizarre old amp up to ten, and it sounded fantastic,' Marco remembers. 'Then Sid sat down and said, 'What are we gonna do?' Sioux said, 'We thought we'd do "Goldfinger". "Fuck that," said Sid. "Let's just make a noise." So that's what we did.'

Having toyed with the idea of ruining The Beatles' 'She Loves You' or a Bay City Rollers song, the young radicals settled on the idea of Siouxsie reciting the Lord's Prayer against an improvised backdrop. Marco was at liberty to toss in a few riffs from his own limited repertoire if he felt like it. That twangy James Bond theme, perhaps, or – for a cheap, punkish, deeply ironic laugh – Deep Purple's 'Smoke On The Water', the rock riff equivalent to breast-milk for every budding '70s axe hero.

Mid-afternoon, Monday, 20 September: the queer-looking quartet turn up at the 100 Club, but nothing much is happening. Boxes of equipment are being carted around to the accompaniment of a long-hair repeating 'One-two' down the PA microphone. Terminal boredom. 'Why don't you take a soundcheck?' someone asks. 'Why? What the fuck's a soundcheck?' They walk past a sign outside the club that lists 'Suzie [sic] & The Banshees' among tonight's entertainment, and adjourn to a pub in Soho's Wardour Street.

'I was wearing an Anarchy shirt with a swastika and Luftwaffe insignia on it,' Marco remembers. 'Siouxsie had the Nazi armband. Steven [Severin] had a white shirt splattered in paint with a Union Jack pinned on the breast pocket. And Sid had a yellow Belsen Babies T-shirt, which he'd customised by ripping out the front and adding swastikas and stuff about Dr Mengele's experiments on the back. We looked like Christmas trees draped in swastikas.' In no mood for reliving a scene from *Cabaret*, the landlord had the awesome foursome hastily ejected.

They return a little later to find opening band Subway Sect midway through their set. Siouxsie And The Banshees had planned to use The Clash's gear, but when manager Bernie Rhodes clocks their dressed-to-kill apparel, he refuses to let them anywhere near it. One of the slogans scrawled across Sid's T-shirt boldly announces, 'I Hate Jews'. 'Not because he did,' says Siouxsie Sioux, 'but simply to wind Bernie Rhodes up.' Life's always a cabaret with old chum Sid around.

The neophytes in Nazi chic walk on stage and help themselves to Subway Sect's equipment. Sid's mates, those pesky Johns from North London, are down the front. 'Sid's a cunt!', they yell. 'Wank-uh!' Sid grins and sticks two fingers up. He works out which of the drums are easiest to hit. Siouxsie strikes a haughty pose but feels like dying inside. 'It's in E!' Marco calls out to Severin, who shoots back a mystified glance. 'The thick string! Just hit the thick string!'

Sid picks up his sticks and begins to thump out a wild, brutish beat. The cymbals and hi-hat remain untouched. There's something superfluous and sissy about them. Sid's loving every minute of it. 'His big joke was to do everything as badly as possible, make it as boring as possible,' says Marco. And what could be more thrillingly monotonous than a beat inspired by The Velvet Underground's cacophonous epic, 'Sister Ray'.

'With miraculous command, [Sid] starts his minimal thud,' scribbles Caroline Coon. Twenty minutes later, having made his point, Sid downs sticks and the rest of the band follow his cue. Johnny Rotten halts his frantic pogoing. The audience cheer, some in amazement, others in relief. Subsequent sets by The Clash and The Sex Pistols sound rockist and conventional by comparison. Though some still insist that the Pistols can't play their instruments, this was something else entirely. Sid, Siouxsie and hastily convened Banshees had taken the DIY ethic to its extreme: pure undiluted punk rock, uninhibited by even the most basic rules.

The Sex Pistols had already managed to divide those who still cared about contemporary rock – and in the sleepy '70s, not everyone did – into pro and anti camps. But the Banshees' inaugural performance (originally intended as a one-off) manages to rupture the apparent unity of the overwhelmingly pro-punk crowd.

Chrissie Hynde and sundry proto-Slits hover proudly around the singer. Nils Stevenson offers to manage the group. Future Banshees drummer Kenny Morris, who volunteers his services immediately afterwards, is 'absolutely thrilled. I don't even remember The Clash or the Pistols that night,' he recalls. Subway Sect frontman Vic Godard still remembers the discordant racket as 'the highlight of the festival'.

Others simply laugh, happy that the punkish prank is now over. A few look perplexed. And there are those who simply refuse to mince their words. 'God, it was awful,' mutters the man from Island Records. 'Shocking!' says The Damned's Captain Sensible. 'Even for punk they were inept. They were shit.'

In London, 1976, shit was good. Bad was good. Good was boring.

3. IT'S ALL BOLLOCKS

IN THE early hours of 2 February 1979, 21-year-old Sid Vicious died and was reborn a legend . . . of sorts.

Two years of intermittent heroin and methadone use, supplemented by copious libations of schnapps and cheap lager, had seen him off. There were other factors too: deep-seated legacies from childhood, the jail sentence he faced for the second-degree murder of his girlfriend, Nancy Spungeon. Above all, there was Sid's unwillingness to withdraw from the threshold of oblivion, a feature of his life since anyone could remember.

Back in London, Nils Stevenson, an intimate of The Sex Pistols back in '76 when the band genuinely meant something, opened his diary and began to write. 'Poor Sid,' he started, 'he believed the myth.' Then Nils downed his pen. Nothing more to say.

It's spring 2004. People have a lot more to say about Sid Vicious today. Some who have not spoken publicly about him before. Others who have recounted their tales many times, for books and magazines, television and radio. If they're lucky, they might have been paid for their memories. No one interviewed specifically for this book has asked to be paid. Some got fed; others had their thirsts quenched. Vic Godard got his customary cuppa and a spare Jamelia CD I had lying around. Two or three whose first-hand reminiscences aren't in the book did invoke a cash-for-questions policy. That doesn't happen when you're researching Syd Barrett.

Perhaps it's a Sex Pistols thing. Sid often demanded money upfront from journalists and photographers, even when he was top of the charts and a notorious household name. He wasn't an empire-builder. Material things or a bronzed future as a tax exile were of little concern to him. Sid simply had immediate needs to fill, his expensive drug habit, for example. Besides, Malcolm McLaren kept a notoriously tight rein on the band's finances. At the height of the band's success, each member received a weekly allowance of £40, just three times what their mates on the dole were drawing.

Twenty-five years have passed since Sid's death. Many interviewees make one of those 'Who knows where the times goes?' remarks. A few also ask, 'Shouldn't your book be on the shelves now?' noting the recent upturn of anniversary tie-in radio documentaries and magazine profiles. 'Nah, myths in popular culture aren't time-specific,' I say blithely. That's not entirely true. Even myths have to wait their turn, and anniversaries (especially when the year ends in 0 or 5) are the turnstiles of the dead.

But Sid is always around, a forever friend in the firmament of lost souls, a 20th century bad boy hanging out somewhere between Valentino and Tarantino. We see him on 'Sid's Not Dead' T-shirts and on 'Sid Is Innocent' badges. In galleries and on television. Sometimes even in record shops. In fact, he can end up in the most unlikely of places.

After two hours spent discussing Sid, *Sniffin' Glue* and Miles Davis over curried eggs and mugs of tea at the Chelsea Kitchen, Mark Perry and I found ourselves in the King's Road branch of Agnès B. We leave clutching complimentary packs of Sid Vicious condoms. Trainee bank clerks now sport Sid-style spikey-tops. Footballers too. I wouldn't know if some 'Sid' or other has had a go at 'My Way' on one of those Saturday night's alright for miming TV shows. But he wouldn't be at all out of place.

Sid Vicious is a name, an image, a brand. He's also a way of life. That's Sid down a dark alley fixing up smack because life's shit or a laugh or useless. There he is again taking a razor to his arm for the same reasons. We can't be sure whether he's trying to cut the pain out or put the feeling back, but it's a Sid thing alright. Likewise that bare-chested, beered-up blockhead bellowing 'Everything's BOLLOCKS!' as he stumbles through the city centre at two in the morning. Sid may be dead, but there are plenty of others still doing his living for him.

Sid Vicious is an icon, a pulp fiction anti-hero, perhaps even a genuine member of the nihilist tendency, who craved attention and crumbled under the unbearable weight of his quick-fix existence. A live-fast-die-young rock 'n' roll cliché of princely proportions, Sid's a cinch to celebrate, easier still to damn. But try finding a fence where it's possible to sit comfortably beside him . . .

'I really hope you don't paint him in morbid and horrible terms,' says fellow SEX shop habitué Alan Jones, who laughed so much in Sid's company that it hurt. And of course there's gallows humour galore in Sid's story, random outbursts of childlike enthusiasm, too. But rarely far from the surface is the dread, the pain and the deep insecurities that fed his mistrust, nourished his denial of meaning and self-respect, and gratified the thirst for oblivion that stilled his long, translucent, hairless body so prematurely. And it's that which rescues him from the blandness of his posthumous, hyperreal existence. As a flat, reducible image – the perfectly imperfect one-dimensional man – there is no rock 'n' roll icon to touch Sid Vicious. But that can't be all there is.

I'M MIDWAY through a lengthy transatlantic telephone interview with photographer Kate Simon, and she's not laughing at all as she describes how Sid threw one of her pals, *Sounds* art director Dave Fudger, down a flight of stairs for no apparent reason. When I tell her that this is hardly out of character, she seems genuinely surprised. 'You mean, when he saw John [Lydon] wearing a T-shirt saying 'Destroy', he took it for real and did that?'

Simon confesses that she finds John Lydon much more interesting ('I couldn't see John ever doing that. This man was a real intellectual'), but agrees to talk about Sid for the book because we have a mutual friend. Interviews often happen this way. John Lydon is not being interviewed for the book because He's A Celebrity And He's Found An Audience Again. Besides, he reckons he's 'said all he's wanted to say about Sid'. I don't think he has, but that's not reason enough for him to dredge up all those old demons again. There's another reason too. As Lydon has aged, the memory, maybe even the guilt, has become more painful. Sid never believed there was anything to learn in life, but evidently there is.

KATE SIMON: 'What's the title of your book?'

MP: ' 'Vicious: The Art of Dying Young'.'

KATE SIMON: 'Okay . . . How depressing!'

Kate was probably being kind. She probably meant to say 'awful' but couldn't bring herself to. It's a tricksy title but 'Sid Vicious: A Life' just didn't seem right. Besides, juxtaposing 'Art' with 'Dying Young' would annoy people, just as Sid, his ever-present swastikas and his oafishness used to annoy people. A book about Sid Vicious ought at least to kick up a little stink.

'Vicious' and 'Dying Young' of course make perfect bedfellows. But 'Vicious' and 'Art'? It's hardly pancakes and syrup. Though his prophetic, vengeful performance of 'My Way' is regarded as a punk rock milestone of sorts, Sid left no genuine masterpieces. But over the course of the past century, art has changed. It's no longer the sole province of the few. Nor is it restricted to a fetishised *objet d'art* one remove from the lived experience. It has become as meaningful – or as meaningless – as life itself. The boundaries have blurred into insignificance. Sid's creation – himself, or a magnification of self – expresses what a gallery full of angst-ridden canvases cannot hope to equal.

The Futurist Manifesto demanded the introduction of 'the fisticuff into the artistic battle'. The ultimate Surrealist act was to fire a revolver randomly in a crowded street. David Bowie took the idea that the work was inseparable from the artist and ran with it. Sid took the idea and turned it on himself.

Sid's fast-track pilgrimage to the rock 'n' roll mausoleum outpaced even that of Brian Jones and Jimi Hendrix and Janis Joplin and Jim Morrison, all of whom – unlike him – had come looking for salvation and found only disillusion in the new art world of rock 'n' roll. Sid's pogo through purgatory was spa-pool pure by comparison. He came to rock with no grand illusions and left with none shattered. Not that he gets much due recognition when it comes to his chapter in 'Those Who Died Young'.

Sid Vicious once slashed journalist Nick Kent around the head with an old bike chain. Several months later, by which time Sid was at least as famous as infamous, the pair made up and sometimes scored smack together. Kent, who lived precariously close to the edge in those days, has written many articles about dead or decaying rock stars. He has an opinion on Sid's legacy, and though it's not a particularly flattering one, it does make sense.

'There is a perverted glory in him dying at 21. It's a Billy The Kid thing but without the talent. That's the thing with Sid Vicious, it's the lack of recognised talent. His talent was the self-destruction. That's what it was. He had a unique talent for it. That's the reason why you're writing the book, and why he's such an icon to young people. When I watch *Jackass*, I think of Sid Vicious. He gave birth to that as a legitimate entertainment form. Fuck the music, let's just be self-destructive. Gob at a crowd and get a bottle in the face.'

Bottle in the face. Lacerations on his arms. Agonising withdrawal symptoms coursing through his mind and body. Sid could feel that all right. But it did help banish the restlessless, the numb impotence that ate away at his being. It was difficult to know which was worse.

'I've been asked to talk about Sid before and I haven't,' says Jah Wobble, who as teenager John Wardle spent a good deal of time with Sid during the mid-'70s. 'That's not because I have any axe to grind about it, but because I find it difficult. I have this sense that there's not that much to talk about. In a sense, that makes him quite a fascinating subject for a biography, this nihilistic, one-dimensional cartoon character and what, if anything, was behind it. God bless his soul and all that . . .'

Simon Barker, one of the so-called Bromley Contingent, has said his bit about Sid, both for Jon Savage's *England's Dreaming* and for my Siouxsie And The Banshees biography last year. One quip he made during our phone conversation – 'You'll probably destroy the myth because you'll not really find anything there' – is worth noting, because I'd been working on the opposite assumption: that not finding 'anything there' would actually keep the myth intact, Sid as the perfect symbol of nothingness.

I did have one suspicion confirmed, though. Sid had an innate gift for winding people up – even his mates. 'He came close a couple of times to getting a pasting off me,' says Wobble. 'We were at my mate's gaffe in Edmonton, this haunted Victorian place, loads of negative energy. John [Lydon] was there too. My mate was supposed to marry this bird, but it had all gone wrong and we ended up with this pile of cans in the front room. Yeah, we could have flogged it to the Tate: 'Pyramid Of Cans, 1976'! Then

Sid starts spitting into this electric fire. I was like, I've brought you here, and this is my mate's gaffe . . . Do it one more time and, woah, here we go. He took it to within half an inch of it getting really fucking serious.'

Annoying people, like getting pasted or enthusing about The Ramones, was one of Sid's most cherished pastimes. And John Lydon just loved that about him. Sid was one of those 'crazy people . . . who don't see the risk . . . He would always find a way to laugh at things,' Lydon recalled in his autobiography. Everything was a joke to Sid. They all say that. But once Sid became a Sex Pistol, the dynamics of his relationship with Lydon, these twin figureheads – Vicious and Rotten – of punk rock, had changed. The smile dropped right off Rotten's face.

Sid's unwillingness to take anything seriously was no longer a laugh but a tedious liability. Sid still didn't care. He started to accuse Rotten of betraying his punk identity, of becoming everything he'd once set out to destroy. He was letting everyone down. In truth, Sid cared little more for his audience – or himself of course – than Rotten did, but he was a punk ideologue of sorts, haunted by the betrayal of two generations of rock idols. He thought and acted with all the commitment of a terrorist, unwilling to see beyond the simplest outline of 'the cause'.

Music-hall luminary Mitch Miller once denounced rock 'n' roll as 'a disease.' That was one of the reasons it was so fantastic. But, said Sid and the new punk tendency, it just wasn't noisy or nasty or stupid enough. rock 'n' roll was about riot and abandon, and of course depravity and ruination were intrinsic to the mad passions it was capable of rousing. Sid believed in the ruins. Can't play, don't give a toss.

Unlike Lydon, supreme being of the heartless put-down, Sid was no bar-room philosopher. But he lived according to a credo of sorts: 'Nothing is more real than nothing.' Perhaps he read it in Ashford, in that book about the Manson family. Perhaps it came to him in odd flashes, when he paused to deliberate on the nothingness of being. For there was certainly something of the void about him, not in that karmic, Zen Buddhist '60s sense, but in a culturally restless, personally insecure and spiritually inadequate way that meant he could only perceive life in terms of defence – and attack. A lone wolf in the grip of a baffling stupefaction, Sid was uncomfortably aware of his alienation. Others noticed it, too.

'It feels very dreamlike recalling Sid,' Wobble says. 'You know when you look into the eyes of a Doberman, and there's something about it, it's not quite looking at you. The dog is somewhere else, not quite getting it . . .

'Many people from that era put up smokescreens,' Wobble continues. 'I can be like that myself. But there's always a point when the cards are on the table and you're like, OK, I'm gonna give you a bit of me. But with Sid you never really had that.'

Over scallops and salad, Wobble wonders 'why [Sid] has become this icon.' He too locates art somewhere in the answer. 'Because it's dark, it's nihilistic, it's unfathomable, it's senseless. Like a lot of modern art. Cutting a cow in half? Why? What's the fucking point? What's that about? There's no empathy. This is exactly Sid. I never got that warm, gut-to-gut thing from him . . . And that sums up postmodernism, and Sid's in there with it. [It says] It's all a load of bollocks, all worthless, all shit, all pointless. I did it My Way. Blam blam. And if he did have a philosophy, it's that postmodernist one: IT'S ALL BOLLOCKS.'

Viewed from another angle, let's say from the high modernist perspective of Mark Rothko, famous for his monumental, wash-of-colour canvases of despair, what might appear blank is in fact filled with meaning. 'There is no such thing as a painting about nothing,' insisted the artist, who committed suicide in 1970. And he's right. I have enough material to write a book four times the size of this one. That's a lot about nothing.

Sid thought art was a load of old Jackson Pollocks. Warhol's outsize Brillo pads and a bunch of arseholes photographed by Yoko Ono? Some turds in a tin cooked up by Piero Manzoni, and Carl Andre's bricks in the Tate? Those boring Old Masters, the Mona Lisa and that Cuntstable? All wank for weeds in Hush Puppies to fuss over and exchange bouquets of fraudulent 'Wuuuunderfuls!' at. At least, reckoned Sid, Warhol didn't take himself too seriously, and the world he created around him was what seemed to matter. But wasn't art simply a sick note handed in by those too scared to step into the theatre of life? Sid saw no option other than to confront life and death head on, not toy with it from the safety of a charmed existence.

Today, Sid Vicious is alive and well and stalking the hallowed hallways of high culture. He is a BritArt icon. Well, not him exactly, but the image of artist Gavin Turk masquerading as Sid Vicious, in a pose adapted from Andy Warhol's 1964 painting – Elvis I – itself inspired by a photograph of the real-life Elvis Presley dressed as a cowboy. There he is, given the title Pop, gazing out from the BritArt portfolio, right up there alongside Sarah Lucas' female form reconfigured as two fried eggs and an open kebab, and Tracey Emin's umade bed, which is of course very Sidney: 'Great laugh!' Pop is nowhere as infamous as Damien Hirst's carefully cleaved cow, but at least it's Sid in the perspex box and not Johnny Rotten.

We know exactly what Sid would have thought about Pop. There is no doubt that he would applaud any likeness of himself – followed by a quip about being 'more handsome in real life'. And, in a voice that sounds like an ungodly hybrid of David Beckham's 'pipsqueak' and Arthur Mullard's 'dullard', he'd eyeball the artist and say, only mock-nastily, 'Gavin Turd. Tosser. Hur-hur.'

What hideous irony! Vicious, punk's Mister Pitiful, at the centre of an academic debate about celebrity and authenticity. (Which is, one presumes, the issues raised by Pop.) Meanwhile, John Lydon slugs it out with creepie-crawlies and celebrity creeps in the Australian jungle and becomes the darling of the Daily Mail's predominantly middle-aged and female readership. Does this really mean that, a quarter of a century on, Sid has emerged triumphant in the battle for the damaged heart and screaming soul of punk rock? That dying young is an art and staying alive is for old farts? Or simply that it is all bollocks, but makes for a good story anyway?

4. JOHNNY VICIOUS

'John Lydon had a functioning brain and a personality that was his own. He was a sophisticated thinker. Sid was not a sophisticated thinker. He was barely a thinker.' – *Nick Kent, journalist*

THREE OF the four original Sex Pistols were in a band to impress girls, to exercise (and maybe exorcise) a little teen spirit, and – so their manager kept saying – to roughen up a moribund rock scene with a bit of vintage three-minute, four-chord attitude. Their heroes were the original Who and Small Faces, The Faces and The Stooges, and all those other wham-bam-thank-you-ma'am merchants that took their cues from Eddie Cochran and Carl Perkins. The fourth Sex Pistol was less reverential to past heroes, and more taken with the idea of roughening rock up a bit. Terrific or terrible, it didn't matter so long as they had impact. Anything mediocre, anything in between was pointless, he groaned.

Anything with that fourth, flaming Pistol, John Lydon, alias Johnny Rotten, out front was unlikely to be mediocre. The musicians in the band weren't half bad either. 'Even taken out of the punk context, the [original Pistols] were a great band,' says Wobble. 'Paul Cook had that dustbin-lid drum sound down to a T. Steve Jones had a classic rock guitar style, and Glen [Matlock] was very musical, all those McCartneyesque runs and that Rickenbacker sound.'

A few years later, at a time when Sid had virtually given up the bass and his life was spiralling out of control, Lydon invited Wobble to join his post-Pistols band, Public Image Limited (PiL). A couple of genuinely frontier-bashing albums later, the pair fell out and Wobble left to pursue a solo career. Nevertheless, the ex-PiL bassist still rates Rotten as a 'phenomenal' frontman. 'John was one of the most charismatic people you could meet. I don't care what anyone says: the Pistols got the best.'

Great rock 'n' roll bands rarely enter into the wider vernacular on the basis of sound alone. 'Heartbreak Hotel' was a stunning piece of music, but it was Presley's lascivious lips and air of defiance that made manifest the sex and notoriety inscribed in the grooves. A fortuitous encounter with the early rumblings of a youth explosion invested the song with added cultural gravitas and momentous meaning. Such a unity of sound, style and social significance is extraordinarily rare in rock. That's probably why the music of, say, U2 or REM exists in some essentially pointless vacuum, while Jimi Hendrix – the music, the man, the icon – is inextricably woven into the fabric of 20th-century cultural history.

Hendrix died at 27, way too prematurely, but at least his reputation was already secure. Sid's legend status is almost wholly dependent on his achieving total self-demolition. It was dying young that transformed Sid Vicious – the boy who looked at Johnny, stole a few key moves, then became a genuine rival – into *the* punk icon, over and above trailblazer Rotten. Sid's hasty, Ziggy-like wipe-out marked some kind of inglorious climax to a movement that had already come remarkably close to choking on its own disgust.

'It had been punk's project to dissolve the boundaries between art and everyday life,' states Jon Savage in *England's Dreaming*, his definitive survey of The Sex Pistols and punk rock. And Sid, the punk purist for whom silver-tongued rhetoric and symbolic refusal were never enough, became the era's just-do-it existential hero. Others were able to say it or play it better. Sid was punk's Action Man, a 'readymade' like Marcel Duchamp's urinal with legs, delighted to piss on everyone's parade. Art is rubbish. Life is rubbish. Let's see action!

Punk's genuinely destructive urges, which ranged from hilarious gestures of cultural bad manners to dramatic acts of self-harm, have been quietly airbrushed out of history. The significance of punk, which reverberated throughout British society and beyond, has now been reduced to a simple shift in aesthetics: the music got louder, the fashions wilder. Was there really no other storyline?

Wasn't punk one final, dog-breath gasp of meaning before the cultural cesspool of the empty gesture engulfed all? Has such a dynamic and socially aware youth movement since grasped British society by its starched collar and roared with such passion and violence in its complacent, collective face?

But all this was Johnny's triumph, not Sid's. When the trembling, shaken nation dared glance back at its tormentor, it wasn't Sid 'fancy a fight?' Vicious who threatened to light fires in their cities, but Rabelaisian Rotten. And that was truly scary. Punch-ups were familiar, comprehendable, part of the fabric of British society. But Rabelais . . . What the Dickens was that?

Malcolm McLaren understood only too well. Rotten was the 'little Artful Dodger' he'd been searching for: genuine working class 'roughage', as defiantly antisocial as he imagined himself to be, and with a toxic tongue to match. McLaren, a veteran of 1968 and student radicalism, remained an angry armchair activist who still harboured fantasies of social upheaval, but he had neither the inclination nor the guts to front a rock 'n' roll band let alone a youth revolt. Besides, he was pushing 30.

The solution arrived one evening in August 1975. Having been spotted by McLaren's fellow plotter Bernie Rhodes, John Lydon was invited to meet both band and manager at the Roebuck pub, across the road from SEX, the shop Malcolm ran with his partner Vivienne Westwood. Adjourning to No. 430 later that evening, Lydon's 'audition' was to stand in front of the vintage AMI jukebox, shower head in hand, and mime to Alice Cooper's 'I'm Eighteen'. Malcolm McLaren's search for an antidote to the present cultural malaise was over. This was the rabble-rouser through whom McLaren would live vicariously for the next two years.

When The Sex Pistols played their first gig, at St Martin's College Of Art in central London on 6 November 1975, Rotten was 19. That made him a virtual infant by the standards of the time, when rock magazine covers were still dominated by a vain parade of monsters in make-up – Dylan, Daltrey, Jagger, Reed, Rod, 30-plus wrinklestiltskins to a man. Bolan and Bowie, the two glam superstars who tarted up the early '70s, were both pushing 30. Even the rising stars of 'young' America, Patti Smith and Bruce Springsteen, were out of their teens by the time of Woodstock in 1969. To cap it all, there was *Rock Follies*, a truly must-not-see television drama series every bit as dumb as its title. It was as if rock had died and its last will and testament – not a fucking penny for anyone! – was being read out in weekly instalments on ITV.

Youth was crucial to punk, but on its own it meant little. If it meant anything in the mid-'70s, it was likely to be The Arrows and The Bay City Rollers, The Wombles and *Watership Down*. McLaren understood that it didn't always have to be this way. He knew that youth was a sleeping giant, an instinctively undisciplined (anti-)social force in dire need of a clarion call to revive its debilitated spirit. That's where Rotten, a rock 'n' roll Robespierre who'd be only too pleased to lop off a few *ancien regime* heads, came in.

Pre-Rotten, The Sex Pistols were three roguish teenagers who belted out roughly-hewn cover versions to an empty rehearsal room. By the soft-shoe standards of '75, that was mutinous enough. But Rotten brought along something else entirely. 'No image. No point. No nothing,' is how the frontman remembers the nascent Sex Pistols: 'Disgusting pub rock'. McLaren's Muppets might well have enjoyed some kind of career with a different singer, but without Rotten The Sex Pistols would never have sparked a subcultural revolution.

Rotten made everyone feel uncomfortable. Steve Jones, the band's guitarist and serial burglar, noted that 'his attitude was fucked.' It was Jones who would soon christen him 'Rotten' on account of his decaying teeth. Drummer Paul Cook reckoned he was a 'bit of a lunatic'. 'Hard work,' adds bassist Glen Matlock, whose relationship with the new singer went downhill from day one. Rotten couldn't sing, at least not by traditional standards, though he mumbled something about 'being able to play a violin out of tune'. If McLaren hadn't decided that Rotten – his hair as green as the Lydon's budgie, his distressed Pink Floyd T-shirt customised with the words 'I HATE' – was right for the group, it's unlikely the others would have given him a second glance.

Rotten was another Presley, another Jagger. The prodigal son, proverbial bad seed, peculiar and compelling. He wasn't some smart-arse Jim Morrison clone or Lou Reed wanabee, either of which could have successfully fronted McLaren's protégés. Rotten regarded the clichéd, hand-me-down rock 'n' roll attitude much like he did everything else. Beneath contempt. The Doors and the Velvets both figured on his teenage musical compass, as did Hawkwind, The Stooges and The Pink Fairies. But so too did many idiosyncratic sounds and maverick characters from rock's outer regions – Captain Beefheart And His Magic Band, ultra-prog hair-puller Peter Hammill, Krautrock rhythm kings Can, Miles Davis' flyaway avant-funk and, by mid-decade, the spatial rituals of dub reggae. John Lydon was by no means your predictable Bowie clone or prog rock bore.

These were crucial, character-building discoveries on Lydon's teenage journey from self-styled 'church mouse' to cultural whirlwind. 'All weird,' McLaren sniped many years later, in a flimsy attempt to tarnish Lydon's reputation by insinuating that he was a closet hippie. Totally wired, totally weird: without Lydon/Rotten fronting it, punk rock may have ended up sounding like a load of old Rolling Stones out-takes played by a bunch of young Keith Richards clones. While in many ways the antithesis of the old glam rock hero, Rotten surpassed both Bolan and Bowie in aestheticising the strange for (a kind of) popular consumption.

With Rotten out front, in his own words 'deformed, hilarious, grotesque', a sinister, Shakespearean Richard III figure for *Clockwork Orange* times, McLaren now had the full complement of young assassins he'd craved ever since hanging out with The New York Dolls a few months earlier. Running a risqué rag-trade clothes shop located in a down-at-heel part of Chelsea had gained him a handful of minor stories in the press, but the 'intellectual terrorism' that rebounded in his head demanded a grander stage. The Sex Pistols – a pop group! – was his best opportunity.

Lydon joined the band with little fanfare. If McLaren's lover and business partner Vivienne Westwood had her way, he wouldn't have joined at all. According to Nils Stevenson, when the rookie clothes designer mentioned that an occasional SEX customer called John had front-man potential, she'd meant the lanky, drop-dead stylish John, not the stooping, withdrawn one. 'Sid just overshadowed John [Lydon] on initial contact,' she told McLaren's biographer Craig Bromberg. 'But Sid had gone off doing something with speed . . .'

Although Sid wasn't with Lydon the day he auditioned for the band, Wobble suspects that he had a role to play in Lydon's recruitment. 'John probably wouldn't have met the Pistols if it wasn't for Sid. He would have had too much pride to walk into McLaren's shop and strike up a conversation. Sid was the one who put himself about.' And made the pair known to the SEX shop staff. Lydon was wary and aloof. 'You wanna talk? Come here and talk to me.'

'I was working at Malcolm's shop,' says Glen Matlock, 'and it was common for some people to float between the shop and ACME Attractions, which was halfway down the King's Road. Sid was one of that crowd, along with John [Lydon] and John Gray. They all dressed in that pre-punk, tail-end of glam rock look, and to a man they used to wear these horrible plastic jelly shoes from ACME Attractions. Cheap as chips and very unstylish. Their crowd were the jelly shoes wearers.'

What 'The Johns' lacked in terms of footwear etiquette, they made up for in sneering, leering attitude. 'In 1975, [Lydon] and his close friends John Grey [sic] and Sid Vicious were the terrors of the King's Road,' wrote Caroline Coon in November 1976. 'I used to go up and down [there] gobbing at the poseurs and pissing around,' Lydon told her, laying it on a bit thick. 'I couldn't stand them . . . They were weeds. Wouldn't defend themselves in any way, even verbally. Spineless.'

While Lydon hissed and spat, Sid made the introductions, and the biggest impression – though not necessarily for the right reasons. Don Letts, then a young dub reggae enthusiast who managed ACME Attractions with his girlfriend (and Lydon's future collaborator in PiL) Jeanette Lee, remembers Sid as a frequent – albeit non-paying – customer.

'He was still known as John back then and he used to get on my fucking nerves,' Letts laughs. 'People came to the shop for one of three reasons: the music – dub reggae – which they heard from outside the shop; Jeanette; and the clothes. In that order. John obviously had eyes for Jeanette, though he wasn't the kind of guy who'd do anything about it. He'd come in, say he was fucking starving for a sandwich, and she used to buy him food and look after him. When he'd occupy too much of Jeanette's time, I was like, 'Right, it's my turn. Fuck off!' '

Despite their mock rivalry for Lee's attentions, Letts was fond of the young hang-about. 'We were mates,' he says. 'Sid was really into his rock 'n' roll. He realised there was something going on, though he never seemed to have his finger on the pulse.' Conversations, says Letts, were hampered by the fact that 'it was almost like talking to a five-year-old. It was difficult to take him seriously, though you could never say that about John [Lydon]. Sid would always complain, 'I went down Chaguarama's [a gay club in Neal Street, Covent Garden, that hosted regular Bowie nights] last night an' they kep' beatin' me up.' Even then, people laid into him. No one took him seriously. He was even more of a dickhead then than when he became Sid Vicious.'

Having tested the patience of the ACME Attractions double act, the hapless Hackney idler would make his way down to World's End, where SEX regular (and an occasional spare pair of hands in the shop) Alan Jones would always be delighted to bump into him. 'He was very much a part of that group of Johns,' he says, 'and Sid stood out from the moment I first saw him. His look was that strong.'

'Sid . . . didn't let anything bother him,' insisted Jordan, the shop floor superstar among McLaren and Westwood's tight-knit circle of subterranean style warriors. 'He never carried troubles on his shoulders. He was happy-go-lucky,' she told Westwood's biographer Jane Mulvagh, 'everyone liked Sid.'

One night, John Beverley turned up at his mother's flat, and it was obvious that something was bothering him. Eventually, he blurted out that his mate – the one, said Anne, who was so shy he'd go beetroot red – had been asked to join a rock band. 'He looked completely crushed,' she remembered years later. 'He believed that he should have been offered the job. He was very bitter about it.'

Even allowing for that familiar whiff of Anne Beverley embellishment, one thing is certain. The day John Lydon joined The Sex Pistols was the day that changed John Beverley's life.

JOHN BEVERLEY and John Lydon met at Hackney Technical College, in Ayresome Road, Stoke Newington, during the 1973-74 academic year. The autumn term began with Wizzard's nostalgic 'Angel Fingers'; exams were completed to the sound of George McRae's falsetto disco floor filler, 'Rock Your Baby'. Not a bad leap forward for a supposedly 'marking time' year.

Both were bored, put-back-a-year O-level students. Lydon was reading Graham Greene's *Brighton Rock*; Beverley preferred Marvel comics and any publication that plastered David Bowie on the cover. Beverley, one year Lydon's junior, later remembered his college pal being 'a balding old hippie with a big pair of platforms on'. The hairy Hawkwind apostle retorted, with rather less charm, that Sid was 'an absolute wanker . . . a poseur, a clothes horse of the worst kind'.

John Beverley was an only child, who hardly knew his father, and had barely had time to know his stepfather before death snatched him away too. A virtual itinerant, who'd attended schools in central London, Oxford, Tunbridge Wells, Bristol and finally north London, he'd not mixed well in the half-dozen or so schools he'd tried his best not to attend. Hackney Tech, with its more liberal attitude towards uniforms and study, better suited him. He wore what he wanted, usually some variant of the latest Bowie persona ('Ziggy', 'Aladdin Sane', a 'Philly Dog' soul boy), and did as little work as possible. By the time he'd discharged himself from the education system, John Beverley had notched up low O-level passes in English Language and Literature, though it was not exam successes that gave him his break. That was down to a mischievous suggestion by his best mate.

'I got on really well with John,' Sid told Judy Vermorel in 1977, 'and with the black kids. They were fucking great, the spades in that college . . . really cool.' (It was while at Hackney Tech that the pair first heard the thrilling blast of the reggae sound system, an experience that had a deep and lasting effect, particularly on Lydon.) Apart from that, he added, 'everything else was shit. I couldn't do any of the work, not because I was unintelligent, but because I wasn't interested.' Sid was 'incapable' of doing anything he didn't want to do.

The popular perception that Lydon has always been his own man and Sid merely a cheap reproduction is not borne out by a comparison of the pair's teenage rampages. Lydon, the eldest son in what he describes as a large London-Irish family of 'shit shovellers', endured taunts of 'Dummy!' after a lengthy spell in hospital for meningitis left him 'backwards in everything'. His tart tongue and cleverly disruptive manner eventually won him the respect of his hard-nut classmates.

A natural outsider, with a Mick Ronson feather cut that was fast becoming as unruly as he was, Lydon found solace in outré rock – he saw Iggy Pop at the Scala in King's Cross in 1972 – and horror films. Soon afterwards, he was expelled from the Sir William Of York Catholic School, with the sound of Alice Cooper's 'School's Out' still ringing in his ears.

Contrary to his goofy reputation, John Beverley possessed similarly lone wolf characteristics. According to Jeremy Colebrooke, a classmate at Sandown Court Secondary Modern for three years between 1968 and 1971, Simon – a name deemed more suitable to the tastes of Tunbridge Wells, where the Beverleys spent a relatively stable six years – was an aloof, vaguely mysterious pupil.

'We never really knew much about him,' Colebrooke says, 'because he didn't have friends out of school. He lived in St James's Road, a street of big old Victorian houses, and you got this sense that he was close to his mother. I imagined that she was very bohemian, someone who wouldn't give him a slap if he gave her a mouthful.'

Colebrooke's instinct served him well. So did his sense of smell. 'One of the reasons I assumed he was from a bohemian background was because he always smelt of garlic. That was rare in 1968. In fact, he was known as 'Garlic Breath', though I'm damn sure no one said it to his face. Not that Simon was a bully. He wasn't, but the bullies didn't bully him because they knew they'd probably lose.'

Sid's psychotic reaction, which landed him in so much trouble during the punk days, was given a dry run during his otherwise remarkably incident-free days down in leafy Tunbridge Wells. 'He had a temper,' Colebrooke confirms, 'but he wouldn't take it out on just anybody. You had to have done something to get it, though if you were on the receiving end, you knew about it. It was like opening a floodgate. Simon would just snap. But only if he was provoked.'

A simmering row with a classmate over the ownership of a Manchester United FC scarf came to an ugly head one afternoon in the street outside the school gates. 'Simon Beverley absolutely hammered this guy,' says Colebrooke, 'he cut him up quite badly. And we're talking about a guy who could really handle himself. Simon was on top of him, kicking, punching, going at him in any way he could. He didn't know how to stop. At one point, a car pulled up but the driver wasn't able to stop him either. A smack in the mouth wasn't enough for him. He'd bloody your nose and blind you in one eye if he could.'

But that only seemed to apply when Simon Beverley felt provoked, affronted, cornered into a situation where there was no turning back. Then, he became fight-to-the-death, psychotic Simon. But, as he approached his teens, that was rare. That incident aside, Colebrooke can remember 'nothing really nasty' about his classmate. Naughty, though. Over the course of the three years they shared classes together, Colebrooke remembers Simon becoming an increasingly disruptive, rebellious presence in the classroom.

'At 11, Simon was like the rest of us. Except that he was a good enough footballer to get picked for the house team. And he wasn't stupid. We were in the 'A' stream together. He did his work, and he always did it in this very neat handwriting. But in the space of a couple of years, he went from being a reasonably normal schoolboy to someone who just didn't want to know.' That's what the ferret was all about. 'He brought it in his duffel bag and of course the bloody thing escaped during a geography lesson. The teacher was almost sweating with rage, but Simon simply smiled, turned around and walked away.'

In spite of this and other crowd-pleasing antics, Simon Beverley never became particularly popular. 'He didn't have a circle of friends in the same way other people did,' Colebrooke says. 'And if he wasn't there, which he wasn't much later on because he'd often play truant, he wouldn't be missed.' In fact, his classmates eventually tired of the daily rows prompted by Simon's refusal to do his homework. 'He got so many bollockings, but he didn't seem to worry about being hit or caned,' Colebrooke adds. 'The kudos was worth it.'

Simon Beverley left Sandown Court in the summer of '71, at the end of the third year, and with his mother moved back to London. 'We never thought anything more about him,' says Colebrooke. 'Years later, The Sex Pistols arrived on the scene and I thought, 'Shit! I'm a prog rocker!' When Sid joined, I remember thinking, 'What idiot calls himself Sid Vicious?' Then I saw a picture of him. The guy can't play, can't sing and he's an idiot – but he does look strangely familiar.

'Occasionally, someone would say, 'Don't you think Sid Vicious reminds you of Simon Beverley?' I thought no more of it until after he died and the *Daily Mirror* ran a photo spread on him that included several schoolboy photographs. That's when we knew for definite that Sid Vicious was actually Simon Beverley.'

Plenty had happened since the nicely turned out 11-year-old with the graceful handwriting walked out the doors of Sandown Court for the last time in 1971. Just as Simon had – via John – become Sid, his looks too had altered almost beyond recognition. The sunken-cheeked, rat-faced Sid of '77 once stood out from the crowd by virtue of his 'small round face and slit eyes that made him look almost Chinese'. 'He was tall and thin, and had shortish, jet black hair that seemed to be tightly plastered onto his head with Brylcream, though I don't think it had,' remembers Colebrooke.

Being different came instinctively to Simon Beverley.

'I first met him at a party in 1974, probably a Hallowe'en do,' says Simone Stenfors, a striking GTO's-inspired proto-goth who later ended up moving in the same social circle as Vicious and Rotten. 'It was at my best friend Martin's house in Temple Fortune, near Golders Green. Everyone still had long hair then, but 'Sid' arrived and he looked like James Dean. His hair was short and swept back, he wore jeans and a T-shirt, had a studded wristband and, I seem to remember, a padlock around his neck. I'd gone dressed as a vamp, my boyfriend Chris [Carter, later in Throbbing Gristle] went as a Swedish au pair, but Sid simply went as himself. I was fascinated by him.'

Around the same time, a group of students at Kingsway College, situated towards the King's Cross end of Gray's Inn Road, barricaded themselves in the building to protest at their subsistence level grants. Mike Baess, an arts and languages student, set up a mobile disco and a crowd sat cross-legged eating sandwiches and smoking roll-ups.

'It was about eight at night,' Baess remembers, 'and there's this banging outside. I went to the door and there was this guy dressed head to toe in black. He asked, 'Is John there?' I'd seen John Lydon about the place but I didn't know that was who he meant. I invited him in and explained what, as students, we were trying to achieve.'

Baess sensed there was something different about the uninvited guest, who didn't formally enrol at Kingsway until the following summer. 'He was not one of us, not your friendly neighbourhood freak,' he says. 'Actually, he was not something I'd come across at all. He had black spikey hair at a time when the rest of us wore it shoulder-length. And there was menace there. Spikey John, which is what we all called him, looked like a cross between someone from Warhol's Factory and a Ted, interesting but slightly dangerous too. I suppose he looked kinda like a rock star . . .'

Inevitably, the 20-minute conversation over a shared joint soon turned to music. 'I was really into Hawkwind, so we talked about them and The Pink Fairies. He liked Roxy Music and Bowie, though I was really impressed when he started talking about Syd Barrett. He didn't look like the kind of guy who would. Then he said, 'Thanks mate', and went off to look for Lydon.'

Kingsway was an arts-based further education college where drugs were common and academic achievement a little less so. 'It was a trendy place where a lot of middle-class kids from Hampstead ended up,' says Baess. 'Kingsway was libertarian and full of long-hairs.'

Of the three Johns – Beverley, Lydon and Wardle – who attended the college, only Lydon, sporting the greasy, centre-parted Lemmy look, was a genuine long-hair. Not one of them was middle class. All understood libertarianism to be something that had to be fought for, not accomplished simply by dancing naked to The Grateful Dead.

'We were outsiders,' says Wobble, 'very dark but all intelligent working-class fellers who obviously weren't gonna go down the apprenticeship route.'

Instead, they went down the pub. The Bell, to be exact, just around the corner from the Sidmouth Street campus. 'It was a rough manor, definitely not posh,' Wobble remembers. 'The pub was full of Scotsmen in Celtic shirts who'd got to King's Cross but never made it any further.'

'The college was bang in the middle of a council estate,' says Mike Baess, 'and there would always be these hookers coming up and asking, 'Fancy action?' I was 17 and I was terrified.'

Ostensibly an A-level student of English Literature and Art, John Lydon's most vivid memory of his time at Kingsway was 'studying pints of ale'. When he enrolled for the 1975–76 academic year, John Beverley eschewed Oscar Wilde and Shakespeare's *Macbeth* for fine art and a course in basic photography.

Art and photography courses were the refuge of the imaginative, the idle or the out-and-out refusenik. John Beverley qualified on all three counts, though his imagination was almost exclusively applied to himself. Other students would take the college equipment off campus and seek out something unusual to shoot. The star of a few streets in north London would stay put and lovingly train the lens on himself.

One surviving shot from his Hackney College days shows the 16-year-old Beverley with an impressive 'Marc Bolan' curly perm. John Lydon reckoned it made him look like 'an old woman', though in truth, it was probably a better option than his own feather cut. However, posing artfully in profile, his arms stretched out theatrically, John Beverley looks every inch the clothes horse Lydon later said he was – a portrait of pride in his baggies and zip-up leather jacket, a ludicrously long white scarf hanging dramatically from his shoulders.

In another shot from the same session, Beverley fixes the camera's gaze with a maniacal look. It's eerily reminiscent of one of those oddly intrusive snaps of Syd Barrett during his post-breakdown period. The ghost-like effect of the teenager's near translucent skin against his mop of curly black hair and dark lips carries a heavy foreboding of white-out.

Once in a while, John Beverley would make an effort and wreak a little artistic havoc on his self portraits. His Bolan-permed, Bowie-posed still, for example, was washed over to create an on-stage effect, his stance artfully dispersed by a penetrating shaft of light. The result is John Beverley, Bowie nut, recast as the Cracked Actor.

Several examples of Sid's fine art work, watercolours and line drawings in a makeshift mix of paint, pencil, Biro or coloured pens, still exist. In fact, they command far higher prices than even his most obscure records do, though that is an endorsement of his celebrity status, not the quality of the work. One colour drawing from 1974 recently sold at auction for a very respectable £1,912.

'It's very adolescent, pretty poor art,' admits ex-Hornsey Art College student Henry Sabini, who was given the piece by John Beverley in the mid-'70s. 'I think it was all about our rivalry for the affection of this girl called Mandy,' he admits. 'John said, 'This is one of my works. Have it!' I unrolled it, looked at it and thought, Hmm, I've got to find something good to say about it. Oh, thanks!'

The 24'x18' illustration, executed in coloured pencils with what appears to be a watercolour wash over it, is a classic work of I'm-an-art-student-and-I've-just-discovered-Dali naivety. 'Sticks hold up decapitated limbs, and there's a statue with a bloated, elongated arm that's come to life,' says Sabini. 'It's total Dali.' He adds that the aspiring Surrealist left a book on the Catalonian painter round at Mandy's and never bothered to ask for it back.

There's a Bowie reference in the drawing too. The anchor tattoo that appears below one eye was almost certainly inspired by the 1972 promo film for David Bowie's 'John, I'm Only Dancing'. Most notable of all is the violence with which the outline of the head that dominates the drawing has been carved with a Biro. 'It goes right through the paper,' Sabini confirms.

'We talked a bit about art, and John said his tutors were all prats. He didn't see why it was necessary to learn life drawing. I told him that once you know how to draw properly, then you really can start playing around. He didn't want to do that step. I just wanna express myself! I don't want the middle part! I want the end result! He was totally indisciplined.'

So much so that at Kingsway, where he collected his grant but rarely bothered to turn up for classes, John Beverley was eventually referred to a college counsellor. 'He asked me if I wanted to go with him because it was a laugh,' Wobble recalls, 'so I did. I remember this man using the word 'movie' instead of 'pictures', and I thought, 'Cunt!' Then Sid – John and the others were already calling him Sid by the time I met him – said 'There's no point in films. I think all films are shit. Everything's shit.' Then the geezer asked me, and I immediately read the situation: how could we frustrate this poor man?'

The triumvirate of – in order of seniority – John Lydon, John Beverley and John Wardle soon won a reputation at the college. 'Lydon had the wit, Wardle the toughness and Spikey John was somewhere in between, but with a little less of either,' says Mike Baess.

John Lydon was far more impressed. 'He'd known Sid from Hackney College,' says Wobble. 'He told me, 'I've got this other mad mate, he really makes me laugh, you gotta meet him.' I met Sid and we began hanging out, though I never felt entirely happy hanging out with him, because you couldn't quite have the conversations you could with John. Sid was just one of these nutty geezers you knew.'

Naive and innocent, soft and feminine: that's how Lydon has always characterised student-era Sid, or 'Sidney', if he felt like extending the joke. Two misfit malcontents, down on the world but high on each other's tragicomic attitude to life, Lydon and Beverley resembled Turner and Chas in the 1970 cult film, *Performance* (a favourite of Lydon's, incidentally), endlessly dipping into each other's personalities until – years later – evolving into a Johnny Vicious blur. Sid regarded everything as 'a joke', Lydon remembered, and that had a liberating effect on the self-confessed 'sombre' long-hair. 'This is useful humour,' he admitted in his autobiography. 'I can use this.'

Still Lydon remained the less approachable of the two. 'He never wanted to be part of the college scene,' says Mike Baess. 'He was this guy with hennaed hair down past his tits, who wore an 'In Search Of Eddie Riff' badge. That was the title of a [1974] Andy MacKay solo album so I knew he liked Roxy Music. We'd nod, but it was obvious he had something else going on.' According to Lydon senior, that 'something else' was shutting himself away in his Finsbury Park bedroom '24 hours a day' listening to records.

Music was already a way of life for the teenage John Lydon. 'He changed completely,' his father reckoned, around the time of those marathon record-playing sessions. For 17-year-old John Beverley, visual panache was at least as important as music in expressing his superiority and disobedience. Lydon has used this as a stick with which to gently beat his mate. Sid was, he states in his autobiography, 'an absolute fashion victim' who'd rather follow than lead. The Hackney faddist might have had Lydon doubled-up in laughter, but Sid's slavish devotion to that 'Dave Bowie thing' irritated the hell out of his mate – especially those crude attempts to put himself through the gender blender. Wrong, wrong, wrong, Lydon complained. Gloss-painted toenails gleefully exhibited in open-toed sandals, hair shot though with red, Aladdin Sane-style streaks, teased skyward with talc and lashings of Vaseline, then 'baked' into place by shoving his head in the oven: the effeminate male just didn't make it in Lydon's man's man's world.

Some time in 1975, John Lydon went through his own stylistic metamorphosis. It had nothing to do with gender-busting, nor with what 'Dave' Bowie was wearing that particular week (probably a '40s-inspired American zoot suit), and yet everything to do with display. Having decided his hard won strawberry-blonde Lemmy look was passé, Lydon hacked off his long, straight locks. He'd first visited Smile, the Knightsbridge salon made fashionable by Roxy Music and used on occasion by him, and later John Wardle and John Beverley. But when he got home, he continued to chop at it. But that wasn't enough. After bleaching it, he rubbed some cheap blue dye into his ragamuffin rough cut, emerging, he said later, looking like a cabbage. His hippie hair was now hacked to pieces and snot green.

It's tempting to see this dramatic anti-fashion statement as an ironic dig at John Beverley's narcissism. If so, it got him more than he bargained for: Lydon's new screwed-up hairdo got him kicked out of his home, and at least as much attention as the dandy long-legs who prowled the streets beside him. This pair of proto-punk peacocks might have had quite different sartorial agendas, but they were now moving inexorably as one into uncharted visual territory. The new world order of Rotten and Vicious wasn't too far away.

THIS TOO is certain. The day Sid Vicious joined The Sex Pistols was the day that changed John Lydon's life.

'You now get this Johnny Vicious character, or Sid Rotten,' reckons bassist Glen Matlock, who was unceremoniously bumped out of the band by Johnny and replaced by Vicious. Matlock is still sore about his departure and you can't blame him. The Sex Pistols are in the history books, and though Matlock wrote several of the key songs and played a huge role in their glorious rise to infamy, he too – like old adversary Lydon – has fallen victim to the legend of Sid Vicious.

Although back in the fold ever since the band's mid-'90s return to the stage, Matlock isn't always regarded as a bona fide Pistol. 'There's always some idiot down the front with his "SID RIP" T-shirt standing right in front of me,' he says, with mild exasperation. 'One bloke was driving me mad at this gig last year [2003] in Milwaukee, so I took off my jacket, gave it to John's minder, and launched into the crowd with my bass. Management read me the riot act the next day. "You can't do that! You'll get sued for a million dollars."'

Initially, Matlock isn't keen to contribute to this book because, while he bears no ill will toward Sid, he still regards his replacement as 'the bane of my life.' For Sid erased Glen Matlock from the Pistols' story long before he began to diminish Rotten's role too. After a few days deliberation, Glen agrees to speak. He's the only Sex Pistol who contributes directly. Perhaps that makes him the nicest Sex Pistol. Perhaps that tells us why Rotten engineered his departure from the band.

There is a peace – of sorts – in The Sex Pistols' camp these days. There's an incredible amount of cash at stake each time they tour, so this quartet of middle-aged men, each with completely different lifestyles, need to get on, at least professionally. Inevitably, a bit of that Rotten/Vicious north London irony seems to have rubbed off on Glen Matlock. I suggest that the decision to replace him with Sid backfired badly on the band. 'Shame that, innit?' he deadpans back.

If Vicious continues to stalk Matlock in the guise of the occasional heckler who demands, 'Where the fuck's Sid?', on the Pistols' never-ending tour, then he must literally haunt John Lydon night and day. As much as this book concerns itself with the facts – fictions too – of Sid's life and times, his death and his afterlife, it's necessarily the story of 'Johnny Vicious' too. For Johnny and Vicious were the Laurel and Hardy of the Hate Generation, terror twins who, despite the fact that half of the double-act is long gone, remain hopelessly entwined. The tragicomic pantomime routine that Lydon developed during the early '80s, and has evolved over the years, is – in public at least – as much Johnny Vicious as John Lydon.

'John realised that Sid was going to be the one who would live on in the way that Marilyn Monroe, James Dean and Ché Guevera do,' insists Alan Jones. 'It might be wrong, but when you think of punk, you don't think of John Lydon. You think of Sid Vicious.'

Past their prime before he'd even joined the band, The Sex Pistols are in some ways now part of The Rise And Fall Of Sid Vicious story. Sid barely played a note on the records, and yet his legend has forced punk's map of meaning to be redrawn. Lydon has taken this on board as much as anyone, dropping his pioneer veneer and adopting some of Sid's more comic book characteristics. Whether he's done this for his own amusement or by some unconscious drive is not clear. Certainly, despite the public shrugging of the shoulders, Sid's death – followed soon after by the death of his mother – left a deeper impact on Lydon than he ever let on.

John Beverley and John Lydon spent many formative mid-teen months together, teasing, mock-fighting and, more important still, nurturing and feeding off each other's idiosyncrasies. It would not be overstating the case to suggest that each was furtively in awe of the other. Reunited once more in The Sex Pistols, and with the heart and soul of punk rock at stake, the pair's tolerance of each other was severely tested. Their profound personality differences grotesquely magnified, and power struggles – Nancy screaming this, McLaren whispering that – raging all around them, they ended up becoming bitter foes. Their last encounter ended with Sid nursing a wound from a blunt instrument, possibly an axe. That healed, but the barely concealed contempt that existed between the pair never did.

Such is the hatred John Lydon has for the myth of the young corpse that one cannot help but wonder whether he protests too much. It is a hoary old myth, as clichéd as a Status Quo riff, but it endures just the same. And it will continue to do so, because as long as the West continues to revere youth and worship the hurried footsteps of escape, there'll always be flowers at the tombs of young martyrs.

In his autobiography, Lydon wraps up his explanation of the fast-track rock 'n' roll cadaver in the dumb seduction of 'fucked up' drug chic. He cannot help but view the procession of stilled bodies in terms of power, condemning those who play Russian roulette with their lives for having lived 'a lie'. Now I don't know whether the life of Sid Vicious was any more a lie than John Lydon's, or Johnny Vicious', for that matter. But I do suspect that Lydon slapped a self-preservation order on himself, some time during his teens, and probably around the same time that John Beverley opened his EXIT doors in case of emergency.

Sid was hypnotised by fantasies of his own death. 'I'll probably die by the time I reach 25,' he told the *Daily Mirror*'s Jack Lewis soon after joining the Pistols, 'but I'll have lived the way I wanted to.' He'd often boldly announce his imminent demise, as if he was the creator and his body the canvas. Twenty-one and I'm off, Sid would say. Few took him seriously. It was punk to live for the moment and fuck the consequences. Punk to trumpet youth and hate the aged. Punk to fixate on the hell of living and the liberating effects of dying. Even without punk's down-at-mouth motivation, it was hardly news that teenagers locked in their own narcissism and melancholy tend to fixate on grand, deathly delusions.

It's hardly inappropriate – or difficult – to summon up an image of Sid reading a report of his own death and laughing uncontrollably. Everything was hilariously funny to him, from run-of-the-mill personal misfortune to the genocidal death camps of Nazi Germany. It would be naive to expect a young man who cared little for himself to treat the misfortune of others, or the world's wounds, with anything other than black humour. That I'M A MESS badge pinned to his leather lapel during the Pistols' January 1978 US tour was not worn for effect but with perverse pride. Punk by its very nature embraced mess, though not everyone took that to mean switching off the self-preservation completely. Not like Sid.

It wasn't punk to grieve for Sid. There was another reason, too, that tears were slow to fall. While Glen Matlock and Alan Jones still saw flashes of that loony-but-likeable Sid as late as summer 1978, to almost everyone else the junked-up Nancy's boy he became soon after joining the Pistols had turned into a complete pain in the arse. In thrall to a woman despised by almost everyone, and addicted to a drug that virtually erased his redeeming qualities, Sid had mutated into a whining, repetitive nursery rhyme of neediness.

For the last 12 months of his life, Sid was about as popular as a leper at a spin-the-bottle party. Hearts sank at the prospect of a visit, or even a phone call. 'What about Useless?' 'What about him?' came the reply. No one cared. It's surprising, then, that Malcolm McLaren, the man most often accused of neglecting Sid during his final free fall into oblivion, has been fairly consistent in his posthumous praise for Vicious. However, that probably says as much about the parlous state of his relationship with Lydon as it does about his admiration for Vicious. Vivienne Westwood, who'd once singled out Sid as the personification of punk rock, has been less charitable as she continues to enamel her punk past. Most telling of all has been John Lydon's response, which has fluctuated wildly since 1979, and his initial nothing-to-say reaction.

Alan Jones, who enjoyed the company of both Rotten and Vicious, is not alone when he says that Lydon has 'reshaped history', that 'what he says about Sid . . . is unbelievably awful.' But Lydon's never been one for the meaningless platitude. His talent, which Sid had a great admiration for, is in the one-line put down. That was him asking, 'What about Useless?' as the Pistols fell apart in San Francisco. And when someone dared to suggest that the Pistols couldn't reform without Sid at the 100 Club press conference in 1996, his 'Sid was a coat hanger' retort was quickly beamed around the world. No one noticed the ghost of Sid Vicious chuckling away in the corner.

Anne Beverley certainly didn't spot him. 'Here [Lydon] is, doing a 'Rotten', giving the punters just what they wanted,' she complained. 'If his love of all those around him is so deep, where was he for his so-called best mate?' Or she for that matter. The truth was that neither Anne, nor McLaren, nor his best mate could ever get close to finding the hotline to her son's better nature. There simply was no magic cure that might have helped protect Sid from himself.

John Lydon's autobiography deliberately – and legitimately – refused to bow to a single viewpoint. However, he was unequivocal when it came to admitting that the death of his friend did not leave him without guilt. 'I could have helped Sid more,' he concluded. Admitting that he'd washed his hands of him 'like Pontius Pilate', he confessed that this was something he'd 'have to carry to the grave'.

In remembrance of things past, Lydon rarely allows old battle wounds to heal. Sid's inability to keep himself alive remains a huge disappointment to him. So does the rash of identikit, Pistols-inspired bands that soon reduced punk to a series of clichés. Today, Lydon can at least reflect on his old pal's basic failings with a degree of humanity, something that was in short supply back in 1979.

'I feel nothing but grief, sorrow and sadness for Sid,' he told director Julian Temple for his Sex Pistols documentary, *The Filth And The Fury* (1999). Twenty years had passed, and those suppressed feelings were fast coming back. 'I've lost my friend,' he continued. 'I couldn't have changed it. I was young. God, I wish I was smarter . . . He's dead, for fuck's sake.'

Bitterness, though, is rarely far away. As Lydon composes himself, his thoughts twist to those [presumably Malcolm McLaren and Virgin Records] who turned Sid's death into a licence to print money. 'Ha ha ha ha. How hilarious for them. Fucking cheek. I'll hate them for ever for doing that.'

Shot in shadow, like some master criminal under anonymous interrogation, Lydon is visibly moved by the moment, his voice croaking under the strain, a hand wiping his eye. 'You can't get more evil than that, can you, Julian. Really you know . . . No respect. Vicious: poor sod.'

Tears have always been a scarce commodity in the tough love world of punk rock. You would have imagined that anyone answering to the name Vicious would rather rip out his own heart than be caught blubbing into a handkerchief. Not so: his emotional waters were prone to breaking more often than most of his contemporaries'. Heartbreakers manager Leee Black Childers stumbled across a strangely lachrymose Sid in the most unlikely of settings.

It was Christmas Day 1976 and various London and New York punk luminaries had been invited to the house in Chesterton Road, Ladbroke Grove, where *Sounds* journalist Jonh Ingham had a room. Hearing the unlikely sound of Jim Reeves' 1960 hit, 'He'll Have To Go', wafting down the stairs, a homesick Childers followed the music until he found 'this little guy, just sitting there crying'. The record stopped, the tears dried up, and the 'little guy' turned and said, 'Hi, I'm Sid Vicious.'

Today, it's 25 years since Sid's passing. It is not a time for tears. Sid Vicious is fashionable again, his anniversary a cause for celebration in the music press. Meanwhile, Johnny Vicious is still very much alive and well and laughing all the way to the bank. The Pistols continue their series of filthily lucrative concert tours despite their uncertain effect on the band's reputation. Quite brilliant in 1996, a little under-rehearsed and more circus-like of late, the reformed Pistols have been tampering with their own mythology. Meanwhile, the legend of Sid, forever in leather and lamp-stand thin, receives a surprise boost in the celebrity stiff stakes. All weird . . .

'Sid's now the James Dean,' says Jonh Ingham, who interviewed the pre-fame Vicious back in autumn 1976. Ingham finds it 'really odd that the one with the least talent has become the figurehead', but he understands why. 'Sid's an easy archetype to grasp. He satisfies that journalistic urge to come up with an easy answer, a soundbite that means you don't have to get into the complexity of what it's all about.'

Johnny = complex
Vicious = cartoon

Complex Johnny Rotten was the critics' favourite because, like Jonh Ingham, they knew he was smart, a mesmerising and convincing orator, one genuine motherfucker of invention. When, as John Lydon, he formed Public Image Limited (PiL) after the Pistols split, Johnny made music every bit as groundbreaking as the mavericks that had helped him through his difficult mid-teens. Whereas since 1976, while countless acts have borrowed from the Pistols' template, there's not been anything quite like PiL's Metal Box because that was music made with brains and innovation as well as raw instinct.

Johnny had brains and that made him the thinking-person's punk. Vicious had brains too but he became the poor man's punk. He had brains but was too punk to let on. Neither was he as sharp-witted or as acerbic as Rotten. Or original. While his fearlessness made him a danger to others as much as himself,

Sid was nowhere near as intimidating as Rotten – as Jonh Ingham discovered when he managed to pin the Pistols down for one of their first major interviews.

'It was spring 1976, and we were in a pub,' he says. 'John arrived late and he just sat there, about 15 feet away, looking bored. The odd thing was that the others continued to talk about him as though he wasn't there. But when he finally opened his mouth there was this torrent of invective about all the things he hated. There was a real intensity to him that nobody else had.'

At one moment an isolated, peripheral figure, the proverbial spare prick at a wedding, the next Rotten would be holding court, in total charismatic control. 'I could say that he was the eye of the hurricane,' says Ingham, 'but in so many ways he was the hurricane.'

He was. Well, at least until he hit on the brilliant idea of bringing his mate into the band. From the moment Sid joined, officially on 3 March 1977, the full impact of Hurricane Rotten began to recede. Punk's agenda was increasingly set by the tabloids. The Pistols had a thousand rivals snapping at their heels. And, no longer the sole focus of the movement, Rotten had a battle on his hands to remain the main focus in the band.

5. IN A BROKEN DREAM

'There wasn't a father figure in Sid's life, so he's looking to see who's the strongest, looking to make a connection. At the same time he's afraid to put a hand out for fear of rejection. So you take the piss. You learn not to show yourself as vulnerable in any way.' – Jah Wobble

IN APRIL 1976, John Lydon, steadily gaining infamy as Johnny Rotten, frontman of the 'so bad they're great' Sex Pistols, interrupted an interview with *Sounds'* Jonh Ingham to declare: 'I hate hippies.' Rotten's quip made a fabulous pull-quote, and served to emphasise the Pistols' rude, antagonistic iconoclasm. In truth, by the mid-1970s a genuine hippie was about as easy to find as Lord Lucan . Love, peace and '60s pop protest had gone the way of the discredited banana-skin high. Now everyone from prominent classical musicians to National Front activists wore their hair long. Hippie had all gone to pot.

The wide-eyed acid trippers of the psychedelic era had been supplanted by a more sober, socially detached subculture sustained by dope, denim and Pink Floyd's bedroom symphony, *The Dark Side Of The Moon*. Once in a while, they'd venture out and congregate in a field in Reading or Windsor, nod out to the sound of Wishbone Ash or Robin Trower (both at Reading Festival '75, which John Lydon attended), then stay up half the night yelling 'Wally!' at each other. More typically, they'd float aimlessly from freak-friendly pub to concert hall, squat to clap clinic, to a soundtrack of Bad Company's 'Can't Get Enough Of Your Love' and Lynyrd Skynyrd's 'Free Bird'. The patchouli-scented vibe of

'67 had grown stale long before punk pissed all over the final, flickering stick of incense.

One evening in February 1975, a typical mix of acid casualties, greasers and curious students congregated on the Roundhouse in Chalk Farm. Hawkwind and the reformed (yet again) Pink Fairies, veterans of the late '60s Ladbroke Grove freak scene, were the night trippers. Both bands were regarded as hippie-era relics, still actively advocating free love and a libertarian attitude towards drug use, but they were conspicuously devoid of the fragrant niceties of flower power. Ladbroke Grove '75 was hardly Haight Ashbury '67, nor were Hawkwind's Lemmy or the Fairies' Larry Wallis likely doves of Love Generation serenity.

'Hawkwind had this reputation as a peace and love band,' says sometime lyricist Michael Moorcock, 'but none of the lyrics were like that at all. It was urban stuff that could have been written ten or twenty years later. I don't see a great deal of difference between that and what the punk people were doing. It was just the same, really, with different haircuts.' Plus the fact that the average length Hawkwind 'sonic attack' went on for at least eight minutes.

Hawkwind's calling card was an unrelenting acid rock mindfuck, built around two- or three-chord riffs and embellished with space-age oscillations and wailing wah-wah sax. Despite the commune-dwelling vibe, Hawkwind's message was underpinned by misanthropy ('We Took The Wrong Step Years Ago', 'Time We Left This World Today'). A rare stab at more earthly social comment, 1973's 'Urban Guerilla', was subject to a BBC ban – prompting the band to mythologise themselves as warriors on the edge of time.

The Pink Fairies were rowdier still, self-styled 'Kings Of Oblivion' with the beat of the street at their dirt-encrusted fingertips. Songs such as 'City Kids', 'Street Urchin', the fearsome 'The Snake' and their infamous call to action, 'Do It', were designed to mug, rather than soothe, the ears.

The Roundhouse double-header was a classic stoner's show. In the audience were two practising drug fiends, Mike Baess and his new pal Spikey John. 'The Pink Fairies were very druggy,' Baess remembers. 'That night, they brought a 20-foot spliff out on stage, and a huge cut-out white pill with MX written on it.' 'MX' referred to Mandrax, a popular barbiturate that cast a sedative shadow over the slumbering '70s. Another of Sid's associates from this time was 'Mandy Pete', so-called by virtue of the generous supply of 'Mandies' he'd liberate from his mother's medicine cabinet.

John Beverley was no stranger to drugs. His mother Anne had long forsaken her casual, beatnik-era dalliance with soft drugs for a heroin habit. 'John [Lydon] and I were round's Sid's place in Queensbridge Road, Hackney,' says Wobble, 'and Sid's there with his mum and they're both using needles. I'm 16, and that's the first time I see someone using needles. I think Sid was banging up speed.'

By the mid-'70s, drugs were no longer predominantly the province of artists, students and counterculture radicals. Anne Beverley and her son certainly weren't living in a cutesy psychedelic palace, cluttered with Victoriana and Eastern relics, where an Ormsby-Gore or a scion of the Guinness family might pop round for lentil bake. 'This was in a tower block, very alienating,' says Wobble. 'It's an overwhelming feeling. You're in this fucking ugly Modernist building, detached from Mother Earth, and you're using needles.'

Queensbridge Road was one of several flats Anne and John inhabited during the '70s thanks to Anne's inability to keep up with the bills. It was hardly the most hospitable of places to call home. 'You get a certain vibe around drugs,' adds Wobble. 'It's different to booze, which is more manic, like, anything can happen in this house. With drugs, with the smack, you can sense darkness. I don't just mean literally, though it wasn't a bright flat. It was metaphorically dark.'

Another of the Johns, John Gray, had a similar experience when he visited Sid's home, a barren place that had a Dansette record player, a pile of Miles Davis albums and virtually no furniture. Despite the poor light, Gray's eyesight did not fail him the day he watched Sid sterilise an old-fashioned metal syringe in a saucepan of boiling water, before fixing himself up with amphetamine sulphate, or 'speed'. 'It's me mum's,' he explained, with little fuss.

John Lydon's memories of Anne Beverley are as 'an oddball hippie' who cooked quiche and devilled kidneys. Anne herself admitted that she was 'quite the hippie', her habit of wandering around the flat naked after taking a bath prompting 'impromptu' visits from her son's friends on wash days.

Both emotionally and materially, there was plenty missing from John Beverley's home life, though the absence of discipline provided some compensation. If 'Sime' didn't feel like school, Anne would always understand. If he wanted to dye his hair, she would be there to help him. 'I didn't mind what he looked like,' she said years later. Anne's philosophy, as she explained it to *Sid's Way* author Alan Parker, was simple: 'You should be able to do what the fuck you like. Just don't hurt anybody else.'

These easily gained freedoms did little to calm the restless John Beverley, who'd never really found peace at home after returning to London from Tunbridge Wells in 1971. He'd moved out briefly at 15, after a short, unhappy spell at Clissold Park School in Hackney. Taking a job as a trainee cutter at Simpson's, a local factory notable for producing Daks trousers, John's inability to apply himself to the industrial cutting machine soon won him a 'Frank Spencer'-style badge of incompetence, a reputation he of course wore with perverse pride. But what amused his colleagues infuriated his superiors, so when a further batch of Beverley-supervised pockets came out the size of a postage stamp, he was sacked.

Although he'd return sporadically over the next two years, even when he was at the height of his fame with the Pistols, John Beverley had left home in earnest by summer 1975. His mother wasn't duly concerned, as she later admitted to Alan Parker: '[I said] it's either you or me, and it's not going to be me, so you can just fuck off . . . I don't care if you have to sleep on a fucking park bench.' 'Sime' fared at least a little better than that, ending up sharing floor space in a room in New Court, a notoriously grim block of flats tucked behind the tube station in Hampstead.

'Hampstead was a desirable address,' says Clash roadie-turned-writer Johnny Green, who lived in one of New Court's two intimidating blocks in the late '70s. 'But New Court, which was two sets of steps up from Flask Walk, was the service block where the fucking servants lived all those years ago.' Green, in common with virtually everyone who has ever set foot in the place, has New Court's strange, oppressive aura imprinted on his memory.

According to Mike Baess, a frequent visitor throughout 1975 and '76, New Court 'was a bizarre place, like something out of Dickens' time. The blocks had these huge 50-foot high chimney stacks and looked like workhouses. Yet up the alley and round the corner was Heath Street, where all the posh boutiques are.'

The grim, Dickensian aspect of New Court chimes neatly with the mythology that surrounds The Sex Pistols. This is where Sid and John shared their infamous squat, where the pair grew to hate 'hippies', and of course where Lydon wrote the lyrics to 'No Future' (later retitled 'God Save The Queen'). But the hellhole of Hampstead wasn't necessarily the dump it's been cracked up to be.

'The flat was on the ground floor in the block on the left-hand side as you come out of Flask Walk,' remembers 'Mandy Pete', then a 19-year-old Mandrax-popping teacher (and only part-reformed Borstal boy). 'But it wasn't a squat. It was leased by the Housing Association to a woman named Barbara, who was in her early 30s. When I moved in during summer '75, Spikey John as we called him was already living there.' Mandy Pete spent the summer months bedded down on the spare-room floor next to John Beverley.

'Barbara, who had a five- or six-year-old daughter Zoe, was the matriarch of the place,' Pete adds. 'She didn't really do drugs, and though she was kind of a festival type, there were no hippie decorations. The flat was very plain and tidy. The carpets were clean and Barbara always washed up.' She also neglected to charge the boys rent. 'She was very much the motherly type, a very calming influence, and John had a great respect for her. Maybe that was his attraction to her. He seemed the kind of guy who needed a mother about.'

To Mandy Pete, his new roommate resembled 'a young Ted with brothel creepers . . . quite brash, somebody with a bit of attitude. His hair was very Bowieish, without the long [mullet] at the back and more sharply spiked on top. It was jet black and spikey against his really pale skin. John was a peacock and he knew it.' Which is probably why he fretted so much over his acne, the only blight on his otherwise impeccable façade.

Despite a clash of attitudes ('We didn't bond at all,' Pete says. 'I was a free festival person and he probably would have spat at me if we'd have met anywhere else.'), the pair shared a mutual passion for music and drug-taking. 'We all did a lot of speed together,' he admits. 'We had parties where we'd stay up for days listening to music, smoking joints, snorting sulphate and doing Mandies. We were careless, didn't give a shit, though we weren't so much seeking oblivion as simply having a good time. As far as I know, John didn't shoot up in those days, though he did a bit of dealing. Everybody did, though you wouldn't think of it as dealing. It was a community thing, helping mates out and making a little bit on top.'

With scarcely more than a change of clothes with him ('I can't remember him washing,' Pete says), Spikey John had to rely on the musical tastes of Mandy Pete, as well as those of frequent visitors such as Mike Baess and Steve England. 'The only time I got close to him was when we were listening to music, though that was more about sharing an atmosphere than verbal exchanges. He was really into Stanley Clarke, the jazz bassist, and I found that extremely surprising. His music was clean, intellectual and very intense. It was also the time of Roxy Music's *Siren* and 'Love Is The Drug', both of which were very bass orientated.' Whether this had any bearing on his future musical pysche can only be a matter of wild speculation.

While a revolving door of pals would drop by the New Court hangout to get high with Mandy Pete, no one ever came round for Spikey John. 'He'd always go out to meet them,' Pete recalls, 'though I never really worked out where he'd go.'

One of Spikey John's key meeting places was the midweek Bowie Night at Crackers, at the Oxford Street end of Wardour Steet. (The venue later turned into popular punk hangout, the Vortex.) 'It was mainly full of Bowie clones and soul boys,' remembers art student turned aspiring musician Henry Sabini. Many Crackers regulars – Siouxsie Sioux, Steven Severin, Kenny Morris, Gary Webb (later Numan) and Mick Jones (London SS, later The Clash) – became active during the punk era. 'The night I met John, as I knew him then, he was with John Lydon.'

Sabini often came across the two Johns at the family home of a mutual friend named Mandy in Eade Road, close to Manor House underground station. 'We'd go out drinking, then take various substances back at Mandy's house,' he says. 'Her parents were divorced and seeing new partners, so we'd often have the place the whole weekend. We'd play loud music and get stoned.'

There was dancing, too. 'John [Beverley] would get totally out of it and do this very strange dance that only he could do. He got a lot of abuse from Lydon for that. Lydon would call him a hippie.'

The Johns were already fashioning their proto-punk look. 'Lydon had the spikey hair first,' Sabini remembers. 'It was gnarled, bleached and streaky, and sticking out all over the place. "Sid" had the Bowie hairdo, sticking up with long bits down the side, and a Teddy Boy quiff at the front.' He'd also had a go at the Crazy Color. 'It was blue and red, but it looked awful 'cos he got it all round his scalp. Mandy was a professional hairdresser, and she'd say, "Why don't you come down and we'll get it done properly." He'd say, "No, that's how I like it."'

John Beverley 'couldn't help but stand out because he was naturally freaky,' Sabini continues. Even without the hair or the outfits. 'He had an awkward way of carrying himself, slightly stooped, which I think was a result of him being so gangly and thin. And his acne was really bad. It used to look purple at times. He'd get depressed when it flared up. I mean, he was a peacock. His appearance meant an awful lot to him.

'I didn't think there was much to him. He seemed nice enough, though I thought he was pretty shallow. And there was something a bit dangerous about him. You never knew when he was telling the truth.'

Cultivating a powerful exterior of sartorial sharpness didn't fool all of John Beverley's teenage contemporaries. 'He wanted to be seen as somebody who was really tough,' reckons Mandy Pete, 'that he had no weak points whatsoever. Yet I still picture him as a big softie. You could tell that he was quite vulnerable, someone with a soft centre, even though he'd always put on this show of bravado.'

'John desperately wanted to belong, to be in a gang,' insists Henry Sabini. 'I suppose he really wanted to be loved. He seemed childlike, vulnerable, and easily influenced.' And often, the butt of the joke. Sabini reckons 'his appearance probably had a lot to do with that.' To boost his frail, attention-seeking ego, John Beverley always seemed to have a dramatic story about himself. 'He was always getting chased or beaten up, but I'm sure at least half of it was pure fantasy. I dunno, maybe it *was* true . . .'

Days before I interviewed him, Henry Sabini chanced upon an episode of *I'm A Celebrity . . . Get Me Out Of Here*. Marooned in the Australian jungle with a motley crew of TV notables, and miles from his reggae records and his wife of 25 years, Nora, John Lydon still dominated the show. 'I thought, he's exactly the same as he used to be. He's not changed one bit! Lydon always did seem quite worldly, as if he was clued up on everything.' Sabini cannot say the same for the teenage John Beverley.

'Lydon was obviously the boss,' he continues, 'and John [Beverley] was one of his followers to the extent of it being embarrassingly fawning. John was already very much what he wanted to be: powerful, confident, arrogant.' John Beverley did his best to keep up. 'Part of him actually wanted to be intellectually sharp, and part wanted to be a big thick thug who could handle himself. When I first knew him, he did aspire to become an intellectual, but it didn't last long. John Lydon told him he was being a pretentious prat, so he used to put all the learning down. But he knew what was going on.'

About the genius of The New York Dolls, or the wrongs of Bryan Ferry's new US GI look, perhaps. But when it came to the heated discussions Sabini and Lydon would have about politics, Sid wasn't interested. 'We'd have passionate rows about the marches, the strikes, [Prime Minister] Jim Callaghan,' Sabini says. 'Lydon would spout his anarchist views ('Marching's for wankers!'), I always took a strong left-wing socialist viewpoint, but John [Beverley] had no take on any of it at all. It was all way beyond his existence.'

When it came to serious talk, John Beverley almost always preferred the company of women. 'Women instinctively understood that he needed mothering,' reckons Mike Baess who, like Don Letts, became aware that Beverley was spending rather a lot of time with his partner. 'I'd started going out with this stunning girl, Carole, who we'd both met at the Hawkwind/Pink Fairies gig. He liked her too though only as a companion.' Really? 'Yes, I don't think he knew how to ask a girl out, how to romance a girl. Carole found him amusing because he was so different to everybody else, but there was no romance there. He looked like he was not looking after himself, and that's what brought out the maternal instinct in women.'

Henry Sabini found himself in a remarkably similar situation. 'To be honest, I wasn't always pleased to see him. He could be a pain in the arse. The bell at Mandy's would ring, you'd look through the glazed door and your heart sank: Oh, fucking hell, it's Sid! You knew he'd be out of it, have loads of drugs on him, and was gonna spend all evening huddled up to Mandy. He used to confide in her a lot.'

One evening, the bell rang, the hearts plunged collectively, and John Beverley walked straight into the sitting room where he collapsed into Mandy's comforting arms. 'He was in tears about something – I seem to recall that he was being chased – and totally out of it. He'd often turn up in a state, and she'd always have to sort him out.'

This was a side he dared not reveal to his peer group, The Johns. 'I never saw him genuinely vulnerable,' says Wobble, who had already begun to notice the incipient close-down, detached junkie vibe about his mate. 'If he did show vulnerability, a large part of it would have been play-acting.'

Wobble has a tale to back this up, which also gives a flavour of the gallows humour Sid was famous for. 'When Sid was in the squats, it wasn't unusual for him to phone up and claim he was in a bad way. One day, he got some girl to call, and she told me that he'd overdosed and had died. That was a very good performance! The funny thing was, I didn't know what to say. A day or two later, he comes on the phone and says, 'Yeah, I had ya! I set the whole thing up.' I was laughing too. I said, 'You know what? After she told me, I went back to watching the telly!' '

Back then, it never occurred to Wobble that his mate might have been lonely. Neither did he question why Sid never had a partner. 'With some geezers you automatically think, 'He hasn't got a girlfriend', but not with Sid. I had a girlfriend, and all I remember was there being this slight gooseberry vibe: 'Sid, fuck off, go away now . . .' Looking back, I think he was lonely. But then, we're human beings. It's not that different to a lot of fellers.'

'Some of us used to think he was gay because he never showed much interest in women,' says Henry Sabini. 'The guys used to say, 'He's bent', because as far as we knew, he never made any advances on Mandy or any other woman. He actually had a very feminine side to him. He liked to talk to girls, but never did I see him take it further with any woman. We thought he wasn't interested.'

'He was never into sex,' insists Mike Baess. 'In the two years I knew him, I never once saw him lust after women. He might have liked my girlfriend but there was never any hint of sex or, 'Cor, look at the tits on that!' He never had any feelings for women in the obvious way. When you think about the music that he liked – Bowie, Roxy Music, The Velvet Underground and Lou Reed – there's a very feminine side to all that stuff.'

Later, when he'd become Vicious, Sid would claim that he'd briefly been a rent boy, even going as far as signing photos of himself with the phrase, 'I'm Hymie, try me'. (The teenage Marc Bolan, similarly style obsessed and from the streets of nearby Stoke Newington, had made similar, more substantiated claims.) Though there was a private John Beverley that few ever got a sniff at, there is no evidence that this particular fantasy was in any way fulfilled. The nearest Sid came to renting his body out was when he enjoyed a brief stint as a model for students at St Martin's College of Art.

'He used to ask me about being gay,' says Alan Jones. 'I'm sure I could have had sex with Sid if I'd seriously wanted to. He seemed to be one of those 'I'll do it to see what it's like' people, the friend to whom you could say, 'Stick your hand in the fire' and he would. Honestly, he would do anything. There were so many times when I saw that in action.'

Mike Baess cannot hear Sid's reinterpretation of 'My Way' – with its intriguing 'I'm not a queer' declaration – without thinking of the conspicuous absence of any obvious sexuality about his mate. Or the supposedly 'Vicious' reputation that had grown way out of hand. 'I do wonder,' he says, 'whether all that anger may have been due to suppressed homosexual feelings. There's obviously a lot of self-loathing there, a recognition of something in himself that he didn't like very much, which manifested itself in beating people up, chucking glasses and whipping his chain out.' Sid would hardly be the first teenage male to utilise a violent machismo as a disguise for sexual uncertainty.

To Caroline Coon, this issue has as much to do with masculinity as it does homosexuality. 'There is this mistake in thinking that the only way to be masculine is to be hard and brittle and unbending. That's a very partial idea of what masculinity is, especially when you're young and both your identity and your sexuality are fluid. That's why Sid had such a difficult time in the punk rock environment.'

This confusion over identity and role play invariably spilled over into the Lydon/Beverley relationship. In autumn 1975, by which time Lydon was already rehearsing with The Sex Pistols, the rookie frontman was already 19, his apprentice a year younger. 'John definitely had this slightly older brother vibe,' says Wobble. John Beverley would have 'brought out a paternal side in Johnny', reckons Mike Baess, who saw that the troubled youth increasingly becoming known as Sid was 'someone who needed looking after'.

Although his patience was severely tested later on, Lydon's loyalty to The Johns – his first, formative pack with whom he emerged to take on the world – has, if anything, grown over the years. There can be no greater accolade from Lydon than when, at the climax of *The Filth And The Fury*, he readmits Sid as 'one of The Johns. I care about every single one of The Johns,' he says emphatically.

Back in the mid-'70s, The Johns presented a formidable collective front. Even today, mention of 'The Johns' can still induce a nervous tic or two. So why was it that the daftest, and in many ways the most immediately likeable of The Johns ended up with all the battle scars?

'I think he was trying to impress Lydon, by pretending to be as hard as him,' says Steven Severin. 'And he clearly wasn't. There were real hard cases around Lydon, the real thing, and Sid needed to live up to those kind of people. That's why he'd get himself in those scrapes and situations, but I don't think it was really him.'

'They were an odd crowd that lot,' remembers Subway Sect's Rob Simmons. 'Rotten and his mates The Johns were more threatening than the rest. They were like the nasty kids in the school who got the cane. I remember Sid being slightly apart from them. You'd often see him on his own. He wasn't a big, hard-nut type.'

'Nearly all of us were having brushes with the law around that time,' Wobble admits, 'being in stolen vehicles, assault, affray, drugs. We weren't villains. We weren't going out with pick-axe handles to beat up other tough guys, not unless they were trying to bring it into your backyard. But you learn not to let people take liberties. It was a hard environment, and that encourages people like Sid. You learn not to show vulnerability.'

Henry Sabini noticed there was 'a lot of sadness' about Sid. 'People would talk about him and say, 'What is the matter with him?' That destructive streak was definitely there by this time. That 'I couldn't give a shit about anything' vibe. Lydon was fascinated by this. I mean, he indulged and everything, but he still stayed in control. Sid didn't.'

What Sid did possess was the instinct, and the necessary absence of self-regard, to emerge as the rogueish clan's clown prince of chaos. 'He was regarded as a bit of a loon,' Sabini remembers. 'He'd do anything to please. And he would get out of it more than the others. He used to get really, completely and utterly out of it – and as quickly as he could.'

While some people are able to use drink and drugs as a pleasant and temporary distraction, Sid's consumption was motivated, in a large part, by the promise of obliteration. 'It wasn't about the pleasure in the process,' says Sabini. 'It was all about getting to the end, to the point where he was completely gone.'

A user through need as much as social convention, Sid would experience more dramatic – and seductive – changes in personality when under the influence. Sid's tough guy within was always more convincing once his fractured psyche had been patched up with drink or drugs. While one or two of The Johns might defend their patch or their honour at the flimsiest of prompts, the vicious, mad-eyed and dangerous part of Sid tended to require a little kick to stir the moral gravy in his head into physical action. As his consumption grew, so too did the frequency of Sid's 'psychotic reactions'.

This tendency to lash out had been there from his early teens, ever since that incident over the Manchester United football scarf, and perhaps earlier still. A genuine warning sign came on 27 May 1974 when, shortly after his 17th birthday, the Hackney College student was charged and found guilty of assaulting two police officers and damaging two windows at Stoke Newington police station after a party.

The police had been called to a house in Coronation Avenue, after reports of a disturbance, and arrived to find John Beverley 'shouting at the top of his voice and appear[ing] to be berserk'. Attempting to restrain him, one PC Pollard was kicked in the face and had a tooth broken. The defendant needed stitches after his shoulder went through a glass door panel back at the station. According to Pollard's statement in court, the defendant 'was very drunk at the time and had gone berserk. He seems to think that someone put methylated spirit in his drink while at the party' – an assertion he duly verified: 'I did notice that the defendant's breath smelt of methylated spirit.'

Sid seized on the king-making effects of cheaply procured drugs and alcohol, and rejoiced in the escapist subculture that surrounded it. 'He used to come round and make out that he knew dealers, and that's how he got his stuff,' says Henry Sabini, 'but we assumed most of it had come from his mum. God only knows what those strange little pills were. They were bloody awful things that made you feel great for a while, but brought you down terribly the next morning.'

'He was always on the ponce,' adds Mike Baess. 'He never had any money, so you'd always find him hanging around to cadge a smoke and nicking dinners from the college canteen. I rarely saw him pay for anything. One afternoon, he asked me to come back to his place, have a smoke and listen to some records, and when we got to the tube at King's Cross, he simply jumped over the barrier, stuck his fingers up at the ticket man and legged it. That was completely normal for Sid.'

Sid's petty criminality also proved useful in more glamorous scenarios. In mid-October 1975, Roxy Music were back in London for two nights at the Empire Pool, Wembley, to promote their new album, *Siren*. 'I met Sid at Finchley Road, and we took the tube together despite not having tickets,' Baess remembers. 'The gig was sold out, and the band were already on stage. I pushed the doors, which weren't reinforced in those days, Sid crept his hand in to lift up the catch on the metal bar, and we were in. I lost Sid immediately because he ran down the front.'

Much has been made of the teenage John Beverley's style-fixated passion for David Bowie. Roxy Music, who, in Bryan Ferry and Brian Eno, featured two spaced-out oddities for the price of one – also occupied a powerful place in the Beverley imagination. And it was Roxy Music that unknowingly gave John Beverley his first whiff of media stardom.

Arriving at the Rainbow one night in November 1973, for the band's show during the Stranded tour, Beverley was among a handful of fans photographed for a *Honey* magazine pictorial spread. The clipping later ended up on the wall of the group's management company's offices, and that's where Jonh Ingham, researching a piece on Roxy in 1976, recognised the 16-year-old John Beverley, all glammed up and with schoolboy mate Vince at his side. 'Sid's wearing a white tuxedo with a T-shirt,' says Ingham, 'and though he hasn't yet got that sneer, the attitude is already there. He's the only one in the entire piece with any genuine presence.'

By the time of the autumn '75 Roxy show, two years later, that Beverley attitude was hardening. While John Lydon was busy with The Sex Pistols, Spikey John was, reveals Mike Baess, relieving Hampstead's wealthy old dears of the contents of their handbags. 'Sid's mugging was legendary,' he says, though floor-mate Mandy Pete has no recollection of this new development. But then, Pete had been away during the autumn, and wouldn't return until the Christmas holidays. 'Barbara knew about it too,' says Baess. 'She'd say, "He's been up to no good again."'

Spikey John was becoming 'increasing obnoxious,' Baess notes. 'In early November 1975, we all went up to Oxford for the weekend because one of my mates was having a 21st birthday party. The house was in a middle class area, and John [Beverley] really started having a go at people. He pissed everybody off. It was embarrassing. Everyone was saying, 'Who the hell is that jerk?' I'm not sure if he nicked any of the family silver that night, but he was notorious for nicking records and anything else he could get his hands on.'

On his return to New Court that Christmas, Mandy Pete also detected a change in his roommate. 'His character seemed to have developed over those few months,' he says. 'He'd become uptight, a real Cockney-with-attitude type person. He wasn't intimidating, but he definitely had a new kind of charisma. A lot of it was bound up with his dress sense and the way he carried himself.

The way he walked and the way he talked was completely different to everybody else.'

Though not quite yet the full 'Vicious', Sid was certainly stirring. Encouraged perhaps by the rhetoric coming out of the downmarket end of the King's Road, he drew a line under his own past by taking a match to a bunch of cherished records and outfits. 'One day he turned up at Mandy's,' says Henry Sabini, 'and told us that he'd had a big bonfire and burnt all his Bowie stuff.' Sabini and his mates did wonder whether this was another of those fanciful Sid stories, though Sid did enough to convince them that this latest escapade was quite true.

'He was always doing things like that, seeking attention as much as anything,' says Sabini. But Sid was also gaining strength in his new-found identity as the sidekick of John Lydon, up-and-coming rabble-rouser of the club scene and, so those shady King's Road characters had begun to whisper, a revolutionary in the making. 'Me too!' Sid wailed, bouncing impatiently on the balls of his feet.

There was, Sabini adds, a second, even more sensational moment of epiphany. 'He used to wear this pink Teddy Boy-style suit with a long drape jacket. And he was so proud of it. Then, one day, he turned up at Eade Road and he'd completely shredded it. That's the first time I encountered what was to become the punk rock safety pin thing. He'd just destroyed this outfit that had been his pride and joy and safety-pinned it back together. He thought it was fantastic. The rest of us were gobsmacked.'

6. ROCK IS DEAD

MALCOLM MCLAREN had been running a retro clothes shop at 430 King's Road with his partner, the ex-schoolteacher turned seamstress Vivienne Westwood, since the dawn of glam rock in the summer of 1971. He shared the two Johns' hatred of 'hippies', dubbing them 'Hippos' with teeth-bared hostility. He despised convention, capitalism and social complacency. Delinquent teenage cults, trashy rock 'n' roll and all forms of imperfection were what excited McLaren. He was like an overgrown Ton-Up Kid with a well-thumbed copy of Guy Debord's classic Situationist text, *The Society Of The Spectacle*, in his jacket pocket.

'McLaren wanted to make an art statement, that was his whole thing,' remembers Nick Kent, who spent many hours with the aspiring *agent provocateur* during 1973 and 1974, even quoting him in his April 1974 *New Musical Express* article, 'The Politics Of Flash'. 'He was a fascinating guy, with a brain and his own agenda, but he hated the '60s. That's where he and I were at odds. I remember us arguing about the relevance of Bob Dylan and Johnny Kidd And The Pirates in popular culture. He was all for Johnny Kidd. Bob Dylan didn't mean anything to him. He liked Gene Vincent, dumb guys dressed in black who made barbaric noises.'

'Malcolm's shop was the hippest place in London,' insists Glen Matlock, who'd manned McLaren's counter since the Let It Rock days. 'Everyone else thought Granny [Takes A Trip] and Alkasura were hip, but Malcolm looked down on them, and we did too. We'd look down on everyone from Keith Richards to [Roxy Music's] Bryan Ferry, all those multimillionaires. We didn't have a pot to piss in – we were a bunch of oiks from Shepherd's Bush and Kensal Green – but we just thought they were wankers.' Stoked on World's End iconoclasm, Sid had even hatched a hare-brained plan to doorstep his one-time hero Bryan Ferry, who lived a short walk from McLaren's SEX shop in SW10. There is no evidence, however, that any encounter ever took place.

Matlock's 'bunch of oiks' were the original Sex Pistols, and they too had a strong Roxy Music connection. Having started out as The Swankers, they briefly named themselves The Strand after the breathtaking opener on Roxy's 1973 album, *For Your Pleasure*. McLaren changed all that, coming up with the incendiary Sex Pistols name ('It makes them sound like young assassins,' he happily told anyone who asked), and plenty else besides.

'The Pistols were fashion models, a way of showing off Malcolm's clothes,' reckons Ray Stevenson, semi-official photographer for the band and the tight-knit coterie of admirers that congregated at SEX throughout 1976. 'He knew a lot about clothes but nothing about music, and it all went wrong because they became a proper band.' Stevenson is another who insists there was a vicarious element to McLaren's 'authorship' of The Sex Pistols. 'He'd have liked to have done it himself, but he didn't have the bottle or the talent to get up there and do it.'

According to Stevenson, McLaren 'always wanted to be Andy Warhol, creating a scene and then saying, 'Look what I did!' ' But while the pop artist and the artisan proved to be great enablers, they were also unashamedly sponge-like, voraciously feeding off all those who hung to the scenes they created. And all around Malcolm's scene were the condemned children of the failed '60s revolution, the semi-cultured miscreants of Anthony Burgess' *A Clockwork Orange*, harbingers of a moral, aesthetic and philosophical revolution that would alter the cultural landscape forever.

'It was classic anomie,' says Caroline Coon, 'not belonging anywhere, and certainly not belonging to society where there aren't any jobs, a society which is fast becoming Thatcherite. That generation of kids was very needy, wanted love, wanted to belong. And punk gave them that opportunity. It was a reaction to the perceived failure of hippiedom, of peace and love. It was a cry of rage, an inversion of peace and love into hate and war.'

Malcolm McLaren was an ideal Svengali for this emerging generation of disaffected youths. He was angry, but neither consumed nor enfeebled by it. Ambitious, yet bored and disgusted by routine showbiz and business practices. A passionate believer in the latent revolutionary potential of the teenager. A dreamer/schemer with a mischievous fascination for all forms of social collapse. McLaren was the classic libertarian landlord, happy to entertain an unruly household as long as he was welcome at all the parties. But very soon the police would be knocking on his doorstep, and the neighbours would be in an uproar.

'Malcolm would come over to the house all the time and talk politics, hardcore politics,' says photographer Kate Simon, who lived round the corner from SEX with fellow American snapper Joe Stevens. 'It put me to sleep.' Alan Jones confirms that 'the ideology was laid on by Malcolm to a great extent', though the 'politics of punk' debate still makes him feel uneasy. 'It was like, "If that's what Vivienne and Malcolm said, it must be right." People learnt to say it parrot fashion, and that's what bothered me.'

'Most of us were in it for the laughs and having a good time,' Jones adds. 'Isn't that what rock 'n' roll's supposed to be about?' McLaren understood that rock 'n' roll had the potential to address more than simple pleasures, that it was at its most powerful when it engaged the wider world, tangled with forces that ran deeper than sex and smiles. McLaren's gleefully apocalyptic update of the De Sadean nightmare of social corruption, meaningless lives and bourgeois morality gave an insurrectionary twist to contemporary cultural convulsions. The Sex Pistols would give that discontent a loud, rowdy focus, and the resulting punk subculture rejoiced in the ability to torture the soul of the society that had produced it.

In August 1975, the month that John Lydon became a Sex Pistol, a batch of SEX's more risque T-shirts, the one depicting two naked and well-hung cowboys, were confiscated by the police. Soon afterwards, in November, the Pistols made their first public appearance. McLaren's long-fermenting fabulist fantasy was starting to take shape, as he explained in a contemporary interview with a London newspaper. 'I've always been involved with cults, the subterranean influence on people,' he told Rick Szymanski. Then he made what was in hindsight a remarkable prediction. 'I think now that kids have a hankering to be part of a movement that's hard and tough and in the open,' he said, 'like the clothes we're selling in here.'

Glen Matlock remembers hearing McLaren describe himself as 'an artistic cretin' who catered for the needs of backward-looking people. That was back in 1973, when McLaren and Westwood's shop was shifting its orientation from the almost exclusively Teddy Boy appeal of Let It Rock to the wider retro feel of Too Fast To Live, Too Young To Die. McLaren continued to flog T-shirts that garishly declared 'Vive Le Rock' over an image of Little Richard, but a new stock of heavily studded leather jackets, glitter boots and a batch of vintage zoot suits opened up the shop to all manner of style freaks. The premises, which Matlock remembers being just like his 'granny's sitting room', was still more 'That'll Be The Day' than 'Tomorrow Never Knows'.

Locked in his museum-like time warp, Malcolm had the air of a parochial man, content to feed off the crumbs of rock culture hand-me-downs. Discovering New York, and more precisely, The New York Dolls, changed all that. Legend has it that when McLaren first heard the Dolls' debut album, in September 1973 while in their home city for a fashion exhibition, he demanded the record be taken off. Two months later, and back in London, he'd had a change of heart. He saw the Dolls' riotous rock 'n' roll masquerade at Biba's Rainbow Room in Kensington, and was bowled over.

'The New York Dolls were kinda effete,' says Nick Kent, who bumped into McLaren at the show. 'The music was raw, but there was a limp-wristedness about what they did; it was still Glam Rock. The Sex Pistols could never flirt with sexual ambiguity. That was never gonna work with Steve Jones or Paul Cook or Glen in the band. But the other ingredients were there for them to pick up on.'

Coming on like the idiot bastard offspring of Andy Warhol's Factory freaks, The New York Dolls dumped all over '70s rock's self-righteousness and McLaren eagerly lapped it up. Infamous for their showy, Stones-style pastiches and exaggerated, ultra-camp glam poses, the Dolls rolled into Paris in January 1975, and superfan Malcolm was there too, delighting as the band threw up, threw Nazi salutes and caused all manner of offence with their decadent embrace of culture's waste disposal unit.

The drug-related death of drummer Billy Murcia in London in 1972 only served to exaggerate the sense of glorious failure that attached itself to the band (amusingly dismissed as 'mock rock' by *The Old Grey Whistle Test* presenter Bob Harris). The aura of decay around the band was virulent, potent enough to prompt Malcolm McLaren to walk away from his shop, and his loveless relationship with Westwood and, in autumn 1974, take off to New York.

Part manager, part stylist, he attempted to revive the Dolls' flagging career by dressing them in red patent leather, and creating a provocative backdrop of pro-Communist symbols and slogans ('Better Red Than Dead'!). The experience he gained in the day-to-day functioning of a rock 'n' roll band was invaluable. The band liked him, too. 'I was always amused by Malcolm,' says bassist Arthur Kane. 'He was an oddball character who almost belonged on the Monty Python show.'

However, by the time McLaren started working with them, The New York Dolls were on the verge of collapse. His thirst for shock and showmanship failed to halt the slide. When the inevitable happened, early in 1975, he returned home to London. Clutching guitarist Sylvian Sylvian's white Gibson Les Paul under his arm, McLaren had hopes that the Dolls' guitarist would follow him, and perhaps even front the bare bones of the band he'd been keeping an eye on back home. Creating a rock 'n' roll band as an extension of the shop, one based on similarly confrontational principles – sex, shock and subculture – seemed entirely possible, especially in the moribund British rock scene where even the music press was torturing itself with a series of 'Whatever happened to the spirit of rock' think-pieces. 'I want a raunchy Bay City Rollers,' McLaren told Peter Perrett, a regular customer and future frontman with The Only Ones.

In McLaren's absence, the shop – renamed SEX in late summer 1974 – had flourished under Vivienne Westwood's supervision. The formidable Jordan, a living work of art in the outré style of a classic Warhol superstar, became the shop's public face, though Westwood too had her own circle of admirers. 'Tim Buckley thought she was heaven good-looking,' remembers photographer Kate Simon. 'Vivienne always wore lavender eyeliner, and Tim liked that.'

Westwood's latest designs – now incorporating a slightly more affordable range of T-shirts emblazoned with incendiary messages – introduced a cutting-edge contemporary vibe to SEX's well-established subterranean reputation. Now 'specialising in rubberwear glamourwear & stagewear', the shop began to attract a different, more pervy clientele, some who came simply to delight in the disciplinarian air created by the mighty proto-punk mistresses.

The prominence of the shop's *femmes formidables* gave McLaren more time to nurture what he continued to tell anyone who'd listen, SEX regular Nils Stevenson included, were his 'new Bay City Rollers'. By the summer, The Swankers – old Shepherd's Bush schoolmates singer/guitarist Steve Jones and drummer Paul Cook, plus SEX shop assistant and bass-playing art student Glen Matlock – had tightened up their act. And they'd found themselves an almost famous second guitarist.

'I rehearsed with them for about three months down at Riverside Studios in Hammersmith,' says Nick Kent, then the star writer at the *New Musical Express*. 'Steve Jones had been playing guitar for exactly three months, though he'd been stealing them for far longer than that.' Kent adds that the group required another guitarist because Malcolm McLaren – already meddling – had just kicked out original singer/guitarist Wally Nightingale.

In addition to impeccable contacts and journalistic clout, Kent also had a pile of pre-release tapes (most then unreleased) documenting the new music then coming out of the New York scene: Patti Smith, The Modern Lovers and Television, plus rare New York Dolls live recordings and Iggy Pop and James Williamson's *Kill City*. 'At the time he joined, The Sex Pistols were little more than a straight '60s nostalgia group with a fondness for Who and Small Faces covers, 'Call Me Lightning' [The Tremeloes], 'Everlasting Love' [The Love Affair] and 'Build Me Up Buttercup' [The Foundations].'

The band had knocked up three originals but, says Kent, 'essentially it was the same song, 'Didya No Wrong'. 'Didya no wrong, going out of my head' – those were the only lyrics.' He was impressed. 'When I first heard that, I thought those guys already had it in the pocket, right there in 1975. They were raw and alive, a young band still in their teens, who could really play rock 'n' roll. That was unique in England at the time. The Stones had forgotten how to play like that. So had a lot of bands, who were getting more complicated, getting into star trips.'

Contemporary stars sucked. McLaren knew that. But he was also aware that no new band, let alone one that might actually mean something, could ever hope to make any genuine (anti)social impact without having some kind of anti-hero out front. When it became obvious that Sylvain Sylvain was staying put, his thoughts turned to an erudite if sartorially distressed young bassist he'd spotted in New York who called himself Richard Hell. But he too had no intention of turning his back on the aesthetic revolution happening in downtown New York. Especially when the alternative was an offer to front a callow, somewhat artless combo with one original song and no obvious audience in a capital city that was a pale shadow of its mid-'60s heyday.

Stick-thin cool, clad in leather and on first-name terms with the small handful of London's heroin dealers, Nick Kent could conceivably have been the one to add some time-honoured rock 'n' roll debauchery to McLaren's West London rascals. 'I moved them closer towards the new punk thing,' he says, but there was a problem. 'McLaren realised that I could not be controlled. I didn't want to be controlled. There was no way he was gonna push me around like he did the others.' Kent was given the boot.

Within a couple of months, McLaren had found his anti-hero, the angry adolescent who hated everything, whose attitude – so perfectly enshrined in his face and demeanour – embodied all of Malcolm's antisocial fantasies in ways that Kent's classic rock 'n' roll outlaw look didn't. 'They wouldn't have been anywhere near as impressive without Lydon,' Kent admits. 'He brought something new to the music.' More than that, he brought something *beyond* music, something that McLaren knew had been missing from rock culture for too long. Within days of Lydon joining, the now deadly serious rock 'n' roll manager was predicting the inevitability of a movement every bit 'as hard and tough' as the clothes that hung provocatively in SEX.

DYING YOUNG and rock 'n' roll make great bedfellows. Just the other night, I heard someone recount a life story that went off the rails at precisely the moment he put drink, drugs and doomed figures such as Jim Morrison together. It reminded me of that summer's day, on 3 July 1974, when I bunked off school to visit Brian Jones' grave. Paying homage to a gifted, woefully misunderstood icon? Not at all: it was death, the great unfathomable that makes lepers of the living, that I'd unconsciously come to worship.

'Jim [Morrison] was prophetic on "Rock Is Dead",' says Doors guitarist Robbie Krieger, 'because right about that time, Jimi died, Janis died and in a way rock was dying. That adagio is the perfect funeral march.'

The Doors' Jim Morrison became involved with rock 'n' roll during the mid-'60s as an extension of his film-making and poetry-spouting pursuits. On 3 July 1971, the leather-clad Adonis of the counter-culture was found dead in his bath, his demise apparently hastened by the pursuit of yet another intoxication-driven, nirvana-chasing pursuit, the orgasm.

'Jim seemed to know that he was gonna die early,' says Robbie Krieger. 'He talked about it quite often. We never believed him when he said that he was gonna die. We thought he'd be one of those drunk Irishmen who hang around until they're 80 drinking a bottle of whiskey every day. He fooled us.'

The rock 'n' roll tombstone inscribed with the names of Brian Jones and Jim Morrison, Jimi Hendrix and Janis Joplin cast a long dark shadow over the '70s. A monument to better times, it compared favourably when held up to what remained: The Rolling Stones parodying themselves; The Doors going it alone without Jim Morrison; Robin Trower reinvented as Jimi Hendrix; the memory of Janis Joplin erased by Linda Ronstadt.

Even those twin peaks of hippie ruin, the Manson murders and the Altamont Festival, seemed more fascinating, more instructive about the darker meanings of rock 'n' roll than the clichéd, cock-rock showmen who'd strut around the mid-'70s rock stages. Rock and pop now existed only to please itself, rather than engage with, or perhaps even enlighten the wider world.

There was a great deal of difference between the '60s rock hero and the '70s punk anti-hero born in the shadow of the former's failure:

Jim	Sid
Hero	Anti-hero
Rich	Poor
Sexual predator	Sexual pygmy
Hallucinogenic	Heroin
Arty	Farty
Genius	Mediocrity
Curly	Spikey
Utopian	Dystopian
Eden	Belsen
Hippie	Punk

United in their willingness to dally with death and, lest we forget, their near-pathological penchant for leather clothing, Sid and Fancy Dan Jimbo would eventually meet in Hollywood heaven (hell?) thanks to that most maligned of movie genres, the rock star biopic.

'I was quite incensed when Alex Cox told me he was doing this Sid and Nancy film,' says Alan Jones. 'I said, I don't want you painting Sid as a horrible person, because he wasn't. But whatever you think of it as a film, the portrayal of Sid was actually sympathetic.'

'Alex Cox got it right, man,' says Don Letts. 'I saw that film [Sid And Nancy] the other day and at times I actually forgot that I was watching a movie. It's so fucking spot on it's unreal. And [Gary] Oldman . . . man, has he got Sid down.' Though shorter than Sid, and at 27, considerably older, most agree that Oldman, another Londoner with a difficult upbringing, was a convincing facsimile of 'Sid Vicious'. Sid's mother Anne sanctioned the film and allowed Cox to use the padlock and chain that had always hung around her son's neck. And though Cox was unable to obtain the rights to use original Sex Pistols recordings, Glen Matlock agreed to re-record versions of old Pistols material for Oldman to sing to.

Others have dismissed Cox's film as distastefully premature, cliché ridden and made irredeemable by a script that was no less painful than Cox's naive claim that the film didn't glamorise drugs. 'I honestly believe it celebrates heroin addiction,' John Lydon stated in his autobiography, making special mention of the climactic scene where Sid and Nancy are reunited and taxied away to screw and score in the afterlife. It was, he insisted with typical sarcasm, a film by an Oxbridge graduate who had missed out on the punk era.

At the time of the film's release, in 1986, Cox claimed that *Sid And Nancy* was 'an anti-drug statement to show that the degradation caused to various people is not at all glamorous'. It was a specious claim, because the Numbskull Sid and Nauseating Nancy portrayed in the film are archetypes that fascinate at least as much as they repel. Besides, not everyone gets all saintly about degradation. Especially not in the mid-'70s, with Brian and Jimi dead, with Iggy and Syd visibly decaying, and with those Angels from Hell and Charlie Manson somehow typifying 'the world as it is today'. Be true to your ghoul.

I'm back at the table opposite Jah Wobble. It's now over 25 years since punk shocked the world, and we still have cause to discuss the end of liberalism and the possible emergence of a hardline new world order. Parts of the conversation remind me of the watershed effect that punk had. 'It's like medieval cosmology,' Wobble says. 'This is what we believe in. You don't even have a debate. Is there an absolute truth? Is this a question of Kantean philosophy? They're like, Fuck you. The will of God. Bang! Don't even think that shit. It's like Colonel Kurtz in *Apocalypse Now*, a great film from the punk days, based on Conrad's *Heart Of Darkness:* "Reason defeats us."'

Sid and Wobble were once infamous for their modern-day displays of medieval-style jousting. Wobble was one of the genuine tough nuts who hung around John Lydon, and was certainly worth his reputation. In fact, Nick Kent is still troubled by the memory of the night Sid and Wobble confronted him at the 100 Club. 'Tell him that I've not forgotten,' Kent urges. 'Tell him this: YOUR KARMA IS MINE.'

So I did. 'Tell the geezer I'm sorry,' Wobble says. 'It's not a nice thing to do.' Then he pauses. 'Actually, I couldn't really give a flying fuck. No one got their head cut off, nobody got killed or ended up in hospital.' These days, Wobble is more prone to philosophising than pugilism. So the conversation drifts back to the death of the Modern.

'That's the thing with Sid,' Wobble continues. 'He was just a little bit of flotsam floating on that final tide of everything that dates right the way back, from the Renaissance, through the Enlightenment to Modernism. And that's where Sid ended up, living in this brutal, fucking Modernist structure in Hackney. People underestimate the power of post-war architecture in London. You don't feel connected. You always feel oppressed. It doesn't let you in. I mean, you can't even find the fucking door! What's that all about?'

Between 1967 and 1977, the doors of perception were slammed shut, the long-haired leather boy wonderkid of British rock journalism had been given a belting, and the grand narrative of rock 'n' roll's – and Modernism's – forward march had screeched to a perplexing halt. Rock wasn't quite dead, but its rulebook – especially those weighty chapters on aesthetics, the sanctity of the canon, technical ability and showmanship – was about to receive a rude overhaul.

* * *

100 Club, London, Tuesday, 29 June 1976

NICK KENT: 'I first encountered Sid at the last Rolling Stones concert during their Earls Court run [27 May 1976]. Every major punk figure was standing outside without a ticket. The Sex Pistols were already playing by then, but all the rest who didn't get in went off and formed groups.

'I was hanging around with Brian James and Chris [Rat Scabies] because I'd just played a gig with them in Cardiff as The Subterraneans. Soon afterwards, they became The Damned.

'That's when I noticed this broomstick-like figure with big black hair. He was dressed in a really ill-fitting suit which made him look like a very tall 16-year-old who'd just been let out of school. They said, "Oi! That's Sid." He was by himself walking through the crowd.

'Two or three weeks later, I saw him again at the 100 Club.

'Sid was down the front talking to McLaren and Lydon. The Sex Pistols were about to walk onstage. I could see them all having a heated debate and Vicious pointing at me. All three of them had these evil grins. Then he came and attacked me.

'It happened during the first or second number. He pulled out a chain and hit me over the head about three times. Half a pint of blood ended up on the wall, because I was sitting on a chair positioned next to it. I was with two record company guys from Island Records, Michael Beale and Howard Thompson, who'd recently signed Eddie And The Hot Rods. There'd been some trouble between that group and The Sex Pistols beforehand that I was completely unaware of, so maybe that played a part too. But they weren't attacked. It was me who got all the fucking action.

'It wasn't Vicious that worried me, because though I was tall and skinny and no good at fighting, I could see that he was no better. He was just on more drugs; he was on speed. I wasn't frightened by him. What I was frightened about was when his mate Jah Wobble pulled a knife and stuck it two inches from my eyes. That's what fucking scared me, 'cos that guy had a look on his face like he really wanted to hurt me. I'd never seen this guy before in my life, man, and he was staring at me with this grin on his face.'

JAH WOBBLE: 'Well, I was the real deal, I suppose. It really was a bit of fucking about. Me and Sid were standing there and these two geezers started pushing us in the back, as I remember it. 'We can't see the band – move!' So we're like, 'Fuck off', but they're not fucking off. They probably thought it was a couple of young punk kids, not realising that by this stage you want them to come in front of you. 'Cos I'm a hot head. I kinda realised they were just a pair of cunts, basically. I didn't know they were music industry guys. They were older. All I know is that they were a bit lairy, and they were probably stoned, giving us stoned vibes.

'Sid had swung and slashed him, and maybe they were still shouting. Maybe I might have said something like, "You really will get hurt if you don't fuck off. You've been told once, now fuck off." I'll tell you this: we didn't just pick on those geezers. It started with us being pushed from behind.'

NICK KENT: 'That attack had a cataclysmic effect on me, though it didn't affect me at the time because I was so stoned when it happened that it didn't hurt. It stung more than it hurt. I remember leaving very quickly with blood pouring from my head. I should have had stitches, but I just went off somewhere. I didn't have a home to go to. Those were bad times for me.'

ALAN JONES: 'Nick Kent was such a cunt. I hated him. I would have fucking punched him in the face myself and I'm not a violent person. We all hated him. And what Sid did, we were all cheering, believe me. The way he looked – leather trousers, leather jacket, scarf round his neck. He looked like a heavy metaller trying to be a punk. He wouldn't go the whole way, and of course those were the ones we hated the most. Of the people commenting on the movement at the time, not many got it right. Caroline [Coon] did her best. Yet when she turned up at the Nashville, she looked exactly the same as she normally did, except she'd put safety pins in a tie. I thought, Take that fucking thing off, it looks stupid!'

MARK PERRY: 'Nick Kent was one of those writers who was virtually a rock star in his own right. I liked that.'

NICK KENT: 'It happened because I was an ex-Sex Pistol and I was Nick Kent. They were so fucking paranoid. They thought I would go around and say some bullshit around them, which I never ever did. I knew from the start that they were gonna be a major group – though I didn't realise how completely earth shattering it was all gonna end up being – and I wasn't gonna get in their way. Once McLaren kicked me out, he just didn't want me around. It became a power struggle between him and me. I went to [Steve] Jones and said, "You gotta get rid of McLaren, the guy's a jerk." Of course, McLaren said, "Get rid of Kent, he's a junkie", which, of course, I was.'

'It was a message to me from Malcolm McLaren to say, 'You're out'. They'd done this T-shirt [You're Gonna Wake Up One Morning And Know What Side Of The Bed You've Been Lying On!, autumn 1974] , and my name's there on the side with all Malcolm's favourite people. So I'd gone from the cool side to the uncool side for doing nothing, man.'

GLEN MATLOCK: 'I dispute that. I can't see any reason why Malcolm would put Sid up to do that 'cos they were quite friendly.'

NICK KENT: 'It's got nothing to do with the press, or with me being a rock critic. It was a personal thing. McLaren used to be one of my best friends, and for about six months to a year around 1974 we were very close. He was a bright guy before he became corrupted. You could sit and talk to him and there was a kindness in his heart, but that just evaporated. I didn't realise what a fame seeker he was. He bought into the image of punk and it became vicious, very nasty. If Marc Bolan or even Keith Richards had gone into that place, they would have been attacked as well. There was this seething hostility to anything that had gone before.'

JAH WOBBLE: 'McLaren pointing him out? I don't know anything about that.'

GLEN MATLOCK: 'Something happened between Nick and [his one-time girlfriend] Chrissie Hynde. Maybe that had something to do with it. After his run-in with her, he stopped coming into the shop. He had problems, too. He was struggling with his own personal demons.'

NICK KENT: 'The resentment may have started with Chrissie Hynde telling Sid Vicious what a cunt I was when I went out with her, and telling him that I'd hit her. But that's pure conjecture. Later on, I asked Vicious himself: 'Why did you fucking attack me?' 'I don't remember,' he'd always answer. And I believed him. He was very out of it on speed that night, and he was looking for any kind of aggression. I think he went along with it because he thought he could get a mention in the music comics by beating me up.'

STEVEN SEVERIN: 'Sid never picked on anyone who wouldn't get him into the papers. He always chose his targets well.'

GLEN MATLOCK: 'That whole run-in at the 100 Club was Sid wanting to get some attention for himself. He craved some of the limelight.'

NICK KENT: 'It was also the seething hostility of wannabes. On one side there was this very healthy element of people wanting to have their moment. That's how youth movements start. But there was also this nasty side; suddenly, the dogs were let out of the cages. The exhibitionist was king. When punk said, OK, musicianship is redundant, it was like whoever takes the microphone has the microphone. That was the basic philosophy. A lot of shit happened and I ended up watching so many drug-addled exhibitionists who had nothing to say because they were too young to have formulated a personality, never mind an opinion.'

JAH WOBBLE: 'What you had there was a certain world meeting another certain world. We were coming from a different world.'

7. ROCK IS ALIVE IN LONDON (AND SICK AND TIRED OF EVERYTHING)

'Rock was supposed to inspire and provoke, be loud and violent and change your life, but it had become toothless. At the same time, there was football violence every weekend, strikes, lots of shit going on. It was a powder keg situation, and that's why we reacted with such force. The audience was just ready to explode.' – Steven Severin

1976: THE YEAR that punk broke. The year that John Beverley, alias Sid Vicious, found a place where he could belong. It was the year of The Sex Pistols' emergence, from bottom-of-the-bill art college makeweights to moral panic merchants, fomenters of what the *Daily Mirror* cordially dubbed 'ROCK CULT FILTH'.

'I fucking loved that band,' said Sid, long after he'd become a Sex Pistol. 'I think I was the biggest fan they had . . .' And dropping his characteristic competitive ribbing for a moment, he reserved his greatest admiration for the King's Road comrade who had beaten him to the lead role. 'Rotten was incredible, like unbelievable,' Sid said. And, like McLaren, he knew exactly why his mate was perfect for the part. 'What made The Sex Pistols different was Johnny Rotten, 'cos he's a total anti-star. He didn't like wiggle his bum or shake his hips. He did robot dances and fucked around, and took the piss out of everybody in a nasty, snidey way.'

The ideological axes that underpinned British punk rock revolved around the unholy triumvirate of Malcolm McLaren (The Manager), Johnny Rotten

(The Face) and Sid Vicious (The Activist). Throughout 1976, with all activity focused on breaking the band and creating an attention-grabbing scene around them, an unspoken alliance allowed the trio to co-exist in a state of boisterous disharmony, based on admiration and rivalry in roughly equal amounts.

In the beginning, there was McLaren, the man who'd accepted an invitation from New York and had returned home certain that he could engender some kind of Warhol-meets-CBGB's scene back in London.

'The band were kids, whereas Malcolm was grown up, a way of getting on stage, a source of money, a way out, basically,' says Ray Stevenson. 'You can't knock the amount of work he did. He was always in the office, on the phone. One of the first things he did was put them in SEX clothes, then take them out to get them noticed. We'd be out 'til two or three in the morning, and yet he'd be in the office at 9:30 the next morning while everyone else was sleeping it off. He had a remarkable work-rate.'

Early Sex Pistols fan and future Subway Sect frontman Vic Godard first encountered McLaren back at the shop during its pre-SEX days. 'I'd never seen anyone like him. He had a unique style that I'd never seen before.' Subway Sect's Rob Simmons who, like Godard, first saw the Pistols in February 1976 at the Marquee, agrees. 'Malcolm McLaren always had a leather case under his arm. He looked like a debauched professor.'

Also at the Marquee was *New Musical Express* critic Neil Spencer, who ended his review with a quote attributed to guitarist Steve Jones: 'We're not into music . . . we're into chaos.' 'That sounds so much like a Malcolm McLaren soundbite,' laughs Jonh Ingham. 'In the early days, Malcolm made you interview him before meeting the band. He sat there for an hour spieling out this manifesto, which all made perfect sense in that it was anti-everything that was going on at the time. You definitely got a sense that this was all about McLaren having an agenda. The others were simply following it through.'

FRIDAY 23 April 1976: Buoyed by Ingham's feature published in *Sounds* earlier in the week, McLaren and the Pistols swagger into the Nashville Rooms in West Kensington. Sid's there too, as he often is. He's been coming ever since the band's debut at St Martin's College Of Art the previous November. Now, journalists have started to join the handful of friends who usually made up the crowd of between 30 and 50 people.

Earlier in the month, a writer from *Melody Maker* had already caught the band at the Nashville. He left complaining about 'this retarded spectacle . . . which did as much for music as World War II did for the cause of peace'. Not so the legendary 'Jesus', concert-goer extraordinaire and famous throughout the land for his tendency to strip while the bands played on. He was photographed – still with his long hair and dog collar – dancing gaily to the Pistols' rough 'n' ready mix of '60s standards and self-penned material.

Tonight's star audience member is a striking, bottle-blonde woman, not far off middle age. With dodgy teeth and a menacing glare, she resembles some peculiar hybrid of Myra Hindley and Sex Pistols drummer Paul Cook. It's Vivienne Westwood, and she's just returned from the bar to find that the chair she'd been sitting on has been taken. A fight kicks off right in front of the stage. The band pile in. Joe Stevens and Kate Simon snap away, and the episode gets major coverage in the following week's music press.

Also captured in the fracas is Malcolm McLaren, tussling with the unfortunate leather-jacketed long-hair. 'Malcolm McLaren being all macho and stuff? Now that was worth capturing on film!' says Kate Simon. 'I thought he was an intellectual.'

While there is no photographic evidence that Sid Vicious threw any punches that night, what Kate Simon's lens did catch was a look of ill-begotten intent that fit his name like an iron glove. 'He does looks pretty mean in the picture,' she says.

'You can see real madness in his eyes in that photo,' adds Glen Matlock, whose nice boy reputation is somewhat undermined by his involvement in the mêleé. 'The retinas look like they're on fire . . .'

In reality, Sid's demon-like gaze was all an unfortunate trick of the camera's unforgiving flashbulb. But with his corpse-like pallor and fright-wig hair, Vivienne's latest 'naked black man' T-shirt creation bulging out of his open gold and blue 'Elvis Presley' faux-Nudie jacket, the effect was one of total aggression.

If scary-eyed Sid has been implicated posthumously, the Pistols were damned at an instant. Was this a rock band, or simply a bunch of troublemakers invading sacred territory? Above all, what did they want? Malcolm McLaren seemed to have the answer. While the idea that he scripted the band's entire career (the 'Swindle' thesis) has long been discredited, there is more than a suggestion that, as with the Kent incident, he clearly understood that a little bit of trouble could go a long way in terms of press coverage.

'We were told to start a fight to get the gig publicised,' insists Henry Sabini, who was there with a mate of his and Mandy's called Mick. 'He'd been around a while and was a bit like Sid, a rough 'n' ready rogue, but with muscles. Mick was short and stocky, and he could handle himself.' Sabini maintains that the call to action came from the top.

If that's true, then most are agreed that the protaganist was Vivienne, not masher Mick. 'She got up and started dancing, and maybe Chrissie Hynde started dancing with her,' says Steven Severin. 'If anything, it was her who was doing the barging into people. Then some old hippie took offence and that's when the whole thing went off.'

Alan Jones saw the incident as a loud-sounding nothing. 'That story was just ridiculous. It was just us being boisterous and having a good time, and people weren't used to it back then. It looks much worse in the pictures.'

'There wasn't even a bad atmosphere at that gig,' says Vic Godard. 'There wasn't any violence at anything I saw, really, except when I saw them the first time and they were being chucked out of the Marquee. But that wasn't crowd violence; that was management wanting them out 'cos they weren't a Marquee-type band.' Neither were they a Nashville-type band after this latest fracas, and another ban swiftly followed.

Incidents such as these were rare at this stage in the Pistols' career. But there was no doubt that muck-raker McLaren and Johnny Too-Bad were hardly Billy Gaff and Rod Stewart types. And violence was in the air, if not necessarily on the dance floor. The band's attack-over-technique approach made sure of that. The Sex Pistols came with an aura of disorder. And Sid, John's daft mate and Vivienne's living doll, had the measure of the Pistols' vibe right from the start.

'He was always hanging around the Pistols,' says Captain Sensible, who first saw the band at one of the earliest Nashville Rooms shows. 'Rat [Scabies] was roadying for them that night, which was supposedly when the gobbing thing started, which Sid was involved in.

'The Nashville was scuzzy, the sort of place you couldn't get chucked out of, but Sid managed it a couple of times. Sid wasn't as stupid as people think, but he was when he was tanked up. When he was straight, he was amicable and witty, though he wasn't a natural extrovert. I suppose that's why he drank so much. By the end of the evening, when he'd had about five or six pints of strong ale, he'd wanna fight. So he'd pick on a bouncer or someone he really shouldn't pick on. He got beaten so often.'

Both Sid and Sensible managed to get themselves ejected from the Nashville. 'I'd see Captain Sensible at punk gigs and he'd be pouring lighter fluid on his head and setting fire to himself, doing stupid things because it was expected of him,' says Nick Kent. 'Different generations have different ways of having fun. In the '60s, it was standing around looking like you were on drugs when you weren't. With punk it was looking for a fight. I'd see people transform right in front of me. It was incredible watching all these people change, how punk affected their personalities. All the guys cut their hair, and had their punk night of the soul.'

Though they'd become adversaries on the Roxy Club dance floor several months later, Sid and Sensible (a less troublesome alter ego than Vicious, though the pair shared a reputation for recklessness) experienced at least one punk night of the soul together. 'We decided to go back to Sue Catwoman's place on Ealing Broadway after one of those early gigs,' Sensible says. 'We'd had a skinful, and there were no night buses in those days, so we decided to walk. Then Sid thought it would be fun to uproot these spiked railings in a car park, and throw them through a car windscreen. Then he gave one to me and said, 'Your turn', so I smashed one too.

'We ran off down the road shrieking with laughter, smashing loads more of these windscreens, then we heard the police siren. We ran for it but got pulled over and ended up in the police station. I don't remember a lot about it, but next morning they got us up at six o'clock, presumably to feed us and give us a cup of tea. But I'd urinated all over myself in this cell, so they took one look at us and kicked us out: no interview, no charges, nothing.'

The damage was not always unleashed on man-made things. One of the more visible manifestations of the darker forces unleashed during the punk era was the proliferation of self-inflicted wounds. A subterranean cult, their limbs sliced like salamis, began to stalk the clubs of London.

'It was really scary that people would want to be that violent about themselves,' says Jonh Ingham, who was first exposed to it at The Sex Pistols' 9 July gig at the Lyceum. 'John [Rotten] stuck his hand out while he was on stage, and clearly visible on the back of it were about four cigarette burns.'

'We were supporting The Pretty Things at an all-night show,' remembers Glen Matlock. 'We'd already started playing, and then John came on, rolled up his sleeve and stubbed a cigarette out on his arm. I thought, That's weird 'cos you don't smoke!

'There's a bit at the beginning of *Laurence Of Arabia* where he burns a lit match down to the end without flinching,' Matlock continues. 'Then the desk sergeant tries to do it and goes, 'Aaargh! You're mad! Doesn't that hurt?' 'Yes it hurts exceedingly,' Laurence says. 'so how do you cope with it?' 'Well, by not minding that it hurts.' John [Rotten] and John Beverley and all their mates were always goading each other to go one further . . . and I think Sid's self-mutilation came from that.'

'Sid often used to cut his arms up,' Henry Sabini remembers. 'That was the first time I'd witnessed this self-hurt thing; it was new in those days. He'd wear a capped T-shirt with his arms exposed revealing all this scarring, especially on the inside of his wrists. But I don't remember him showing off about it, or bothering to explain why he did it. You wouldn't talk to him about anything deep.' Besides, Sabini, Mandy and their mates had learned not to take anything Sid said at face value. 'When he used to turn up and say he'd been beaten up, we'd look at each other and think, I wouldn't be surprised if you hadn't done it to yourself.'

'You can't get much more punk than stubbing cigarettes out on your own arm, can you?' says Marco Pirroni. But maybe Sid didn't always do it as a matter of punk rock brinkmanship. Maybe he simply wanted to feel. Maybe he wanted to feel a pain greater than the one that tugged at his insides. Maybe he was cutting out the hurt from within his body.

'You definitely did wonder with Sid where it was all going to lead,' says Jonh Ingham. 'He and Johnny would have contests over who could stub out the most cigarettes on the back of their hands, but Sid took it further. I saw him cut himself with a razor. A lot of it, I think, was self-hatred, hatred of who he was as a person and his inability to do anything about it.'

'This group of kids utilised their self-abuse and their depression to the extent that they were cutting themselves, burning themselves, and using that as a heroic form of decoration,' says Caroline Coon. 'Kids would come to shows having slit their wrists, then decorated their clothes in their own blood. It was the ultimate death protest staged by kids who were heroically struggling against their anomie.' Though she doesn't use the phrase, Coon's explanation – 'a death protest' – sits comfortably with what I've turned on its head and called the 'art of dying young'.

'A while back,' says Wobble, 'a mate was talking to me about some geezer up in Islington who knew Sid. I said, "I must know him". He said, "No, he never met you, Sid told him to keep away from you". I was like, Sid, you've betrayed yourself. Twenty years on, I've just found out: you noticed something. Sid never normally made a comment like that, or showed having any interest other than in something that was determinedly nihilistic. It was bourgeois to pass comment.

'Sid was so resoundingly narcissistic. And when you're dealing with someone that wrapped up in themselves, it's kind of mental illness territory. It's all ME. GIMME SOMETHING. I'M FEELING AND I DON'T WANT TO FEEL. And YOU? Do I have any interest in you and how you behave? I DON'T FUCKING CARE. That's why it was strange to hear of him looking out for somebody else.'

Famously a man of relatively few words, Sid found it easier to express himself through style, through action and, at Sex Pistols shows, through a boisterous new dance movement called The Pogo.

No one quite remembers how or when it began, though most agree that The Pogo belonged to Sid. The movement certainly had his 'Keep Off!' stamp all over it. 'It was completely self-contained,' says Subway Sect's Rob Simmons. 'Sid would literally bounce up and down on the spot.'

Malcolm McLaren propagated many myths in *The Great Rock 'n' Roll Swindle*, his post-split take on the Pistols' story, but few doubted the veracity of his pen-portrait of Sid. 'Then there was Sidney. What a natural terrorist, working in the pubs, making sure every gig the group played ended up in the most unpredictable bloody mess. He invented The Pogo.'

JONH INGHAM: 'The first time I saw Sid, he was standing in front of John at the 100 Club – probably in May '76 – bouncing up and down with 20 people around him. He was this guy down the front, with a padlock and chain around his neck, bouncing up and down and twisting his head to the side. It soon caught on.'

MARCO PIRRONI: 'I didn't know him when I saw him pogoing at the 100 Club. Then about a week later I was in the shop, and so was he, so Jordan said, 'Do you know Sid?' I said, 'You're that bloke who jumps up and down, aren't you?'.'

ALAN JONES: 'I remember Sid doing it. I don't remember him being the first to do it. He apparently invented it, but it's like, who invented the plastic bag look? I know it was definitely going by the time of the 100 Club, because I always sat on the speakers there and looked out over the crowd.'

VIC GODARD: 'I only remember Sid doing it. It was basically him trying to annoy anyone who was within a ten-yard radius. It happened well before the 100 Club.'

STEVEN SEVERIN: 'The first time I saw him do it was at Bangs in Charing Cross Road. He was simply trying to see the band. If you take it a bit further than craning your neck, you're jumping up and down on the spot. The whole concept of charging into everybody else came a lot later. Yes, he was tall, but he would usually be somewhere at the back with us. We'd never go right down the front. No one went right down the front!'

'He looked great at the start,' says Rob Simmons, 'and not many people looked good at those early gigs. I only remember Sid standing out: very tall, very thin and with a Dennis The Menace hairstyle that looked like it had been chopped at with a pair of shears. Sid, Siouxsie and Mick Jones stood out most. But while Mick looked like a Keith Richards clone, Sid had something of his own.

'He was a very imposing, intimidating figure,' Mick Jones agrees. 'The first time I saw him he had on a full-length rubber coat down to his ankles, no socks, brothel creepers and shades – and a totally shaved head. He looked fantastic.'

Despite hacking his hair right back a couple of times, Sid gradually evolved a consistent look as 1976 progressed, slowly dropping the flamboyant drape-style dinner jackets and full-length rubber coats for a look more closely aligned to that of his latest heroes – The Ramones.

SUNDAY 4 July 1976: Watergate and the ignominious withdrawal from Vietnam temporarily forgotten, America celebrates 200 years of independence from Britain with characteristic stars-and-stripes aplomb. In London, it's the hottest night of the year thus far, and four young Americans are in town. They sing about punks and Nazis, about the CIA and the SLA, about basement drug highs and beating 'the brat with a baseball bat'. Their flag is more mangled than star-spangled.

One and a half thousand sweaty young souls, among them Sid Vicious and many other future punk rock luminaries, are jammed into the Roundhouse. Some of them were here a few weeks earlier, watching Patti Smith's thrilling warning shot, a performance that was primitive yet artful, poetic yet full of punkish intent. There is no poetry reading tonight. Nor do The Ramones wear Keith Richards T-shirts. Young, loud and spotty, they grunt petulantly into the microphones, rattle out their set at breakneck speed, stopping only to remove their leather jackets, and leave the stage to loud cheers after half an hour. 'Moronrock,' enthuses Max Bell in *New Musical Express* the following week. The phrase doesn't catch on, but the sound and style does.

Unlike Patti, high on the rebellion of Rimbaud and reggae, The Ramones revel in their unvarnished white trash status. Everything about them is shockingly simple: matching names (Joey Ramone, Dee Dee Ramone, etc.), identikit street style, songs that blur into one another. Dressed in cheap sneakers, worn and torn drainpipe denims and tight-fitting T-shirts, The Ramones adopt a legs-apart-knees-bent pose, their gaunt, unsmiling faces revealing little. Max Bell reckons Dee Dee, boldly sporting a so-crap-it's-good bowl haircut, is 'possibly the most half-witted specimen' he's ever witnessed on a stage. Dee Dee plays his bass so fiercely that he cuts his finger. Dee Dee becomes Sid's favourite Ramone.

'Sid didn't hate everything,' says Marco Pirroni. 'He loved The Ramones. I remember a conversation about their hair. We hated their hair. Sid had great hair; they didn't. But he did get his ripped jeans and leather jacket look from The Ramones.'

It was the rudimentary Ramones that gave Sid the confidence to pick up a musical instrument. 'He was the world's number one Ramones fan,' remembers Captain Sensible. 'I'd be round Sue Catwoman's house and there'd be this terrible noise. I'd go upstairs and there'd be Sid jamming along to The Ramones' first album – which kick-started the whole UK punk thing – on a bass guitar. That's how he learnt.'

Bassist Dee Dee Ramone remembered the cloying attentions of his young English fan. 'Sid Vicious followed me all over the place,' he told Legs McNeil and Gillian McCain for *Please Kill Me*, their definitive oral history of New York punk. He added that, contrary to his reputation, star-struck Sid was 'very nice and very innocent'.

A few days later, The Ramones played Dingwalls. This time, The Sex Pistols, who were in Sheffield on the night of the Roundhouse show, showed up too. They didn't come quietly. During the course of the evening, one of their crowd hurled a bottle at Joey Ramone, then bashed a door in, earning an instant ban for the band. Another Sidney misdemeanour?

Not necessarily. 'I'd been to the Roundhouse show, but because this was before I'd done the first *Sniffin' Glue*, I didn't know anybody there,' says Mark Perry. 'I met Shane McGowan that night. He was my first friend in punk. My diary records that I'd met this really wacky Irish guy who kept threatening to throw himself in front of a train. We went to the Dingwalls gig together and that's where I met my second person in punk, [The Damned's] Brian James. I'd finished my drink during the first song, and instead of just dropping it down, I attempted to chuck it in the gap between the band and the crowd. Before I knew it, I was lifted off my feet through the crowd and literally thrown out, ending up on my arse in the street.'

Sid managed to survive intact all the way to the after-show party. 'Everybody was bombed,' Dee Dee recounted in *Please Kill Me*, who remembers 'disgusting' mountains of puke 'in the sink, in the toilets, on the floor'. Sid still hadn't had his fill, so he asked The Ramones bassist for something 'to get high'. Generously stocked up with speed, Dee Dee offered some to his protégé. 'Sid pulled out a set of works, put a whole bunch of speed in the syringe, then stuck the needle in the toilet with all the puke and piss in there and loaded it.' Though a Class A user himself, Dee Dee was shocked by Sid's recklessness. 'I'd seen it all,' he told McNeil and McCain. 'He just looked at me kind of dazed and said, 'Man, where did you get this stuff?' '

The Patti Smith and Ramones' Roundhouse shows were both sell-outs. Meanwhile, The Sex Pistols were still playing the 100 Club and various out of town venues to between 20 and 150 people. Punk, common currency in describing the New York scene for well over a year now, was already being used to describe any music that was guitar-based, rocked hard and didn't outstay its welcome. In the summer of '76, it signified a broad spectrum of musical sound. By the end of the year, punk suggested an entire way of life.

Slowly, though, a genealogy began to emerge. For Nick Kent, all roads led back to Iggy Pop. 'The Stooges created punk. Iggy Pop is the Robert Johnson figure. The Velvet Underground played art rock with studied incompetence. I mean, John Cale came from the Conservatory! That first Stooges album had that real dumb simplicity; anyone could have written "1969". And Iggy's performance was crucial to it all too.'

While The Johns were still wandering aimlessly up and down the King's Road, and Sid was boyishly coveting Jeanette Lee in ACME Attractions, New York's Bowery district was already awash with stickers proclaiming prophetically: 'Watch out! Punk is coming!'

The binding force was youth, energy and attitude. That aside, there was little else to unite the groups emerging out of CBGB's and Max's Kansas City. 'The Ramones were the only band that embraced the punk label and direction,' says Television guitarist Richard Lloyd. 'Every other band was trying hard to get away from that. It was a bunch of very different bands in the same clubs. And it wasn't just musicians hanging out. There was a whole scene – painters, journalists, photographers, filmmakers. It was a cultural explosion.'

When the CBGB's set came to London, and collided with the nascent homegrown punk rock scene, the cultural explosion that followed wasn't restricted to artful creatives. In a country where the final embers of a working class tradition were still smouldering, it was this politicised, quasi-revolutionary dimension that gave UK punk rock a significance that went far and beyond anything that the self-pleasing Manhattan misfits could have achieved. Johnny Rotten's extraordinary claim to Jonh Ingham in *Sounds* back in April – 'I want people to see us and start something, or else I'm just wasting my time' – turned out to be more prophetic than he could ever have imagined.

'The economic situation was much more precarious in Britain at the time, and you have a tradition of being very vocal about political opinions and dressing up,' says Debbie Harry. 'Politics in Britain has always been expressed in fashion. It really isn't an American tradition.'

While there were echoes of New York's artful posing, the emerging British punk subculture tapped into something more meaningful than simply banishing creative ennui. 'It was more nihilistic than in the States,' says New York photographer Bob Gruen, who looked up Malcolm McLaren when he visited London in autumn 1976. 'These crazy looking kids were in your face. They had writing all over their jackets, hypodermic needles and Nazi emblems hanging off their clothes. In New York, a T-shirt and jeans would do.

'When I went to SEX, there were these trousers and shirts with straps around them which allowed you to tie people's legs and arms together. I remember looking at them on the wall and thinking, 'That's the dumbest thing I've ever seen. Why would you want to tie your legs together?' When I came back to England six months later, all the kids were wearing them.'

Despite its energy and creative ambition, the New York scene still saw itself as part of the Great Tradition. The bands cranked out sleazed-up variations on 12-bar rock 'n' roll, while most of its audience still thrilled to the spectacle of the traditionally wasted rock idol. Narcissism and hard drugs were endemic to the scene.

London was different. Malcolm McLaren and his cabal of provocateurs – among them designer Jamie Reid and Marx-spouting Bernie Rhodes – seized the moment and dreamed up new ways of putting revolt into style. The Sex Pistols and their champions punched their way on to the front pages of the rock press, which seemed increasingly desperate to champion anything that might consign 'Rock Wankman' or 'Steel Shite Pan' to the dustbin. Above all, what gripped London, and very soon the rest of the country, was a moody iconoclasm that refused to acknowledge that dog-eared and dreary rock 'n' roll rulebook. That's why so much domestic punk came out so thrillingly jagged and hamfisted, why the nation's photocopiers soon whirred to the sound of a thousand hastily assembled fanzines. Music and style were overturned as much by shot-in-the-dark necessity as by artful design.

As a genuine believer in nothing much at all, Sid made a perfect punk ideologue. He hated everything: the cruelly stratified society in which he had no stake; the elders who taught him nothing; and most of all, rock's old guard, those proverbial Boring Old Farts, who had reneged on their promise of teenage revolution.

'He always had an opinion,' remembers Jonh Ingham. 'We'd talk about the first Ramones album, because it was the only thing around, and I remember him saying, 'If The Ramones were smart, they'd break up now.' Everyone else went, 'Eh?' He said, 'That first album's perfect. How are they gonna get better? The only thing they can do is make it all over again.' He was clearly very, very smart.'

The Ramones were the ultimate punk rock band, reckoned Sid. Unlike the Pistols, with their McLaren-induced rhetoric and Rotten's bile and anger, the New Yorkers had no obvious social or intellectual agenda. They were smart-dumb and funny, so perfectly Sid. 'There was never any point to what Sid did,' says Marco Pirroni. 'It was just stupid, so stupid it was funny, a celebration of dumbness.' John Lydon was a little less fanatical in his admiration for The Ramones. 'Lydon was sharper than Sid; they were two completely different characters. I understood Sid a lot better because he came from the same musical background as me. He was a complete glam fashion freak, really.'

Unlike Lydon, whose Rotten persona stamped itself indelibly on the psychopathology of British punk, the comic clothes horse looked to others for approval and self-esteem. And as a 'punk' mindset began to take hold during the summer and autumn of 1976, his peers demanded acts of more punkish abandon. He fought. He threw glasses. Yet Sid could still be hilarious, taking the piss out of the Old Farts, out of Rotten for getting his mug in the papers too often, out of the part-time punks who'd pin a safety pin to their lapel and hit Louise's in the hope of meeting a Sex Pistol.

Poly Styrene was another early, thrill-seeking malcontent who became swept up in punk's first flush of iconoclasm and creative liberation. She sold trinkets and second-hand clothes, formed X-Ray Spex and wrote some of the era's most incisive songs about consumption, identity and casting off the old ways ('Oh, bondage, up yours!'). Then, in 1978, she famously turned her back on it all.

'Punk was all about communication of energy and ideas, and what a messed up screwed up world we're living in,' she says. 'But that was all quite negative. Yeah, it's not a nice world that we live in. Terrible things are happening. And that's 100 per cent what punk was about. But we can't just keep criticising, and become a helpless victim unable to do anything.'

Under the presssure of all those isms, all of punk's negative rhetoric, Poly Styrene bowed out and took off in search of a spiritual awakening. For Sid Vicious, spiritually adrift and desperately seeking respect from wherever he could find it, that option was unthinkable. Once he had that Manchester United scarf in his mind, he had to have it. Once he launched himself, James Cagney-like, into a fight, he was unable to extricate himself. Once he'd become the dandy of the punk underworld, he threw himself into the role with a vengeance. When it came to tunnel vision, Sid was impeccably short-sighted.

Punk was loud, demanded to be noticed, was all about the big gesture, and that's just what Sid excelled at. That's what gave his life meaning, made him 'whole'. 'I've been thinking of what to say to you for weeks,' admits Henry Sabini, when we finally get together to speak, 'because it was so difficult to get to know him. He was kind of hollow, whereas all the others from that time had something about their character that sticks out. Sid was 'The Hollow

Man', though you could never say that about Lydon. Sid was kinda empty, he really was . . . pretty vacant.' Well, someone had to say it.

'A lot of the punks became victims, really,' says Poly Styrene. 'Look at what happened to Sid Vicious. They got into the age-old habit of getting drunk, smoking, taking drugs, ruining their health, doing exactly the same things as the generation before them did. They weren't that much different from their parents.'

Unlike the hippies, who attempted to show the rest of the world a different way and failed, the punks held themselves – and everything else that was debased and rotten – up to society as a more brutal, honest and effective assertion of teenage power. Though spiritually bereft, Sid had a mantra of his own that he repeated often: 'People are rubbish.' 'That was one of his favourite lines,' says Steven Severin, 'that everything was rubbish, worthless.'

A refuge for the damaged, for strays, and of course, for those to whom violence came naturally, punk was founded on a necessarily pessimistic view of human nature, a subcultural hard hat that afforded protection and a safe place from which to attack.

'We all adopted a certain macho stance,' admits Alan Jones, who then speculates whether this trickled down from the mischievous mind of McLaren. The Pistols' manager certainly understood the value of a few fisticuffs and an antagonistic attitude towards the parent culture, but one man – or even one band – alone couldn't have engendered such a shift in attitude.

According to Caroline Coon, punk coincided with a crisis in masculinity: 'By 1976, there was a huge masculine backlash against the emerging women's liberation movement. All the men in rock 'n' roll were talking about women as slags, boilers, slappers and whores. To a man, those journalists were virulently homophobic. Remember the phrase 'Brickies in satin'? This idea that working-class men couldn't be gay too . . . it's a myth. It's a male hysteria against homo-eroticism. They couldn't cope with the idea that strength could also be female, that you could wear skirts and make-up and still be heterosexual and masculine, and love women, love fucking . . .

'It's a mistake to think that the only way to be masculine is to be hard and brittle and unbending. That's a very partial idea of what masculinity is, especially when you're young, when your identity, your sexuality, is fluid. And rock 'n' roll, in the tradition of theatre and ballet, is a place that whatever your sexuality was, it could be expressed freely.

'The paradox for men who became rock 'n' rollers was that being a rock star on stage is a passive, 'feminine' thing to be. If you are a man who thinks that the epitome of masculinity is to be a truck driver or a miner, the paradox that you are actually on stage playing a guitar creates quite a conflict within your psyche. So what you get in rock 'n' roll is hyper-macho.

'For a time, it looked as if the hippie male was going to introduce a new kind of sexuality. Jimi Hendrix was the epitome of a gender blur. Jagger and Bowie flirted with the gender blur, began to talk about their bisexuality, but the male culture was so hostile to it that they quickly backed off. The male culture in rock 'n' roll is so homophobic that they have to disavow it.

'Sid was a beautiful-looking youth, and absolutely unaware of it, which is part of what beauty is. And of course to talk about beauty was also part of the psychopathology of being masculine. You can't be beautiful. Johnny and the others made themselves look as ugly as possible in order to be masculine.'

At one remove from 'phoney' humanistic values, punk shunned love, tolerated violence and delighted in making a nuisance of itself. 'It's great the way all this is getting up the old farts' noses,' said drummer Paul Cook that summer. At the second Manchester show, later that month, Rotten tore off his shirt for the encore and tore into a new song, 'Anarchy In The UK'. Days later, *Melody Maker* splashed a fight scene from a Pistols' show on the front cover, coupled with a large print prediction by Caroline Coon: 'Out of the gloriously raucous, uninhibited mêlée of British punk rock will emerge the musicians to inspire a fourth generation of rockers.'

Almost immediately, the rock world experienced a moment of epiphany: everything was either before or after The Sex Pistols. The group's impact began to be felt beyond London and into the provinces. New songs were added all the time. One night, after sharing the bill with the Pistols, Joe Strummer quit his pub rock combo The 101'ers and set about forming his own 'punk rock' band. The Clash, and dozens of others like them, began to spring up in the Pistols' wake. Unsurprisingly, Sid too wanted in.

During 1976, Sid had become an itinerant, moving from New Court in Hampstead to various squats in Islington and King's Cross, and into the burgeoning West London squat 'n' roll scene from which The Clash sprang. By October, he was back in Hampstead again, a fly on the wall while Johnny Rotten wrote out the lyrics to a new song, 'No Future'. Also that month, having been fired up by his stage debut at the 100 Club, he attempted to knock a band of his own into shape.

While dossing at the maisonette squat in Davis Road, where the nascent Clash were living, Sid was surrounded by aspiring musicians. Some, such as Mick Jones and Keith Levene, were innately gifted; others, including future Slits guitarist Viv Albertine, had no better idea how to tune an instrument than Sid did.

Among punk aficionados, The Flowers Of Romance have become a band of mythic proportions. But unlike The Slits, The Pop Group, This Heat, Throbbing Gristle, Kleenex or any number of punk-era cult heroes, there is absolutely nothing to substantiate the legend. In truth, they have more in common with the fictional punk combo, The Moors Murderers. Great name – bittersweet, and also used for an on-stage Sex Pistols noise-jam. So good, in fact, that its author, John Lydon reactivated the name for the third Public Image Limited album. Pity, then, about the legacy: no tapes, no reviews, nor even any positive testimony to lend support to the group's apparent greatness. Truth is, The Flowers Of Romance barely managed more than a handful of cursory rehearsals.

According to Viv Albertine, who became close to Sid in autumn 1976, the group attempted to play a few Ramones songs. Recalling the makeshift combo to Jon Savage for *England's Dreaming*, she admitted that The Flowers Of Romance were simply 'a bunch of interesting looking people [who had] never done anything and could hardly play.'

Viv had a stab at the guitar, Palmolive, a fearless young émigré from Spain, bashed the cymbal-free drum kit, Jo Faull and Sarah Hall (girlfriends of Sex Pistols Steve Jones and Paul Cook) fiddled about on guitar and bass respectively while Keith Levene would sometimes drop by to show everyone how to tune up. At the helm of this intentionally female-dominated band of hopefuls was Sid, who hovered idly at the mike stand wondering what to sing when the bare bones of a song materialised – which wasn't very often. Despite his outward confidence, and the vast quantities of speed he was now consuming, Sid wasn't a natural out front. That's why he'd not turned up earlier that summer when Rat Scabies and Brian James asked him to audition for The Damned.

Uncertain of his role, Sid decided to restyle himself as an English Dee Dee Ramone. According to Anne Beverley, he practised 'for a month solid, 18 hours a day . . . I had never known him put so much into something,' she told Simon Kinnersley. 'He was going to form a rival band to The Sex Pistols.'

Applying such sustained dedication to anything, even the chance to compete with his mate Rotten, didn't much sound like Sid. Chrissie Hynde's recollection that he spent two or three days playing along to The Ramones' album sounds far more feasible. Legend has it that the sum of Sid's learning was mastering a few basic moves on the E string one night while out of his head on speed.

Sid saw no mystique in musicianship. 'You just take a chord, go twang and you've got music,' he'd grunt punkishly. The technically gifted had had it their way for too long. Now it was the turn of the musically illiterate, those diamond dogs who would giggle at the mention of a G-string, and not give an F about the other five either. But even trying to assemble a punk band took some organising, and when it came to rehearsals Sid was hardly the world's greatest disciplinarian.

The Flowers Of Romance sounded great in Sid's head. Trying to make the group happen was rather less fun. Jo Faull quit, Sid sacked Sarah, and then got rid of Palmolive. By the time he'd returned from his autumn one-night stand with the Banshees and short stretch at Ashford, the group revolved around the nucleus of Sid, Albertine, Steve England and Steve Walsh. His intriguing idea to lead an all-women backing band had been scrapped.

During the winter, future Banshees drummer Kenny Morris also sat in on a few sessions. 'It was in The Clash's rehearsal room, and it was more cold in there than it was outside. We'd play a few Ramones covers and a few of Sid's songs like 'Belsen Was A Gas' and 'Kamikaze', but everything would always break down.'

Around this time, The Flowers Of Romance were interviewed at The Clash's rehearsal studios in Chalk Farm for the *Skum No 1* fanzine. Even by the standards of the time, Sid's responses to interviewer Paul were pure punk fundamentalist :

Sid on singing: 'I just scream down the mike.'

Sid on why he formed the band: 'I don't know about the rest of them but personally I don't have any views on anything.'

Sid on fame (if it beckons): 'I'm not into the superstar trip . . . select places or bodyguards. I'll just be the yob I am now.'

Sid on musical ambition: 'If I ever get the urge to do something like that, I'd consider myself to be a total cunt and I'd blow my brains out.'

Sid on politics: 'I'm not prepared to write about dull, tedious nonsense.'

Sid on Sid: 'I'm totally numb . . . I'm more of a robot than a person. I don't work on an emotional level.'

Sid on why he started playing: 'As Jonathan Richman said, 'Cos I'm Lonely'. That was true once with me, but now it's not.'

Sid's favourite colour: 'I haven't got a favourite colour.'

Sid didn't give a fuck about politics, about the needs of others, or what concerned liberals and leftists thought of his abundance of swastikas – which even found their way down to the front of his underpants. Taken with the bondage trousers, the proliferation of padlocks and safety pins, the repetitive pogo dance, the temporal and technical restrictions in the music, the radical rhetoric, and the nihilism that pervaded the scene, the swastika expressed all the bad-tempered visual noise that punk could muster. Sid loved his swastika. He hated virtually everything else, especially those 'fascists' who tried to tell him that his swastika was in 'bad taste'.

Sid's sole legacy to the art of the popular song is 'Belsen Was A Gas'. One of a handful of originals he'd written for The Flowers Of Romance – the others were 'Brains On Vacation', 'Postcards From Auschwitz' and 'Piece Of Garbage', further exercises in schoolboy misanthropy – 'Belsen' was later deemed suitable for The Sex Pistols. Written during an era when aborted foetuses were being thrown on stage, and faeces and menstrual blood were becoming acceptable tools for the contemporary artist, it was perfectly pitch-black humour that left The Ramones' Nazi-chic 'Today Your Love, Tomorrow The World' standing.

Sid wrote his lyrics out in neat, girlish handwriting, meticulously dotting each 'i' with an open circle in flamboyantly flower-power fashion. But this was no ode to a nightingale, or to the nice girl next door. 'Belsen Was A Gas' aspired not to high Romanticism but instead reflected the grim, gallows humour of the streets, where even the most awful tragedies – Aberfan, Biafra, the death of Marc Bolan – invariably prompted a wave of jokes that spread virus-like throughout every pub, office and factory floor.

The song's catchphrase, 'Oh dear!', was heartless enough. The verse that Johnny Rotten chose to omit for the Pistols' version of the song was bleaker still:

> Belsen was divine
> If you survived the train
> Then when you get inside
> It's Aufiedersein [*sic*]

Punk could niggle and shock and wag an admonishing finger. But still it was found wanting when held up against the chamber of horrors that was everyday life.

Junk

'I wish I was a baby
I wish I was dead.'

'Cold Turkey' (1970),
Plastic Ono Band

1. I'M WITH THE BAND

'The line-up is much more handsome now. That is a fact. And we play songs much faster now.' – Sid Vicious, 1977

Buckingham Palace, London, Thursday, 10 March 1977

SID VICIOUS was lying in his favourite position: comatose, on his back, on the floor. A small television crew loitered aimlessly, amid the bodies and the beer cans, hoping that someone might speak to them – or at least spew up for the benefit of the cameras. It was late at night in The Sex Pistols' Denmark Street rehearsal studio/crash pad and nothing much was happening.

It was especially quiet around The Sex Pistols' new recruit who, recalled Malcolm McLaren, was 'totally out to lunch'. Then the barely conscious bassist – though the public had yet to hear him play a note – raised his head, blinked long and hard, and uttered a few priceless words of gratitude. 'I've had the greatest time of my life,' he slurred. 'This is my first day and as far as I'm concerned it's great being in The Sex Pistols.' Then, finding Steve Jones' bed, Sid flopped out. It had been a long day. It sure felt good to be barely alive.

Little over 12 hours earlier, at around ten past ten on an overcast early spring morning, the four Sex Pistols, together with manager Malcolm McLaren, had gathered outside Buckingham Palace to sign an historic treaty. In truth, the real signing had taken place the day before, in the offices of Rondor Music, the publishing wing of the Pistols' new label, A&M Records.

But with the band's winter-long front-page status on the wane, and the public demanding a fresh line in sensationalism, McLaren decided to pit his so-called 'nightmare of British culture' against the greatest symbol of the class system – the monarchy.

As the band flash V-signs to the waiting press corps from the Daimler that circles the appointed, palace-facing traffic island, a table is hastily erected to receive them. Standing beside it is the A&M managing director Derek Green, in suit and tie, and a couple of security men. After the Pistols emerge from the car, a police constable arrives to check out the uncharacteristic early morning activity. He finds four youths, all hung over from the previous night's celebrations, dressed in swastika-festooned 'Destroy' T-shirts, mohair jumpers and leather jackets, giggling and gurning for a gaggle of photographers. The constable asks the gathering to leave, and – as photos are taken – everyone makes their way to the Regent's Park Hotel in nearby Piccadilly.

The press conference isn't scheduled to start at the hotel's Apex Room until eleven. The band arrive a quarter of an hour early so they help themselves to the 'hospitality'. Sid grabs himself a large bottle of Bacardi, which he polishes off over the course of the next hour or so. With a skull and crossbones on his heavily studded leather jacket, his customary padlock and chain around his neck, and his hair now spiked to even greater heights, Sid the new boy with the ready-made reputation is already competing with Rotten as the focus of attention.

The event, which is attended by the national press and even a handful of international music journalists, was introduced by A&M's Derek Green, justifiably proud to have signed the most newsworthy band in Britain for a snip at £150,000 over the next two years. Introducing Sid as 'the one with his flies open', Green then takes questions from the floor. Someone quizzes him about the band's behaviour and whether he has any control over them. As Green opens his mouth to answer, Sid leans to one side and farts loudly. Sid swigs hard at his Bacardi bottle, which prompts this most Swiftian Sex Pistol to expand his repertoire with a few belches and, of course, the customary stream of profanities.

A woman from the *Daily Express* directs a question at him. He is roused to his feet. 'Why are you asking me that dull fucking question? Anyway, didn't I see you at a party last week stuck on so-and-so's cock?' It's the cue for the band to begin firing off soda siphons at the assembled throng. Vivien Goldman, *Sounds* magazine's reggae enthusiast and a pal of Rotten's, is also on the receiving end of some abuse from punk's supposedly femme-friendly male.

In a lull between questions, Sid slurs: 'What's wrong with you? Don't you want to say anything to us?' For fear of public humiliation, they don't. *Melody Maker* reporter Brian Harrigan later describes the band as 'ugly, shabby and exceedingly unpleasant', three quick reasons why many of the journalists feel intimidated. Asked why they chose Sid to replace Glen Matlock, the new boy jumps in with a proud 'Because I beat up Nick Kent.' When it is revealed that The Sex Pistols are going to play a benefit show at the King's Road Theatre at the beginning of April, someone asks whether it is a benefit for the beleaguered Rolling Stone guitarist Keith Richards. 'I wouldn't piss on him if he was on fire,' Sid deadpans.

After the press conference, Brian Harrigan introduced himself to Sid, whom he memorably described as 'looking a little like a corpse freshly fished from a river after about ten days of floating around. Tall, thin, spikey-haired, with the complexion of a slab of Polyfilla he had an expression of congenital idiocy, and eyes like razor slashes.'

With just two inches of rum remaining in his bottle, Sid spoke briefly about McLaren. 'I think he's a great manager,' he explained in what Harrigan called his 'zomboid' voice. 'I like him. He never gave me my wages last week. He said I was naughty. I don't care anyway.' If being 'punk' meant dumbing down, then Sid certainly passed his first test as a Sex Pistol with flying colours. 'I'd love to see him on Mastermind,' Harrigan concluded.

Afterwards, the group – carrying all the booze they could salvage – were driven to Wessex Studios in north London, where Chris Thomas was mixing the next single, 'No Future', now more provocatively retitled 'God Save The Queen'. Sid and Paul Cook began to fight (about who was the toughest Sex Pistol, McLaren later claimed), a flurry of fists that became more serious on the journey back to A&M's offices in New King's Road, where they were supposed to decide on a B-side. Sid lost a shoe and cut his foot, Paul Cook (an 'albino gorilla', taunted Vicious) got a bloody nose and in the mêlée, Johnny Rotten's watch – a Christmas present from his mother – also got smashed.

At A&M, things turned from bad to worse. The band were introduced to the staff, one of whom got more than she bargained for when Steve Jones escorted her to the office loo. Sid's encounter with a record company lavatory was somewhat less pleasurable. Jamming his foot down the loo in an attempt to clean his wound, he broke the bowl, fell back and put his elbow through a window. Returning to the press office, Sid ranted and raved: 'My foot's bleeding. Can you find a fucking plaster for me, you bitch!'

After being bandaged up, Sid nicked some more red wine, threw up on the carpet and passed out in the boss's chair. Someone placed a daffodil in his lap. Someone else threw up on a rubber plant. Things slowly quietened down. 'No Feelings' was selected as the forthcoming B-side. Sid was woken up when someone hurled a glass of red wine in his face, the cue for the band to head off to the Speakeasy – though not in the Daimler, whose driver refused to take them any further – before heading back to Denmark Street.

As Sid said, it's great being in The Sex Pistols.

SINCE 1 December 1976, when a brief, expletive-strewn television appearance on the *Today* show provoked a national outcry, McLaren's idle fantasy – releasing a cultural virus that would have the country shaking to its foundation – was exceeding even the wildest fantasies of his wayward imagination. The Sex Pistols, and the punk subculture that had grown around the group, had created a genuine moral panic, the greatest threat to the nation's morale since the doodlebug. But one weak link in the chain gang had emerged. No matter that Glen Matlock was the band's chief songwriter and the most musically gifted Sex Pistol, his relationship with Rotten had become increasingly untenable.

Back in November 1976, Rotten had told Caroline Coon: 'People have blown our involvement in violence right out of proportion. They want to associate us with violence . . . It makes us out to be just crude, ignorant and loutish. Which means we aren't a threat to them.' It was extraordinarily perceptive, but at the same time, violence, or at least the vicarious thrill of it, was a defining characteristic of the Pistols' milieu. With new 'punk' bands popping up daily throughout the autumn, the Pistols needed to maintain their sense of superiority, their reputation as supreme architects of the new disorder.

Glen Matlock has no beef with the man who replaced him. But as someone who was 'the tunes of the band, with a bit of the lyrical stance as well', it galls him to think that those who don't know better still regard him as an imposter when he takes the stage at Sex Pistols reunion shows.

'Even Steve and Paul now recognise that they made a wrong move,' he says. 'steve has even said that the day we appeared on the Bill Grundy [*Today*] show marks the beginning of the end of The Sex Pistols. That's when it went from a band that were their own men, and who could play, to some media exercise with a built-in shelf life. We were already front-page news when I was in the band.'

In the wake of the 100 Club Punk Festival, the Pistols had moved out of the music press and into the tabloids. A deal with EMI was swiftly followed by a debut single, 'Anarchy In The UK', in November. The record chugged along, not unlike Hawkwind's 'Silver Machine'. But while it was slower than the impatient punk audience might have liked, 'Anarchy' conveyed – thanks to Rotten's snarling delivery – the necessary message of social disorder. Matlock didn't, at least according to Rotten, who had him marked as a well-fed, grammar school-attending mummy's boy hung up on musical heritage and unwilling to embrace punkish abandon.

Antagonism between the pair had been long simmering. Matlock, with his muso Rickenbacker bass, and Rotten, drunk and lairy after a pre-show piss-up with his mates, fought on stage at the Pistols' first 100 Club performance at the end of March. The rivalry between the band's musical head and its non-musical heart intensified as fame – or at least infamy – beckoned.

'As soon as he got his boat race in the paper, John totally changed,' Matlock says. 'You can't have a working musical relationship with somebody when it's all one way. His persona was fine for the public. But when you're in the back of a van with somebody . . .'

There was also the important question of intra-band politics. While publicly revelling in his outsider status, Rotten, now sensing the bit between his teeth, remained isolated within the group – not a good thing when there were important decisions to be made. 'For all his strengths, when John joined he upset the balance a bit, and his whole idea was a political thing. He always thought it was Steve, Paul and me against him, but it wasn't like that. It was Steve and Paul, then me, and then John.' By January 1977, after the band returned from a short tour of Holland, it was everyone – McLaren included – against Glen Matlock.

'Malcolm was stirring it up,' Glen recalls. 'He's got a short attention span and likes to keep everything on its toes. He was playing this game, pitching me against John, sending a lot of false information between us.' Momentarily anxious at those 'THE FILTH AND THE FURY' headlines that erupted the day after the *Today* show appearance, the manager's nerve soon steadied and he gloried in the Pistols' bogeymen status. Music became a secondary consideration.

'Malcolm didn't want a musician,' says Marco Pirroni. 'He wanted someone who could cause trouble, cause chaos! He wasn't interested in managing a band and sending them to America, doing deals and merchandising and taking his 20 per cent. That's work. That's *boring*!'

Jonh Ingham remembers 'this wonderful quote that Malcolm once said: 'I never think until I open my mouth. That makes things far more interesting.' Ever since his association with The New York Dolls, Malcolm wanted to have a famous band, but the fact that he was dealing with people's lives never really entered into the equation.'

'I wanted a band like The Who or the Stones, not necessarily to sound like them but to have some kind of career,' Matlock says. 'I didn't wanna be in a band to toe the line worse than if you were bottom of the rung working at some carpet factory. I wanted to be in a band 'cos I wanted to be me, not pretend to be somebody else.

'I thought punk was forward-looking, not about falling into the same traps and routines of the old superstars. It was a bit of an art movement. Then Sid came along and totally blew all that. Malcolm had been pitching this whole idea that we were his puppets, which was a complete load of baloney, and Sid just played right into Malcolm's hands and the whole thing became a cartoon strip. Apart from the fact that the songs were great, it was like The Bay City Rollers with the knobs turned up to 11.'

'Lydon wanted his mate in the group,' reasons Nick Kent. 'Paul and Steve went way back, so John wanted his mate too. And John got him because Malcolm liked the way Sid looked. Sid was controllable. He couldn't play very well, but Malcolm wasn't stupid. This thing ain't gonna last. I wanna explode it. I'm getting bored. When McLaren brought Sid into the group, it was like giving a mentally challenged 18-year-old a gun and inviting him to rob a bank with you. You know there's gonna be victims.

'McLaren knew that when this guy was let loose in a room, he's gonna start hurting people, people he'd never even seen before, for no particular reason. This is a guy who threw a glass at a pillar and blinded a girl. He should have been jailed for that. But punk needed a real psychopath. That's what McLaren really liked. I got the real thing here, man! The guy was a pimp, wilfully immoral in what he did and he knows it. I've spoken to him about it. I've looked into his eyes. I know how haunted he is.'

'Malcolm wanted to make them as unruly as possible,' affirms Alan Jones. 'He definitely knew that Sid was more malleable than John. You could talk Sid into doing anything, whereas John would always question things. If he didn't wanna do it, he wouldn't do it.'

'That's a convenient way of explaining it all away,' says Steven Severin. 'I think it's more complex than that. It's quite possible that in social situations, he could be wound up and become the centre of attention by getting involved in a fight with someone or getting himself ejected from somewhere. But this would only happen on his terms, if he could subconsciously see it would benefit him. I can't imagine Sid simply being told what to do.' Especially within earshot of his best mate. 'John Lydon was saying the complete opposite: Be yourself. Sid adopted that forceful personality where he'd say, 'Everything is rubbish', and to have him then manipulated by McLaren . . . I find that hard to believe.'

Caroline Coon insists there's a crucial difference between McLaren's knowing, manipulative nihilism and the romantic, self-destruct button that was at Sid's disposal. 'What you're meant to do with youth at that age is to hold them so that they can grow enough to recognise their destructive patterns, and with any luck they'll come out the other side. You really need to take care of those kids.' Except that this was '77, not '67; destruction was *de rigueur*, caring was only for delicate hippie types.

There was no soothing invocation of the magic phrase 'musical differences' when, on 28 February 1977, McLaren dictated a telegram explaining that Sid Vicious was to replace Matlock.

'GLEN WAS THROWN OUT OF THE SEX PISTOLS SO IM TOLD BECAUSE HE WENT ON TOO LONG ABOUT PAUL MCCARTNEY STOP EMI WAS ENOUGH STOP THE BEATLES WAS TOO MUCH STOP SID VICIOUS THEIR BEST FRIEND AND ALWAYS A MEMBER OF THE GROUP BUT UNHEARD AS YET WAS ENLISTED STOP HIS BEST CREDENTIAL WAS THAT HE GAVE NICK KENT WHAT HE DESERVED MANY MONTHS AGO AT THE HUNDRED CLUB LOVE AND PEACE MALCOLM MCLAREN.'

Shortly afterwards, McLaren summed up the change more succinctly: 'The playing is not the big deal,' he said. 'That comes afterwards. It's the attitude that counts.'

McLaren was right. Too much emphasis on technical ability had killed rock as a force for social change and instead transformed it into a masturbatory exercise in aesthetics. The politics of messthetics is what mattered now. And if the uncouth and the untrained could take over rock 'n' roll, which in spring 1977 was looking distinctly possible, then who knows what might happen if such an (anti)social subculture began to impact on society at large?

Unfortunately for McLaren, The Sex Pistols had already grown used to the idea of being a tight-knit rock 'n' roll combo. Cook and Jones took great pride in their technical advances. 'Paul and Steve rehearsed every day,' says Pistols roadie John 'Boogie' Tiberi. 'Steve was obsessive about it.' Having Sid along meant that more burning matches were applied to hair and bottoms on the tour bus, but his limited bass-playing skills stopped the band's musical development dead. Worse still for those trying to hold it together, Sid made a virtue of his limitations. Pissed or stoned, usually both, he'd rather play the audience than his instrument. When the others attempted to cajole him into playing properly, Sid insisted it was the performance that mattered, not the music. This was just what McLaren, already courting Hollywood with an idea for a full-length Sex Pistols film, wanted to hear.

Alan Jones agrees. 'Sid picked the bass up, plucked away, and he was hopeless. But he didn't need to do anything. Sid simply looked fabulous, and had bags of charisma. He was a pop idol.'

Subway Sect's Vic Godard reckons that, contrary to legend, Sid did possess an instinctive musical ear. 'I thought he was a real expert. We were in The Clash's rehearsal place, some time after the 100 Club Festival, and Chrissie Hynde showed me how to roll a joint, and Sid showed me how to play [The Heartbreakers'] "Chinese Rocks" on an acoustic guitar. I went home thinking, 'Two great new things I know how to do now!' As a guitarist, Sid was in a different league to us. He also taught me how to play Eddie Cochran numbers like 'Nervous Breakdown'. He was talented.'

'It wasn't that he couldn't play,' insists Subway Sect's Rob Simmons. 'When he switched to bass, he just wanted to play in that simple Ramones style, keep hammering that single note. Sometimes, he'd sit in and play bass with us, and it was embarrassing because he could play really well. He would hear a song, then pick up a guitar and play it. I think Sid could play it by ear.'

'In *Sid And Nancy*, there's one scene toward the end where Gary Oldham as Sid takes some speed, he sits in the chair and goes, doo-doo-doo-doo, Ramones style,' remembers Marco Pirroni. 'That's exactly what Sid would do, lean up against a wall and play 'Blitzkrieg Bop'. Simple basslines. When he joined the Pistols, he wanted to be good, he was conscientious. I dunno what happened. Maybe the heroin got in the way.'

2. ENTER THE DRAGON

PISTOLS GUITARIST Steve Jones ripped Johnny Thunders' guitar licks and on-stage moves. Sid Vicious picked up his chronic heroin habit, and the ex-New York Doll's total enslavement to the art of falling apart. Both Sid Vicious and Johnny Thunders are dead. Thunders' inspiration Keith Richards, rock's most 'elegantly wasted human being' according to the '70s stylebook, riffs on.

'All this stuff really starts with Keith Richards,' says Dead Boys guitarist Jimmy Zero, who hung out with Sid during his last days in New York. 'Actually, it goes back a long way before that, too, but Keith is the person that Johnny was copying, and Sid and the rest of us we were all picking up on Johnny's thing.'

Never underestimate the death instinct in rock 'n' roll. It's so strong, in fact, that Bob Dylan once faked his own, and others faked Paul McCartney's for him. Like a sneeze, or a drink or drug binge, rock at its most powerful can take on the status of a little death, the proverbial eargasm, a sensory escape into an exotic otherworld, a cloud nine refuge from flat earth hell. Loud and intense, repetitive and angry, punk had the ability to derange the senses more intensely than other music genres.

Punk nourished Sid, nurtured his barely concealed craving for self-destruction. Like a pint that refused to settle, he became the movement's effervescent problem child. Bolstered by beer, by whatever drugs he could lay his reckless hands on, by constant noise and by the gang mentality that inspired him to ever more outrageous acts, he skidded wilfully into a fragile omnipotence.

17-year-old John Beverley (far right) partying in north London, Halloween 1974. 'It was fancy dress,' says Simone Stenfors, 'but he simply went as himself.' (photo courtesy of Simone Stenfors)

(Top l–r): Simon Cowen, Steve England and party host Martin Shapiro. Short-haired Sid (bottom left) was already perfecting his punk attitude. (photo courtesy of Simone Stenfors)

Sid's first public duty as a Pistol, outside Buckingham Palace, 10 March 1977. 'The line-up is much more handsome now,' he claimed.

'Beastly' Sid with punk matriarch Vivienne Westwood. The aspiring designer regarded him as the ultimate punk, the perfect Sex Pistol.

Pistols on the run: By summer 1977, the band's rabble-rousing antics had provoked a huge social backlash against the punk rock movement.

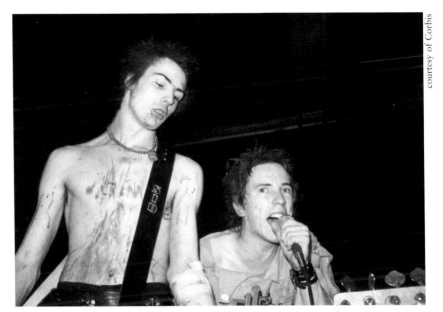

Theatre of cruelty: Sid's self-inflicted wounds were not so much punk bravado as a visible manifestation of his chronic lack of self-esteem.

L–r: Paul Cook, Johnny Rotten, Sid, Steve Jones. As 1977 progressed, Sid eclipsed Rotten as the most newsworthy Sex Pistol.

Sid and Nancy in Paris, spring 1978. Their reliance on drink and drugs was already taking a visible toll on the pair.

Glen Matlock salutes the man who replaced him in The Sex Pistols at the 'Sid Sods Off' gig in London, 15 August 1978.

Nancy joined Sid on stage for his first solo appearances, but invariably her microphone was switched off.

Sid and Nancy with Motörhead frontman Lemmy, one of the few famous faces he didn't try to punch out.

Sex Pistols manager Malcolm McLaren flew into New York after the death of Nancy Spungeon, but was back in London working on his own court battle when news of Sid's death came through on 2 February 1979.

Before heroin, before Nancy, even before he joined The Sex Pistols, Sid was already losing some of his boisterous, boyish charm in his bid to become the New Wave's king of oblivion. 'The night in Louise's when he told me about joining the Pistols he wasn't very Sid,' remembers Marco Pirroni. 'He wasn't funny for a start. Any humour or loveableness had completely disappeared.'

That Christmas, while Sid was in tears at a maudlin old Jim Reeves song, the party Jonh Ingham and Caroline Coon arranged for London's punk rock waifs and strays was rapidly disintegrating into an orgy of disrepute. The reason, says Coon, was the arrival of Johnny Thunders, his fellow Heartbreakers and a few stateside associates.

'We arranged the whole English Christmas spread, the tree, mince pies, and for four hours it was wonderful. The Clash were there, the Pistols, people coming by the house, chatting, music playing. Then in walked The Heartbreakers. They were older, they came with heroin, and the whole idea basically was to wreck the joint.'

'Johnny Thunders came in literally bouncing off the walls because he was so fucked up,' Ingham remembers. 'The first thing Johnny did was pick up a phone and dial New York. And almost instantly the competition had started, who was more punk than the other. They came with a real chip on the shoulder. These were the guys that had started it, and now they were being outclassed completely.'

Earlier that day, Johnny Rotten had given Sid a Christmas present, an 'Auntie Sue' doll customised with safety pins and torn clothing – a sweet reference to the protective relationship Sid enjoyed with Sue Catwoman. Now, as Sid was upstairs having a quiet cry, all hell was breaking loose elsewhere.

'Paul and Steve were having fuck contests to see how many girls they could screw,' says Ingham. 'Steve stole some guy's fur coat and that all got very emotional with this guy pulling out a switchblade and throwing it at a door. I'd locked the door to my room at the top of the house, and that had been kicked in and people were screwing on the bed.' Sid, too, managed to rouse himself into action. 'I found out later that Sid had done a shit in the towels in the linen closet. He'd left a nice big stool there.'

This goodwill-free collision of New York and London punk marked a turning point, at least for Caroline Coon. 'It was the punk Altamont,' she insists, 'that same kind of moment when the movement went bad.'

Everyone has their punk Altamont moment. Things were never quite the same after the 100 Club Punk Festival for Subway Sect and Mark Perry. The Pistols' 15 November 1976 show at Notre Dame Hall killed it for The Bromley Contingent. The furore in the wake of the Bill Grundy interview invariably attracted a different type of audience to the scene. But The Heartbreakers, at least two of whom had deadly heroin/methadone habits when they arrived in London (coincidentally, on 1 December 1976, the same night as the Grundy broadcast), certainly get their fair share of the blame.

'The Heartbreakers brought motorcycle jackets and heroin to London,' says Marco Pirroni. 'Before they arrived, it was mostly dope and speed, what Sid used to call 'far out and decadent drugs'.' In their early days, the New Yorkers were often billed with the amusing legend: 'Catch 'em while they're still alive.' For once, it was no empty rock 'n' roll hyperbole.

STEVEN SEVERIN: 'In the mid-'70s, you could go into any pub in London and buy blues or hashish or tabs of acid, but you could not get heroin. It was the grown-up drug; you had to be in the know. It was hardcore. Heroin was taboo. Then The Heartbreakers arrive with their habits and suddenly there's heroin around.'

GLEN MATLOCK: 'We were rehearsing for the Anarchy tour in Harlesden. The Heartbreakers had flown in that morning. After we finished our set, they got up and did their set. And they looked fantastic. They had a whole new look. It was nothing to do with The New York Dolls. They'd got stuff from Malcolm, mixed in with this Italian, New York cool thing.

'After they'd finished, Jerry Nolan sat next to me, and I told him I particularly liked that song, 'Chinese Rocks'. 'What's that one all about?' He looked at me like I was an idiot and said, 'Herowine, bwoay!' And then it all changed.'

DON LETTS: 'It was really simple. Nancy and The Heartbreakers came into town. Smack came into town. Johnny did look cool. He had the smack chic thing going before everyone else did.'

JONH INGHAM: 'The Heartbreakers ruined everything by introducing heroin into the whole scene.'

NICK KENT: 'Heroin was already there. The Heartbreakers just made it glamorous. Johnny Thunders became such an ardent advocate for heroin that it seeped into his image until it couldn't be detached from who or what he was.'

Even in New York, The Heartbreakers were veterans of the intravenous lifestyle, says scene-maker Eileen Polk. 'Johnny Thunders and Jerry Nolan were the first people who were known for using heroin on the New York scene. The Heartbreakers were the core heroin-using bunch. And Dee Dee Ramone.'

'Everything we did was based around drugs,' Jerry Nolan admitted in *Please Kill Me*. 'There would be no rehearsal without drugs. Everything we did, we had to do drugs first.'

It wasn't only decadence and heroin that The Heartbreakers brought to London. While the angular riffs and make-do amateurism of the domestic punk groups had marked a genuine breakthrough, The Heartbreakers were old school in more ways then their long-held junk habits.

'I saw the Heartbreakers play on the Anarchy tour,' recalls Rob Simmons, 'and I was really disappointed. They were just like a professional rock group. I liked the early Pistols when everything was falling apart. The Heartbreakers had longer hair, dressed up a bit, were really tight with a powerful sound, and they knew how to work the audience.

'It felt like punk was about to tear away that traditional rock thing, but The Heartbreakers epitomised it. Johnny Thunders was made into this big, drugged-up hero, which had all been done before with Keith Richards anyway. Here we were in England, wanting to end rock 'n' roll, and along come The Heartbreakers making it all big again.'

The antagonism between the Pistols' camp and The Heartbreakers was barely concealed. Jerry Nolan regarded the Pistols' show as 'an act', and bragged that they got scared when 'the real nitty-gritty' paraphernalia of junk began to materialise. According to the band's manager Leee Black Childers, quoted in *Please Kill Me*, Johnny Rotten was nothing more than 'an awful little poseur – phoney . . . had no soul. He just didn't get it. He wasn't rock 'n' roll at all . . . There was nothing real, nothing musical about Johnny Rotten.'

Nothing rock 'n' roll? Nothing real? Nothing musical? Too right! The genius of Rotten – and so much British punk – in a nutshell.

THE ARRIVAL of The Heartbreakers in December 1976 had been greeted with ambivalence. But that was nothing compared with the response reserved for Nancy Spungeon, a well-known New York hustler with the hots for Heartbreakers' drummer Jerry Nolan.

'She was vile, absolutely vile,' says Steven Severin. 'I'm sure everyone will tell you that. So brash, so vulgar and New York, an ugly character. She just whined.'

'Jerry Nolan had left a guitar round her house or something, and she used that as the reason to track him,' says Glen Matlock. 'He knew she was bad news, and gave her the bum's rush. Then she hooked up with Sid.'

'I walked into Louise's and, to the left as you went through the door, there were these seats. And there they were,' remembers Marco Pirroni. 'Someone said, 'Sid's got this American girlfriend.' I thought it was bizarre. Sid doesn't have girlfriends! He said, 'This is my friend Nancy'. I thought, "Who's this dumpy thing? Horrible hair, terrible make-up and a nasty plastic jacket with safety pins in." It was all a bit shit. She got it completely wrong.'

The Pistols still come over all Anglo-Saxon when they're asked about Nancy. 'I thought of her as a filthy cunt, which of course appealed to Sid,' John Lydon said of the woman he describes in his book as 'screwed out of her tree, vile, worn, and shagged out'. Initially Nancy made a beeline for Rotten but was hastily rebuffed. So she set her sights on Sid. Lydon still holds her partly responsible for his mate's hasty downfall.

Unlike Lydon, Steve Jones, the Pistols' serial shagger, did once take up Nancy's offer of a knee-trembler in a public loo. But he too has only contemptuous memories of her, as he explained in *The Filth And The Fury*. 'She showed up with Sid and I was thinking, 'Who the fuck is this cunt? This is a horrible person.' I've never felt such negative energy from someone.'

Caroline Coon feels that Nancy's reputation has been unfairly discoloured by the rampant sexism of the era. 'She was a magnificent young women. I thought those women who sought to be with musicians were honorable, exciting and intelligent. They sought out the fucks that they wanted, much to the horror of the men who called them groupies. The hypocrisy was gross. All those boys – The Damned, The Clash, the Pistols, every band on earth – said the reason they're in a rock 'n' roll band is to pull girls.'

It's a fair point, but the dislike of Nancy Spungeon was also spurred by a subtle anti-Americanism – this is a country that eschewed glam in favour of The Eagles and Linda Ronstadt – and the fact that you only needed a few seconds in her company to realise that she was a Grade A problem child.

One cliché that needs busting is the one that portrays Nancy Spungeon as the archetypal dumb blonde. Much of the surviving footage of her simply shows a stoned, babbling mess, a ceaselessly chattering bubble perm whose puffy face and incomprehensibly outsized lips screamed 'GIMME GIMME GIMME!' Even her name oozed neediness. Some gentlemen may have preferred dumb women, but Sid was no gentleman and Nancy, with her chestnut-brown locks, was no blonde. And she was no dumbo either.

Nancy Spungeon seemed to be in pain all her life. Reading *And I Don't Want To Live This Life*, Deborah Spungeon's harrowing, honest account of her daughter's life, doesn't necessarily make her any more likeable, but it's difficult to resist the sense that if anyone ever entered this life cursed, then Nancy did.

The eldest child of a solidly middle-class family who lived in a four-bedroom colonial house in the Philadelphia suburbs, Nancy Spungeon was prescribed her first drug, Phenobarbital, at three months in a bid to stop her constant crying. Shortly before her fourth birthday, the girl with the abnormally high IQ – and uncontrollable tantrums and mood swings – underwent the first of many psychiatric evaluations.

By the age of ten, Nancy Spungeon was a 'pint-sized hippie', who'd lost her heart to psychedelic rock, from *Hair* to The Beatles' *White Album*. More alarming still, she was reading the *New York Times*, *Rolling Stone* and Sylvia Plath's troubled verses. Within a year, Nancy was running away from home, screaming 'I wanna die!' and committed to a home for disturbed children.

Complaining that people were trying to steal her Jimi Hendrix albums, she ran away from one establishment and landed herself in another. By the time she was 15, in 1973, she was attempting to self-abort with a coat hanger, tripping regularly on acid, attempting suicide by slashing her wrists and making plans to move to New York City.

A self-styled 'sickie', Nancy nevertheless found herself at 16 studying marketing and journalism at the University of Colorado. Her brief moment of happiness there was rudely curtailed when she was expelled for stealing. Shortly afterwards, she wound up again in a mental hospital before being released to her parents, whom she tormented with her violent rages and increasingly worrying drug habit.

She also looked towards men to make herself happy, tottering backstage at gigs in her platform boots, Spandex slacks and silver nail polish and offering her services to bands such as Queen, Bad Company and Aerosmith. One day, her mother returned home to find The Pretty Things and their entourage entertaining themselves. While her parents exercised a tolerance that bordered on heroic, Nancy of course blamed them for everything. 'They couldn't handle it,' she said later. 'I just couldn't stand them.'

Late in 1975, and with the full blessing of her parents ('We think you should give it a shot,' was the unfortunate turn of phrase, according to Deborah Spungeon), Nancy was living in New York City with every intention of getting into the music industry. Instead, she wound up as a topless dancer and giving ten buck hand- and blow jobs. 'There wasn't anything to it. I just give good blow jobs,' she later explained.

Nancy put peroxide in her Crufts-style curls, hung out at Max's Kansas City and CBGB's, entertained Richard Hell and got matey with Debbie Harry and shaggy-dog-haired super-groupie Sable Starr. By the following spring, she was in the grip of a full-blown heroin addiction and had signed up for the first of several methadone cures she'd endure over the next few years.

'The cliché is that a lot of us came from broken homes and dysfunctional families,' says Eileen Polk, who'd first met Nancy shortly after she arrived from Philadelphia. 'We were all outcasts in a way.' Just as John Beverley found a home in the London punk scene, Nancy Spungeon had discovered her true family. And she celebrated. Hard. 'Nancy was surrounded by rock 'n' roll music,' says Polk, 'and she became friends with the bands.' And got herself a reputation.

Eileen Polk clearly remembers Nancy sometimes being referred to as Nauseating Nancy. 'There were a number of women on the scene that didn't like her, especially some of the girlfriends of boys in the bands, because they thought she'd show up with drugs and seduce them to put a notch in her belt.'

Many of the stories were true. Some, insists Nick Kent, were distinctly second-hand. 'I spent three months in LA in the mid-'70s and I went out with Sable Starr. She'd stopped being a groupie by that point, but she was still pretty wild. And Spungeon would write to Sable; she was her Philadelphia wannabe. Sable used to tell me, 'She's fucking crazy, this girl.' When Spungeon came to London, she told all these wild stories about how she'd had sex with Keith Richards, Jimmy Page and all these people, but she was stealing all of Sable's fucking stories! Some Dolls and Aerosmith? Yes, but that wasn't hard. She was a hardcore groupie from a very early age. She's seen that lifestyle as the be all and end all of existence.'

Wracked by pain all her life, it's hardly surprising that Nancy Spungeon seized whatever sex, drugs and rock 'n' roll she could in a bid to escape the pretty hate machine that kicked hard inside. And it's no less surprising that she began to deal in other people's pain. 'She worked as a dominatrix in one of those role-playing brothels,' remembers photographer Bob Gruen. 'She'd tie up German bankers and whip them for a while. One night, she was telling me and [ex-New York Dolls singer David] Johansen about the different fantasy rooms they'd have there – a little girl room, a nurse room – and said, 'You guys, any time you want, you can have it on the house!' For ages afterwards, we'd be driving around at four in the morning wondering what to do. One of us would say, 'We can always go get beat up by Nancy.' But we always kinda passed on it . . .'

The dirtier, the sicker the music and the attitude, the more Nancy loved it. 'I liked The New York Dolls,' she said later, ''cos they were nasty and mean and they wore make-up and they didn't give a shit and they played godawful rock 'n' roll and they had good names and good hairdos.'

Then she heard about The Sex Pistols. 'I read the review, which was shit, and I said, "I gotta get over there." I wanted to see something exciting.' The turning point came in the wake of The Heartbreakers' departure for London. By February 1977, Nancy grew impatient. They weren't coming back. She'd slashed her wrists pining for Jerry Nolan, who claimed he'd tapped Nancy for cash but had turned down her sexual advances.

'Jerry's there . . . That's where it's all happening,' Nancy told her mother. Deborah Spungeon rustled up some cash for the airfare, and in the first week of March – and free from heroin and methadone – Nancy Spungeon left for London.

3. NANCY'S BOY

SID'S SELF-destructive tendencies had been briefly curtailed as he prepared for his grand unveiling as a Sex Pistol. Despite his firm belief in the very non-musicality of punk – 'THE DAMMED can play three chords. THE ADVERTS can play one. Hear all four . . .' ran one tour poster that spring – Sid did make some effort to apply his rudimentary, sub-Ramones playing to the band's songs. For a few days at least, during February and early March 1977, Sid was holed up with his white Fender Precision attempting to get his fingers moving around the big, thick strings. More important still, he learned how to let the bass swing really low while throwing out his best legs akimbo in a Dee Dee Ramone pose.

According to Deborah Spungeon, Sid and Nancy met on 11 March 1977, the day after the Buckingham Palace signing. In truth, it probably happened a week or so later. The point is that Sid hardly had time to take in his new role as a Sex Pistol before finding the life coach of his self-destructive dreams: a woman who was grossly overqualified in harbouring pain and resentment, had a complete lack of self-regard, and was permanently in thrall to the fuck-up.

Nancy had met her match: a fuck-up on two legs who was the rising star of the most fucked-up band in Britain as well as that clichéd instant, access-all-areas passport to the London scene. Sid recognised that Nancy was someone with the capacity to be more nauseating than himself, a fellow sufferer with whom he could plunge into his own death-driven fantasy world.

The recognition was instant. Very soon, this deeply wounded and emotionally wary couple were blissfully adrift, detached from the rest of the world by virtue of their chronic codependence. Their love had quickly become obsessive, a fact not unconnected with the heroic helpings of neediness that both so conspicuously displayed. Too preoccupied with themselves to let anyone else into their lives, the pair quickly morphed into a lethal unit called Sid 'n' Nancy, which rolled off the tongue as easily as the pair whined their way into infamy. And when they whined, which was often, it was the desperate scream of the iron butterfly, flightless and acutely aware that summer would soon be gone.

Nancy Spungeon was the deadly drug buddy for whom the light was always green. The destination was still Nowhere, but that didn't matter. Sid no longer travelled alone. Trust in the conventional sense of the word may not have been Nancy's calling card, but she had a big black heart that Sid instinctively trusted. Punk's puny, loose-limbed Action Man fell happily into her welcoming, loose-fleshed arms.

Nancy bore an uncanny resemblance to Max's Kansas City's favourite drag act Wayne County, which may have had something to do with why she was able to initiate Sid into the joys of sloppy physical pleasure. 'It was like first love,' says Alan Jones. 'She was a good looking girl, nice tits. I'm sure she was a good shag.' And, apparently, she was Sid's first.

Unlike Sid James, his 'crumpet'-obsessed namesake, Sid Vicious was a veritable male eunuch, in his own words, 'one of the most sexless monsters ever'. He once told Jonh Ingham that people were 'very unsexy', which made it easy for him to share beds with people without becoming aroused. 'I don't believe in sexuality at all,' he said in September 1976. 'I don't enjoy that side of life. Being sexy is just a fat arse and tits that will do anything you want.'

Leee Black Childers, who briefly tried to manage The Flowers Of Romance, told the *Please Kill Me* authors that Sid would sleep with him, 'cuddled in my arms', but that they'd never have sex – something the self-styled 'old reprobate' now regrets. 'Sid didn't know what his sexuality was,' he continued. 'We talked about that a lot.'

Nancy was certainly no sweeping swan maiden in the manner of a '60s Beatles wife. Quite the opposite. Yt there was something distinctly old school about Nancy that upset the punk cognoscenti. 'She was a typical rock chick, and that's why others didn't like her,' Alan Jones says. 'More Granny Takes A Trip than SEX and the Pistols. She was hardly a Jordan or a Debbie [Juvenile]. There was a lot of snobbery.'

London's goth queen Simone Stenfors first met Nancy on 15 March. 'The Heartbreakers had just played at the Speakeasy, and I'd gone back to their flat in Pimlico with Nils [Stevenson]. We walked into the living room and there was Nancy, Johnny and Jerry all smacked out of their heads. Johnny was playing acoustic guitar; Nancy was fat and really loud. Nils said, "It's Simone's birthday today", and immediately she was going on about herself the whole time. When everyone had gone to bed, there was this knock at the door, and Jerry got into bed with me in the living room. He said, 'I'm not being strange or anything', but he seemed genuinely scared of her.'

A few days later, Simone ran into her again, this time at the Music Machine. 'She came over and her wrists were all bandaged up. She said, "I was in hospital last night 'cos I slashed my wrists." That was it: I ran away! Even though I was a walking disaster myself, there was something about her that made you not want to be involved with her.'

Nancy didn't need The Heartbreakers to spread the word that she was bad news. She was quite capable of doing it herself. After she walked into SEX, Malcolm McLaren said he considered fumigating the place, and described her as New York's revenge on the London punk scene. After she'd been booted out of The Heartbreakers' flat ('She's a junkie groupie,' recorded Nils Stevenson in his diary) she ended up at Linda Ashby's place in Victoria, a popular stopover for The Bromley Contingent and assorted Sex Pistols. According to Simon Barker, who stayed there that spring, Nancy nauseated everyone so much that her belongings were tossed out of the window and her heroin was cut with talc and flour.

Even hardened New Yorker Leee Black Childers sensed the bad vibrations as he bumped into her in Carnaby Street. 'It was like the devil arrived,' he says in *Please Kill Me*. 'If The Heartbreakers brought heroin to England, then Nancy brought it to Sid,' he told Jon Savage for *England's Dreaming*. The day he heard that she'd hooked up with Sid, 'A cold chill ran down my spine . . . from that day on, Sid was no longer the person that I knew.'

Only the she-devil was bad enough for Sid Vicious. 'Everybody would pick on her,' Anne Beverley recalled. 'Sid felt sorry for her, he wanted to help her. That's how it all started.'

More than that, Nancy fulfilled a need that Anne was never quite able to: she provided him with the dominant maternal figure he'd been forever looking for. Unlike Rotten, Nancy was able to give him ego-bolstering support without posing some subconscious, male-related threat. Trouble was, her support was in providing the same fucked-up answers that he'd been giving himself all along. Now the pair of them could slide to where they were heading in double-quick time.

'He had never been part of the gang,' Anne Beverley told Alan Parker, 'and was always something of a loner right through school. [But with] the punk scene, suddenly his world was full. From day one, he felt very much like he belonged.' But the sense of belonging that punk had given him was not enough.

Deadly aware of her own inner void, which she'd fill with junk and a series of failed relationships, Anne Beverley recognised that same lack in Sid. 'I admit Simon was never a very loving sort of person,' she said. 'He didn't reveal himself to people, and he could be very cold, but he loved Nancy very dearly.'

While delighted that her son could express love, and had found someone who seemed to care for him, she had a grim premonition about his choice of partner. 'If ever two people shouldn't have met it was 'Sime' and Nancy . . . From the minute Sime met Nancy, everything changed. Heroin was now their drug of choice because it was her drug of choice . . . The world gained a Sex Pistol, Nancy got a rock star boyfriend and I lost a son.'

Pathologically unwilling to face himself for fear of what he might find there, Sid found someone even lower down the food chain, someone who made even more of a public stink than he could and who was weighed down by so much baggage that Hannibal appeared to travel light by comparison. And on the plus side? Well, Sid 'n' Nancy's emotional first-aid kit amounted to little more than a pack of hypodermic needles (not necessarily clean) and an increasing intolerance of anything that existed beyond their hermetically sealed world. The portents did not look good for this exclusive, just-the-two-of-us self-help group.

Despite their neat psychological fit, Sid 'n' Nancy's early lives couldn't have been more different. She'd been born into a comfortably numb middle-class existence – breast-fed, pretty in pink and seemingly safe within the belly of the nuclear family. Sid's back pages turned with amazing regularity, with locations changing more often than his name. And, unlike the Spungeons, who did everything to try to understand their demonic child, the only rule in Anne's household was that there were no rules.

While it's more important to pull the donkey out of the ditch than to understand why he got there in the first place, the absence of a living beast of burden in this story springs the focus back to the root of Sid's journey.

'He was never in a stable situation,' Anne Beverley told Jon Savage, adding that this was 'like a mirror' of her early life. Very little is known about the Beverley family background, other than that Anne had been abandoned by her mother, also a single parent, when she was 12.

Who knows whether Anne subconsciously let go of her son at around the same age. Certainly, the forces that shaped John Beverley's early life began to manifest themselves in increasingly antisocial behaviour at around that same age.

There are three potential reasons for John Beverley's future resentments. The absence of a father-figure; his mother's unwillingness to adopt an authoritarian role against which he could rebel; and the Beverleys' itinerant status, which instilled a sense of perpetual impermanence in his life. Though none of these is inherently problematic, it's clear that each played an important role in creating the wrecking-ball of uncertainty that was Sid Vicious.

'Sid was very needy of love; most youth, male and female, is needy of love,' says Caroline Coon. 'And the English aren't very good at parenting. England is a very interesting culture of unparented children wanting to be loved, wanting an identity. One of the reasons why the counterculture in Britain is so strong is that teenagers are desperate for identity and so join and create these incredible countercultural identity groups.'

Anne Beverley (née Randall) was also very much a lost soul desperately seeking something after an unstable childhood. She'd already been married by the time she was wooed by John Ritchie, a dark and strangely handsome Lothario with a Tony Curtis hairstyle. She was midway through a short stint in the RAF; he was a member of the Royal Guard who, 20 years before the Pistols' mischievous anti-royal exploits, did service outside Buckingham Palace. Although Anne insisted she never married him, the pair's son, born on 10 May 1957, took his father's name: Simon John Ritchie.

The boy inherited his father's looks and colouring, and his mother's wayward spirit. For the first years of his life, John Ritchie junior lived with his parents in a semi-basement flat in Lee Green, southeast London. In photographs, the blubbery baby with the thrifty, postwar haircut seems content enough, naked in his grandparents' garden in Dagenham and surrounded by pots and pans. There is an apocryphal story of a neighbour hearing the boy singing 'That Old Black Magic', inspired by Anne's love of Ella Fitzgerald.

Music failed to heal a broken household. The duty-bound John Ritchie, now a publisher's rep, was often away, leaving Anne to struggle with little money and occasional handouts from Simon's paternal grandparents. By the end of the 1950s, John Ritchie had walked out, and the following summer, mother and son were on a one-way trip to Ibiza. This sleepy Mediterranean island off the eastern coast of Spain, where the indigenous *mujeres* still wore black and an assortment of Americans and bohemians travelled to get away from it all, was a far cry from the grimy back streets of London.

Mum liked it hot. Her hair razor-cut into the gamine style made fashionable by Audrey Hepburn, Anne cut a fine figure in her tight jeans and skirts that fell two inches above the knee. Modern jazz would fill the balmy night air, and she would dance, smoke the occasional joint and keep 'Sime' happy with cups of orange curacao. The boy would keep Anne's fellow partygoers entertained with the occasional swear word – in English and Spanish. But with no maintenance money, and little work beyond the occasional typing job, bike-riding Anne and her dungaree-wearing son eventually tired of their extended holiday in the sun, and by early 1961, they were back in London.

That didn't stop mother and son from continuing their wandering existence. With little or no support network, they resembled urban peasants, Anne in her radical dress, her son prone to profane outbursts that didn't find as much favour in Balham as they had done in Ibiza. Anne worked nights at Ronnie Scott's jazz club in Soho, leaving Sime with the landlady.

By the time he'd reached school age, they'd moved again, to a cold-water flat in Drury Lane, with an outside lavatory and holes in the walls. There were no aspidistras in the windows, nor did the doorstep shine. Anne had other things on her mind – an inexorable journey into drug addiction. As life became more difficult, harder drugs were needed to help her through it.

'He was born addicted to the stuff [heroin],' Nick Kent maintains. 'His mother was addicted when she went into the hospital to deliver him. Well, that's what he told me anyway.' It was almost certainly a fanciful exaggeration, an excuse so that he wouldn't have to take full responsibility for his predicament. But Anne did eventually succumb to heroin. A piece of broken-off needle was permanently embedded in her arm.

A neglected child and starved of love herself, Anne nevertheless carried some guilt about her son's upbringing. When Deborah Spungeon published her book, Anne said she was 'sickened' by it, describing Nancy's mother – somewhat unfairly – as 'self-righteous'. Anne never tried to portray John Ritchie's early life in any way other than in plain English. Unlike the Spungeons, she'd not been thrust unwillingly into the world of psychobabble.

Had the infrastructure been in place, perhaps she may have been. At his first primary school, St Peter & St Paul in Great Windmill Street, Soho, the ever-fidgeting Simon Ritchie attracted the unwanted attentions of Lionel, the school bully. Anne wanted her son to be different, special: that's why she'd first installed him in a progressive Rudolf Steiner pre-school. But already his inability to mix easily was landing him in trouble. They moved, and she got him into a school in Farm Street, close to the American Embassy in Grosvenor Square. His school report stated that while he was a bright boy, he lacked concentration.

'He was a very happy child,' Anne told Simon Kinnersley years later. 'He used to laugh a lot, and he was fascinated by music, but being an only child meant that he was very wrapped up in himself.' Sime had kicked balls on beach, worn his mother's shoes, and graduated from Noddy and Big Ears to cowboys and Dan Dare. By the mid-1960s, he knew all the names of the baddies in *Batman* and *Doctor Who*. As a ten-year-old, he was blissfully unaware of flower power. 'I didn't even know the Summer Of Love was happening,' he told Jonh Ingham. 'I was too busy playing with my Action Man.'

Junior school Simon was no longer watching his mother. She'd taken her eye off him too, marrying middle-class Chris Beverley in February 1965, after a whirlwind romance she'd begun late the previous year. In a surviving wedding photo, the groom, bespectacled and with a faint air of the intellectual about him, looks mildly incongruous next to plain, crop-haired Anne. At the front of the small family grouping is seven-year-old Simon Beverley, his shirt open, his hands stuffed in his pockets and a house key on a chain plainly visible around his neck.

But the latch-key kid wasn't Simon Beverley for long. By August, Chris Beverley was dead, his presence now reduced to ghostly late-night visits to his graveside. Although Anne and Simon were taken into the Beverley family, staying close to them in Tunbridge Wells for the next six years, the tragedy further stained Anne's world view. Although lazily characterised as 'a hippie' during the punk era, Anne Beverley was a young mother whose experience of the Swinging Sixties was beset by misfortune. The oppressive vibe that greeted Wobble when he walked into the Beverleys' London flat several years later already had been a feature of young John's life for many years.

'I would guess that Sid was fighting acute depression, and had a sense of wanting to escape, which you could actually call suicide,' says Caroline Coon. For much of his teens, that feeling lay dormant, masked by his sartorial disguises, his bold, aggressive front, and the ease with which he slipped into an existence propped up by an increasing dependence on drink and drugs. By spring 1977, with his damaged goddess Nancy Spungeon by his side, that depressed, escapist, suicidal Sid was willed into full bloom.

4. THEATRE OF HATE

'Punk rock became an excuse to be stupid. It went right back to basics so that even stupid people could understand it. They weren't gonna get the SEX shop, or Situationism, or the juxtaposition of swastikas and fetishism and rock 'n' roll. But they could understand a leather jacket and being stupid.' – Marco Pirroni

SOPHIE RICHMOND ran the offices of Glitterbest, Malcolm McLaren's management company. Her diary, reproduced in part in Fred and Judy Vermorel's *Sex Pistols File*, reveals the almost immediate effect that joining the band, meeting Nancy Spungen and getting involved with heroin had on Sid Vicious:

14 April: 'Sid really ill.'

16 April: Sophie takes Sid to St Anne's Hospital in Tottenham. He is suffering from hepatitis, an illness commonly associated with intravenous drug users. A young doctor lectures him on needles and drug use, and Sid is kept in under supervision.

18 April: The ward sister calls and suggests that Sophie should pay Sid a visit.

26 April: She visits him again.

3 May: 'One big worry is Sid.'

13 May: Sid is released from hospital. He's 'sounding OK'.

16 May: Sid is now 'looking good' and is well enough to add his signature to The Sex Pistols' new contract with Virgin Records.

Sid got off to a fine start with his first public duty as a Sex Pistol, a long-distance telephone interview with LA's leading Anglophile DJ, Rodney Bingenheimer. When the DJ took exception to Sid's claim that everyone was repressed in Los Angeles, he replied with characteristic Sid-ness: 'Yes you are. Mentally repressed.'

At a party at the Roxy Club to mark hi joining the band, Sid celebrated by bottling four people, including Nils Stevenson. Violence was becoming the norm in and around the punk subculture, and Sid, the man Malcolm McLaren called 'the knight in shining armour with a giant fist', was virtually obliged to ensure that The Sex Pistols were always at the centre of it.

One punch-up with significant repercussions took place at the Speakeasy, London's premier traditional-rock watering hole, little over 24 hours after the public A&M signing outside Buckingham Palace. 'It was a tiny subterranean place where people like The Glitter Band would hang out,' says Steven Severin. 'It wasn't really our place. You were almost in enemy environment.'

Hours earlier, Sid had admitted to *Sounds* reporter Brian Harrigan that he wasn't a fighter. 'But if someone starts, I say, 'Ooh, take that you beast', and slap them right on the nose.' At the Speakeasy, and with Wobble by his side, Sid dropped his camp façade as *The Old Grey Whistle Test* TV presenter Bob Harris walked past. 'When are the Pistols gonna be on the Whistle Test then?' said Wobble, bumping into 'Whispering Bob', who – bearded and balding – looked every inch the proverbial 'Boring Old Fart'. 'You're just an old cunt,' said Sid, the cue for one of Harris' crowd to wade in with a punch. Then all hell broke loose. Someone said they'd 'kill' Harris, who received cuts to his back and was left 'more scared than I'd ever been in my life'. Engineer George Nicholson took the brunt of the attack, needing 14 stitches to a head wound. The assailant with the broken bottle in his hand was Sid Vicious.

As a direct result of the attack, The Sex Pistols' contract with A&M was terminated days later, on 16 March. 'We weren't the nice boys they thought we were,' Sid said later. 'We were nasty little bastards.' The label's managing director Derek Green, who took full responsibility for the matter, felt the real blame lay elsewhere. He concluded that the man with whom he'd conducted business was at the root of it all. Describing Malcolm

McLaren as 'Satanic', he added that 'his manipulation of everyone looks like no fun at all',

Manipulation was breaking out all over the place. McLaren and the band. Rotten and the band. Rotten and Sid. Nancy and Sid. McLaren and the media. The media and the Pistols. SEX and the city kids. McLaren, significantly older and widely regarded as the ideologue of the movement, tends to attract most of the criticism.

'The guy's become such a caricature of himself that now it's virtually impossible to see what first motivated him,' says Nick Kent. 'But there was something real there and it wasn't just money. He created the name, and he was the guy that held it all together. Most importantly, McLaren didn't take drugs at all. So he was always together and that's important.'

Caroline Coon is adamant that the culture of manipulation that began to engulf The Sex Pistols was inextricably linked to the hurt that ran deep through the punk movement. 'They're gonna hurt each other,' she says. 'Before Sid was in the band, he was the kind of kid that was cruel to animals, a youth whose psyche is getting emotional reward from cruelty to others. But while he is hurting other people, he is hurting himself, and that's a kind of fascist masculinity. You see the same thing in early Nazi training. They slid into a totally destructive, self-denying lack of self-esteem, which is very dangerous.'

As we sit surrounded by walls filled with her paintings, and with evidence of her continued commitment to progressive causes scattered around the room, Coon has little hesitation in pointing a determined finger in McLaren's direction we cast around for the villain of the piece. 'If you're an adult, financing a group of people who are ten years younger than you, there are certain responsibilities. And it's not politically revolutionary or funny or radical or interesting to destroy a group of human beings.

'So Sid's caught in this maelstrom. Of course he's going to numb his feelings even further with whatever drugs he can, which is classic addict stuff. But his violence is encouraged by people like Malcolm McLaren and Vivienne Westwood. She would attack people as often as Sid did, and Sid admired her a great deal. OK, he might have had a propensity to get into fights to test his masculinity, which he might have been uncertain of. But that was glorified by older people around him who claimed that that was a revolutionary gesture. Vomit-making.'

'Sid wasn't helped by the fact that he had a professional music chick hawk like Malcolm McLaren as his manager,' says Nick Kent. 'What I mean by that is someone who pimps off children. And Sid was a child. I know that Sid Vicious was 21 when he died, but mentally man, the guy was 14 . . . no, 12.'

Kent and Coon's disgust with the elders of the punk scene is not necessarily misplaced, though few of the leading lights fully accept the idea of a one-sided and abusive relationship. 'Malcolm didn't want a musician,' says Marco Pirroni. 'He wanted someone who could cause trouble, cause chaos! Malcolm wasn't interesting in managing a band and sending them to America and doing deals and merchandising and taking his 20 per cent. That's work. That's boring.' So he let his puppet do his dirty work for him? 'No, I don't think McLaren had to tell Sid to do anything,' Marco continues. 'That's why he wanted him in the band.'

Marco also recognises that a rampant and aggressive individualism was intrinsic to the punk aesthetic. It may have been exploited by those who better understood its potential consequences, but that doesn't alter its grass-roots proliferation. 'No one said anything good about anybody,' he says. 'And Sid's the one who took being obnoxious on board – totally. He was doing that before the heroin, before joining the Pistols, but it seemed to be endearing then. Things like stealing Jordan's sunglasses out of her bag while she wasn't looking.'

Siouxsie And The Banshees bassist Steven Severin also has his suspicions about the master/puppet theory. 'Sid could be wound up into getting involved in a fight or getting himself ejected from somewhere, but only if he imagined it could benefit him. Remember, he's looking up to John Lydon who is saying the complete opposite – be yourself. Sid created that forceful personality where he would say that everything is rubbish. To have him then manipulated by McLaren, well, I find that hard to believe.'

Sid was manipulated as much by his own expectations, and those of his times, as he was by individuals. However, there is no doubt that his own wanton amorality would have been nourished by the examples of both

Rotten and McLaren, who were positively revelling in it at the time of Sid's joining.

Now a fully fledged Sex Pistol whose actions could create instant headlines, Sid was aware of the new power at his disposal. No one was immune from his wrath if he felt like showing it. 'I saw him at an early Slits gig at the Scala Cinema,' says Ray Stevenson, 'and I shot a few pictures of him. Suddenly, he's got hold of my lapels and he's pinning me against the wall. 'Never take pictures of me unless I say so.' Ten minutes before, we were friends. I was really frightened, 'cos he's got his reputation, and Wobble was standing behind him ready to act if I did anything.'

Stevenson is sure he knows what prompted the change in Sid's behaviour. "I am a Pistol. A celebrity. And you are a photographer.' If I'd shot something embarrassing of Lydon, he'd have said, 'Don't use it, you cunt.' There wouldn't have been a physical threat at all. Sid had this concept of punk as violent, that hitting people was a really punk thing to do.'

On another night out, Stevenson remembers Sid hitting Billy Idol at the Marquee for the crime of being in Generation X. Billy Idol thumped him back. 'Sid said to me afterwards, 'I really respected him for hitting me back.' Yeah, right! There was a lot of crap around at that time.'

That spring, Sid courted trouble wherever he went. 'I was in the Vortex one night with Adam Ant,' says Simone Stenfors. 'Sid came down the stairs, picked up this fire extinguisher, and Adam just gave him this look. Sid beat a hasty retreat. Adam said to me, "I hate that guy, he's a bloody coward."

I asked him why and he said, "Sid beats people up while they are asleep.' He did that to Adam once."'

There was no such thing as a learnt lesson in Sid's vocabulary. With the court case arising out of the 100 Club incident still hanging over him, he still couldn't help launching missiles when the mood took him. 'We were in the Star Bar in the Music Machine,' says Kenny Morris. 'It was a little bar for VIPs, and one night, they wouldn't let Sid and Nancy up there. He just took his empty pint glass and threw it at them.'

The person who was most in danger of Sid Vicious was of course Sid himself. 'It was quite common to see Sid falling over in front of you at the

Roxy Club,' Simone continues. 'He always seemed to be the one that got beaten up. I never saw him win a fight. He always had blood on his face, or else he'd simply get drunk, break a glass and start cutting himself.'

This was the Sid that Nancy Spungeon could relate to, an emotionally volatile, fucked-up youth propped up by big, spot-lit supports – fame, a wide circle of acquaintances, booze, drugs – all built on nothing but sand. The more Sid became aware that none of this was able to 'fix' him, to deliver a Sid – or even a John Beverley – freed from his eternal restlessness, the more desperately he relied on these crutches.

Sid Vicious joined The Sex Pistols and hooked up with Nancy Spungeon at a time when the initial enthusiasm that had propelled the punk movement into the headlines had waned, giving way to melancholy, even anger. Marc Bolan, a rare punk enthusiast from the older generation, had reckoned, 'It's all related to violence in the mind, not the body.' Things were changing. 'The incidence of fights has increased, and the original, playfully aggressive punk-front has disintegrated into senseless spite,' wrote Caroline Coon in March 1977. John Cale was beheading chickens on stage; Slits singer Ari Up was attacking Paul Cook with a knife, herself having been knifed in a sexist attack in Islington; and the competition between the groups had grown ugly. Violence was becoming a badge of punk conformity.

Although initially an unlikely alliance of misfits from across the class and racial barriers, the combination of beer, loud music and fisticuffs brought a largely white and dispossessed working-class audience to punk during 1977. Inevitably, a few foot soldiers of the far right began to regard the movement as a fertile recruiting ground, prompting headlines claiming that punk was 'ROCK'S SWASTIKA REVOLUTION'.

This outraged many of punk's original adherents, most of whom dropped the swastika once its shock connotations had been hijacked by something more sinister. 'It's a loser's emblem, because the Nazis lost the war. It's ridiculous to suggest we are involved with fascists,' Rotten complained. 'All my best friends are black, gay, Irish or criminals!'

Sid was an unreconstituted swastika-wearer whose fascination for the horrors of Nazi Germany extended to writing songs about dying in concentration camps. Nevertheless, matters of style and humour had, he insisted, nothing to do with conventional left/right politics. 'We should call the next single, 'We Hate The National Front',' he said as the furore over punk and politics broke. 'I find the idea of being shot to pieces by a million bullets from the National Front really unromantic.'

He then made an interesting leap from the genocidal politics of the extreme right to his own self-extermination. 'We're all gonna die from alcohol poisoning anyway,' he said. 'I like getting drunk. I like getting out of my brain. It's good fun. Ordinary life is so dull that I get out of it as much as possible.' Even being part of The Sex Pistols, rapidly regarded as the most important band to emerge since The Beatles, couldn't save him from that.

LATER IN the year, and prompted by Judy Vermorel's persistent questioning, Sid's perception of stardom had changed considerably. 'It's fucking full of shit and I hate it all,' he complained, 'but there's nothing else to do.' It was, he decided, simply the lesser of two evils: 'It's better than doing something I don't want to do.'

The last vestiges of idealism had been banished from Sid's brain long before he joined The Sex Pistols. Even at the end of that long first day, after he had at last been presented to the public, Sid's declaration that he'd had the 'greatest time of his life' came not from the heart but from the bottom of several empty bottles. That set the tone for his brief tenure as a Sex Pistol, an 11-month blur beset by intra-band wrangles and interminable power struggles, musical uncertainty and a personal descent into the dark abyss of addiction.

Sid's essential contribution to The Sex Pistols was a mythological one. His streamlined, easily-aped image, coupled with the comic simplicity of his name, earned him instant infamy. Apart from that, he had very little to do. Anyone who imagined that by joining the band, Sid might acquire a sense of purpose and be distracted from his self-destructive tendencies would be severely disappointed. So infrequently was Sid pressed into service as a member of the most talked-about band in the world that the events can be summarised in point form:

21 March 1977 – Sid debuts with The Sex Pistols at a secret show at Notre Dame Hall, central London.

After the attack on Bob Harris and his friends, the Pistols were hastily dropped by A&M. Aware that the group had been inactive since playing a handful of shows in Holland in January, Malcolm McLaren arranged this 'meet the *new* band' showcase at this offbeat central London venue, where the Pistols had played a sold-out show the previous November.

'The owners wanted to cancel it because it was the Pistols, and they were worried about their reputation,' remembers Ray Stevenson. 'So they put a ridiculously tiny limit on the door of, like 50 or 100 people, and there was no atmosphere at all. They came on, played a set, then everyone went home. It just didn't work.'

Sid walked out in his tight-fitting Vive Le Rock T-shirt, denims with the knees ripped out, pumps, studded wristband and his white Fender Precision bass. He looked more like one of The Ramones than the model for SEX clothes that McLaren had originally intended.

Three of Sid's favourite women were in the audience to witness his Pistols debut. Vivienne Westwood, in a reverie, hopping from one foot to the other. Anne Beverley, who thought that John and Sid looked like the 'band-leaders'. And Sid's new squeeze, Nancy Spungeon, with scary, Charlie Manson eyes, a thick lipstick pout, wild peroxide hair and a collision of hippie, glam and punk threads. It was pure visual insanity, as if a demented poodle had been dressed by the future Duchess of York.

'I remember seeing Sid there with Nancy and being absolutely devastated,' says Simone Stepfors. 'It was probably the first time anybody realised he was with her. Steve English turned to me and said, 'What's he doing with that bint?''

As debuts go, the first Pistols show without Glen Matlock wasn't the disaster some had been expecting. 'I dunno whether Sid ruined them as a musical unit or not,' Matlock says. 'I never saw one of their gigs. Presumably the bass wasn't that high in the mix. I'm not disagreeing that Sid didn't look the part. He kinda did.'

The day after the show, McLaren packed the band off to Jersey where they found themselves subject to a strict search, then a police escort. Sid celebrated his first trip abroad since 1960 by farting in the face of an overzealous customs officer. When they arrived in Berlin days later, a plan to cross the Berlin Wall into East Germany was abandoned because bottle-swigging Sid didn't have the right passport.

3 April 1977 – The Pistols perform at the Screen On The Green, Islington, north London.

After holding it together for the Notre Dame show, Sid's nerves got the better of him, and he took to the stage stoned and unsure of his parts. Reviewing the show for *Sounds*, Jon Savage noted that 'Vicious stands legs astride, playing adequately, but he looks the part.' Others were less generous. 'He was really crap,' says Marco Pirroni, who remembered Sid being so out of it for the show that he failed to recognise him when they bumped into each other in the gents.

Others noted that Sid was at least as nervous as he was stoned. 'The Slits were on, and Sid sat with us in the stalls and said that he was absolutely shitting himself,' says Simone. 'He was about to go on stage and he couldn't remember any of the songs. 'I don't know what to play', he said. 'I actually thought he was really good when he got on stage.'

After the gig, Sid disappeared with original Clash guitarist (and future PiL member) Keith Levene, hunting for heroin. 'Then he met Nancy,' says Pistols roadie John Tiberi, 'and they went off for three nights.' It was, he continues, 'the first clue of [Sid's] chemical dependency. He couldn't fill the hole post-gig. He had to go out there and get stoned.' When Sid finally turned up, he'd already contracted the hepatitis that hospitalised him just over a week later.

While Sid remained in hospital, The Sex Pistols returned to the recording studio. Though a group member in name, Sid's latecomer status and limited contributions always made him feel like an outsider – which is how it had been all his life. Steve Jones played his bass parts. Johnny Rotten didn't get to visit him at all. It was Sid's women, once again, who took care of him. The Slits'

Ari Up brought him a television. And the one person who visited him regularly was Nancy Spungeon.

Sid remained in hospital for the best part of a month. This suggested that his condition was more serious than a simple dose of hedonism. It was as if illness was a physiological response to stardom. When he came out, Sid was asked by McLaren to stay away from Linda Ashby's Victoria flat, because his manager could already see that the temptations of a busy central London lifestyle were having an adverse effect on Sid's health. That, and the fact that another regular there was Nancy Spungeon.

'Luckily, he had hepatitis at the time,' was Steve Jones' verdict of Sid's contributions to the Pistols' recording sessions. There were occasions when Sid did make it down to Wessex Studios to join the band. He even laid down rough bass lines for the new songs, 'Holidays In The Sun' and 'Bodies', though these were invariably smothered by a Steve Jones overdub. 'Sid was too fucking drunk,' Lydon reckoned. As at the Screen On The Green show, Sid got smashed in order to mask his inadequacies. 'He could not hold a tune,' said Lydon in his autobiography, 'I think it was fear of the whole situation.'

Rather than suffer endless playbacks, Sid amused himself by wandering, vodka bottle in hand, through the studio building. One day he bumped into Freddie Mercury, who greeted him with a disarming 'Ah, Mr Ferocious!' Although Sid closely resembled rough trade from a leather bar in Earls Court, the encounter passed without further incident. On another occasion, he was found riding a bike on the roof of the building. 'You'll kill yourself!' called out one of the assembled throng, as Sid cycled desperately close to the edge. 'Is that all?' he replied.

There was, Lydon claims, one success story with Sid in the studio, a version of 'Submission' that he insists was 'a hell of a lot less musical, more chaotic and important'. It stayed in the can.

7 June 1977 – The Sex Pistols' Boat Party, River Thames, central London.

That a rock group possessed the power to upset the cosy celebrations for the Queen's Silver Jubilee would have been unthinkable 12 months earlier. And that, in essence, remains a lasting testament to the combination of McLaren's vision and the band's nerve. Sid Vicious had little to do with any of it.

It has been claimed that Sid played bass on 'God Save The Queen' (hung on a riff not unlike Bowie's 'Hang On To Yourself'), but the final production is far too tight to imagine that anything remained of his performance on the record. He even managed to avoid arrest on the boat trip organised to promote the record, despite a number of scuffles and the eventual arrival of the police. Having played a short set with the band, Sid – looking more gaunt and pale than usual – stayed on the lower deck where he did drugs with Nancy.

He was only marginally more lively a couple of weeks earlier, on 24 May, for the 'God Save The Queen' photo session, which took place in Notting Hill near the offices of Virgin Records. 'Sid held one of those kids' windmills in front of his face all the time because he had a spot on his nose,' says photographer Barry Plummer.

Back at the record company offices, Sid's customary wit was in evidence, though this was interspersed with comments such as 'I'm so fucking ill I'm gonna puke.' Slumped on a couch, he occasionally roused himself to reel off a few names of people he'd like to give 'a good kicking', demanded free records ('or else we'll steal them'), and asked the photographer to come closer because 'I can't gob that far in my present state.' On the spot reporter Alan Jones also overheard Sid telling Steve Jones about the spot on the end of his nose: 'I know, it's because of all that fucking pressure I'm under. I'm too fucking sensitive to put up with all this.'

He also reported the following conversation:

JOHNNY ROTTEN: 'Malcolm is a good manager, but he wouldn't dream of telling us what to do.'
STEVE JONES: 'He wouldn't dare. We'd turn Sid on to him to give him a good kicking.'
SID VICIOUS (with eyes closed): 'Fucking right.'

McLaren's last great act as Sex Pistols manager came at the end of June when he arranged a short tour of Scandinavia. In the wake of the furore over

'God Save The Queen', Rotten, Paul Cook and assorted Pistols associates had been attacked in a number of separate incidents. This was the true summer of hate. War broke out between Teddy Boys and punks. 'PUNISH THE PUNKS'-style headlines gave way to gloating picture captions such as: 'JOHNNY ROTTEN . . . a backlash victim – with more to come?' 'The pop world fears the slashing is only the start of a savage backlash against punk rock groups,' claimed the *Daily Mirror*, delighted to stir the shit.

When asked about the trouble caused by the single, Sid remained adamant: 'What do we care about their dismal opinions, the idiots.' But with a nation whipping up the hatred, and its most brutal henchmen coming at them with knives and machetes, paranoia gripped the Pistols camp. Sid, who'd managed to escape attack on this occasion, put in desperate early morning calls, both to Sophie Richmond, and then to McLaren, demanding that the band be sent out of the country. Rotten – who'd once told Caroline Coon, 'Why people are so frightened of violence I'll never really understand' – made a similar plea.

The Heartbreakers, then seriously considering a name change to The Junkies, were highly amused, and decided to exact a little revenge in a new song, 'London Boys'. 'You talk about faggot/Little Mummy's boy/You're still at home, you've got your chaperone.'

Becoming a Sex Pistol promised fame and freedom from the drudgery of everyday life. But by summer 1977, the private lives of the most exciting band in Britain had taken on a sepulchral tone. Bounced around from squats and friends' floors to grubby shared flats and, at the height of Pistols-mania, even back to his mother's smack-pad, Sid found little stability at precisely the moment when he most needed it.

He explained his grand ennui to Judy Vermorel. 'When I was ten years old, I used to think, what a wonderful life Marc Bolan must have. If only I could be like him, gosh, just think of the things he must do. And he probably did exactly the same thing as what I do now – sit in my mummy's front room . . . I don't have anywhere to live, you know what I mean?'

Sophie Richmond recorded with some disappointment in her diary that Sid 'just seems to be farting around with Nancy'. He'd joined the band, he'd fallen in love both with a girl and with heroin, and he continued to booze himself into a persistent vegetative state as often as he could. The newspapers called him the rising star of punk rock. Those who knew him better could already see him free-falling into hell. 'Once Nancy came on the scene, Sid was always off with her in Maida Vale,' says Don Letts. 'It was a smack thing, and they went off to hide in a hole somewhere.'

With their two bleak, black hearts beating as one, it was becoming impossible for others to penetrate Sid 'n' Nancy's private, mutually dependent world. They briefly shared a cockroach-infested flat with Rotten in Chelsea Cloisters (Sid called it 'Chelsea Closets' on account of its cell-like appearance) before being kicked out for not paying the bills. Rotten despised Nancy, whose tights, he recalls with grim delight, seemed forever stained with white track-marks of piss. That didn't stop the trio from moving into a flat in Sutherland Avenue in Maida Vale later that summer. (Unfurnished and with only a seven-year lease, it was perfect for Sid, said McLaren. 'He'll be dead by then anyway.') It was at Sutherland Avenue where, one night, Rotten and his mates decided to use Nancy's needles to clean the grime from under their fingernails. The singer had been subjected to that whining 'Oooh, Sid' once too often.

By the autumn, Rotten had his own place in Gunther Grove, a short walk from SEX. And he also found a girlfriend, Nora, 15 years his senior, whose strong German accent – and calm, intelligent nature – was in marked contrast to Nancy Spungeon's heroin-fuelled histrionics. She was one of the most unloved creatures on the punk scene, but Sid was convinced he'd found a true kindred spirit, and was delighted to remain locked away in Sutherland Avenue with her.

Deborah Spungeon was rather less impressed by the union. Catching her daughter's new beau on television that summer, she reckoned 'he had to be the creepiest-looking young man on the face of the earth . . . My daughter was living with Frankenstein's monster.' No, he's not, assured Nancy during one of her infrequent, fund-raising transatlantic calls. 'He's the biggest rock star in the world! And he's all mine!' Then she'd pass the phone to Sid. 'Hello, mum,' he'd deadpan, before telling Deborah that he'd just bought Nancy shoes and fancy underwear. Then he'd say, 'Can you send us some cash?' Mrs Spungeon found it surprising that a world-famous musician would be so strapped for cash. But Sid's £35 weekly allowance didn't go far with two increasingly desperate heroin habits to feed.

'The thing that annoyed me more than anything else,' says Glen Matlock, 'was that – regardless of the fact that he took my place – Sid was in the most happening band at the time. And all he had to do was keep it together, but he couldn't even fucking do that. Everything we'd begun to achieve, being forward-looking and on the case and hip he blew away in one fell swoop. It just became a cartoon.'

Sid is a convenient figure to blame for the slow, inexorable demise of The Sex Pistols, but other factors besides a perpetually stoned bass player were creating friction within the group.

13 July 1977 – The Sex Pistols fly to Copenhagen for a two-week tour of Scandinavia.

For the first time since Sid's joining, The Sex Pistols were forced to behave like a coherent four-piece for a sustained period of time. It wasn't easy. There were constant rows. Rotten was becoming increasingly paranoid and aggressive, according to Sophie Richmond – and plenty others too. Sid was becoming 'impossible' and, says Lydon, 'a Johnny Rotten clone', constantly playing up, but with additional harridan/heroin complications. Fed up with the pair of them, Paul Cook and Steve Jones looked towards Malcolm McLaren to hold together the fragile peace. But while the band were playing to boisterous Nordic audiences, the manager was back in Los Angeles trying to raise money for The Sex Pistols film he'd been trying to get off the ground since the beginning of the year.

Prior to the tour, Sid had cleaned up and was making tentative noises about leaving Nancy. But even a heroin-free Sid was hardly a paragon of togetherness. He turned up at Heathrow without his passport, and spent much of the tour in a marijuana-induced daze. When the band alighted at Stockholm Airport, star-struck Sid spotted Agnetha and Anni-Frid from ABBA and demanded their autographs. The Sid-phobic Swedes screamed and legged it.

John Tiberi, who managed the tour in McLaren's absence, regarded Sid less as a pest than 'the guy who sort of kept the spark alive'. When he was able to resist plunging himself into a stupor, which wasn't often because that's what he thought a genuine punk rock anti-star should do, Sid could still be entertaining to company. Especially when he was pulling out the one-line put-downs.

Sid on Paul Cook: 'Rick Wakeman with short hair.'

Sid on Steve Jones: 'A slob, we hate him.'

Sid on Iggy Pop: 'He's just a fart.'

Sid on Bowie: 'He's just a fart.'

Sid on Joe Strummer: 'He makes me laugh. I watch him whimpering across the stage – like a big pubic hair wafting about.'

Sid on The Damned: 'They aren't even funny. They're just quite sad. I want to cry when I see them.'

Heroes?: 'Jefferson Air-o-plane.'

Sid on sex: 'My girlfriend fucks me with a dildo. So what?'

Away from the crates of free beer and the intra-band rivalry, Sid could be nicer still. When asked about the tour some time later, Sid's mind turned not to the nights of on-stage mayhem, but to 'two littl'uns' he'd spent a day with in Sweden. 'We had really good fun. They took me out and bought me sweets,' he said. The Buzzcocks fantasised about being 'Sixteen Again'; Sid's salad days were rather earlier than that.

To add to Sid's sense of separation from the band, he was obliged to fly back to London midway through the tour for an appearance at Wells Street Magistrates Court relating to the incident at the 100 Club ten months earlier. Sid arrived in the early morning of 26 July dressed in a black suit, and 'this really corny shirt my mum got me about five years ago'. The Clash's Paul Simonon and Mick Jones, and journalists Caroline Coon and Jonh Ingham testified on his behalf, but he was found guilty and fined £125 for illegal possession of a flick knife. The prosecution had not gathered enough evidence to press a more serious charge in relation to the glass throwing.

While the band were away, Capital Radio broadcast a pre-recorded edition of 'My Top Ten' featuring Rotten. Among his chosen artists were Captain Beefheart and Magma. 'We can't all do it,' Rotten complained when the band ribbed him about his starring role during an interview that summer. Everyone laughed. But beyond the laddish show of public unity, the cracks were real. Johnny was beginning to question each uncomfortable step the band now took, while the rest were all too aware of his unease and increasing aloofness. Having erected a determined boundary between Old Fart and New Wave, The Sex Pistols were nevertheless susceptible to the age-old divisions between uppity frontman and heads-down backing band.

Sid scrambled the picture. Within the group, he was a proverbial wooden leg, a liability on stage and a hindrance in the studio. More mascot than musician, he was the court jester, taunting Rotten's growing ego, dismissing Cook and Jones' demands for musical tautness as 'not punk'. But beyond the Pistols' inner circle, Sid Vicious was fast eclipsing Rotten as the face – nay embodiment – of punk rock. The name, the look, the 'Wild One' expression, those classic, punkish 'I hate . . .' one-liners – Sid had refined what punk was 'about'. Where Rotten had been all twisted and angular, Sid Vicious was symmetric and democratic. More than anyone else, he reduced punk to a type, one that sat more easily with the classic icons of rebellion – from Brando and Dean through Elvis and Jim Morrison to, with deadly consequences, Keith Richards and Johnny Thunders. Sid simplified the punk 'look', making it seem as orderly and as ritualised as that of a Chelsea Pensioner.

As early as autumn 1977, Rotten was publicly airing his discontent, itself a veiled condemnation of the 'Vicious effect': 'They became clone-like . . . They allowed the *Daily Mirror* to dictate a uniform – the leather jacket, the safety pin, the torn jeans, the bovver boots, the spikey hair. And it became hideous.'

Nothing had done more to launch Sid into the public consciousness than 'Pretty Vacant', the third Sex Pistols single, issued just prior to the Scandinavian tour. Although the song had been around since early 1976, its title and anthemic qualities fitted Sid Vicious perfectly. Rotten, in dark glasses, 'DESTROY' bondage shirt and carrot-coloured hair, dominated the promotional film, a goading, cackling spectacle whose awkward movements brought to mind a Gerry Anderson puppet baddie come to life. When Sid came into view, the meaning was simplified, clearly understood on society's terms. Here was punk ugliness given a beauty makeover. A halo of light gave a Christ-like caress to his punk-perfect spikey-top, lending him a presence that was iconic, almost blissful. And that was just not in Rotten's nature.

'Pretty Vacant': the legend stuck to Sid like herpes. You'd have thought this mirror-fixated Bowie acolyte would have been grateful. But even the joys of stardom, whether seized upon like Cook and Jones, or stolen furtively like Rotten, provided no panacea for Sid's ills. At the end of the Scandinavian tour, Sid asked Barbara Harwood, the group's driver and student of homeopathy, to take him away and clean him up. For a brief moment, he glimpsed another way of life. Like Syd Barrett, perhaps he could turn his back on the whole rotten lot and go find a cellar somewhere. Unlike Barrett, Sid Vicious craved company, craved recognition, craved that never-ending stream of fixes – whether a knock-out punch of booze and heroin, or simply the opportunity to tell everyone how bored he was.

By August, punk and a glut of affiliated New Wave artists were rapidly transforming rock and the wider cultural landscape. No longer a perilous, windswept archipelago, the movement had become legitimised, the accelerated sound and stylistic anarchy of urban Britain. Great British Eccentrics. And, conversely, more normalised every day. The *Daily Mirror*'s old social conscience spoke of a 'punk future'. Steven Berkoff's *East*, a 'punk play', was staged at London's Regent Theatre. Even Sid was being eclipsed by a blond, more sanitised version, complete with curled lip and bags of trad attitude. Yes, that's Generation X's Billy Idol on the cover of *Sounds*.

19 August 1977 – The Sex Pistols play the Lafayette Club in Wolverhampton, the first of six 'secret' gigs commonly known as 'The SPOTS Tour' (Sex Pistols On Tour Secretly).

The perils of fame and overindulgence, of drug abuse and a troubled, concealed sexuality, all of which prompted ugly outbursts of uncontrollable violence, were beamed across the world on 16 August 1977. Elvis Presley had died.

The King keeled over in his loo, said Sid, because he 'forgot what he was about and people had to tell him. He was too stupid to know any better.' Sid knew better because he was a punk, and punks were pure and hardline, and they'd never forget what they were about. 'We're not like that,' said the True Believer.

Rotten was more preoccupied with personality and self-preservation than ideology. 'I don't want to become a fat, rich, sick, reclusive rock star,' he said. 'I don't want to die. Elvis was dead before he died, and his gut was so big that it cast a shadow over rock 'n' roll in the last few years. Our music is what's important now.'

Three days later, the Pistols were driving round the country making guerrilla-like stops in various towns to avoid the bans that had been slapped on them during the Anarchy tour the previous December. Back on home territory, Sid played up badly throughout the tour, trashing hotel rooms, falling sick and hogging the limelight at gigs, where he'd stand, bare-chested and centre stage, encroaching on Rotten's territory. The singer wasn't pleased, especially when his old mate would stop playing midway through a song and play up to the audience instead. 'I didn't know what a useless monster he would turn into,' he later complained. For Sid, it was the performance, the effect, that mattered. It was for Rotten, too, but he'd grown used to a tight backing for his cues.

Once again, the tour ended with an exhausted Sid asking Barbara Harwood to help him 'get himself together'. No assistance was forthcoming. Punk professed self-reliance and libertarianism. Only the toughest love of all was valid: Do It Yourself.

Sid was becoming a pain in the neck, but he was, when all was said and done, one of The Johns. Rotten spent many nights trying to extricate his mate from what William Burroughs once called 'the algebra of need' that is heroin addiction. But neither talk ('It's for losers, Sid!') nor locking him away from Nancy and the dealers had any lasting effect. Sid's will was weak, and besides, he was no longer listening to his one-time mentor. The antagonism between the pair was exacerbated by Sid's constant companion. '[Rotten] didn't like me 'cos I was a junkie,' said Nancy Spungeon. 'He tried to keep me and Sid apart for months.'

If Rotten had become punk's Joycean figure, famous for his diarrhoeic flow of well-chosen words, Sid still believed in old-fashioned Defoe-like derring-do. 'Sid eclipsed John in that he was the easy one for the press,' says Jonh Ingham. 'He doesn't give difficult answers, doesn't give a stroppy attitude other than the archetype. John's venom was articulate.'

And, at times, genuinely mean. 'I didn't feel that Sid was eclipsing Johnny Rotten,' says photographer Bob Gruen, 'but Johnny did. Johnny was certainly an unusual person, very caustic, and someone who really didn't care if people didn't like him. The other band members were generally affable, but Johnny was kinda nasty!

'Sid wasn't nasty like that. Sid was funny. He'd say something insulting, or be obnoxious towards somebody, but not with that underlying level of meanness. Sid was more like, let's insult this guy and all my mates will think it's funny.'

Sid's willingness to please others also fed his need to take the negative aspects of punk's philosophy to the extreme. 'Lots of kids say they might not live past a certain age,' Nils Stevenson told Alan Parker, 'but for Sid there was no red light, only ever green. He bought the whole thing and in the end it was all he needed to destroy himself because he thought that's what people expected from him.'

Rotten saw the increasing manifestation of Sid's death drive as a weakness, and the more acute it became, the less tolerant he became of it. Like Paul Jones in the 1967 film, *Privilege*, a dated but nevertheless clear-sighted study of power and the pop process, Sid was behind locked bars. He'd let himself become a victim, a vehicle for old corrupt ways.

Back in March 1977, at the so-called Palace signing, Rotten had told *Melody Maker*: 'We're fighting bureaucracy, hypocrisy and anything that ends in a 'y'. Most people just want a cushy life. They don't want to fight for anything.' Rotten was, at heart, a pavement philosopher. Sid, meanwhile, was already getting comfortable in the gutter.

Sid, who seemed to regard the exercise of the imagination as girlish, or a sign of weakness, was too wrapped up in his own needs and desires to conceive of himself above and beyond them.

JOHNNY ROTTEN: 'Sid's the philosopher of the band.'

SID VICIOUS: 'I'm an intellectual.'

JOHNNY ROTTEN: 'He's also an oaf.'

SID VICIOUS: 'He's just jealous because I'm really the brains of the group. I've written all the songs, even right from the beginning when I wasn't even in the group. They were so useless they had to come to me because they couldn't think of anything by themselves.'

Still instinctively able to resurrect the banter that was vital to their early friendship, the humour nevertheless masked a vast gulf between the pair that now threatened to tear the band apart.

'They were too alike,' reckoned Anne Beverley, who must have been talking about the pair's mutual love of the instant put-down rather than strength of character. 'One minute, they would be great friends, the next, worst enemies.'

The growing antagonism between the pair wasn't helped by the presence of other enemies within the Pistols camp.

28 October 1977 – The Sex Pistols album *Never Mind The Bollocks, Here's The Sex Pistols* is released.

This record should have been released months earlier. The band knew that; the public did too. But Malcolm McLaren had been too busy chasing bigger glories, spending much of the year working on a script for a Sex Pistols film, and flying back and forth to Los Angeles in a bid to raise the big-money backing required to transform his young assassins into Hollywood anti-heroes. Trouble was, none of the band was particularly impressed, least of all Sid and Johnny.

Although he had little to do with its making, Sid exercised his punk purist role during discussions about the running-order of the album – which he took great pleasure in calling 'Never Mind Your Helmet'. He fought against the inclusion of the two summer singles, 'God Save The Queen' and 'Pretty Vacant', which he felt would be ripping the public off. He was outvoted – though there was some compensation when he was included in the composer credits for the two new songs, 'Holidays In The Sun' and 'Bodies'.

Sid spoke passionately about creative control on several occasions. 'If nobody else in the whole fucking world likes it I couldn't give two shits,' he told Judy Vermorel. 'We do what we do for ourselves, not for some fucking creep out there. That's not what it's for. It's specifically not for those arseholes.'

While spiralling out of control on a personal level, Sid was still able to rail against the projected Sex Pistols film. The script was weak, there was no story; it was simply 'a cheap attempt to make money', Sid complained. His suspicions were magnified when, in July, American sexploitation filmmaker Russ Meyer was brought on board to direct the film, provisionally titled *Who Killed Bambi?*. 'He said that he wanted to make a film that would be good for the box office . . . and make a lot of money,' Sid told Judy Vermorel. 'I said, 'What about making something that you're genuinely interested in?' He seemed a little puzzled by that.'

Sid's idea of an honest bit of movie-making was a film that showed the reality of his own life, 'like a day in the life of a pop star, right'. Get up at three, go to the office to hustle up some cash, then 'going somewhere and waiting hours to fucking cop some dope'. It would be, he said, a film about the most boring thing on earth.

Meyer later commented that while Sid didn't object to the scene in the film where he had to fuck his mother (Marianne Faithfull was earmarked for the part), he didn't want to be seen shooting up on screen. In truth, he hated the whole movie-making process, which he believed was a bogus, passive art form.

Sid concluded his tirade against the movie with what was probably the most articulate and honest expression of his own rage on record: 'I've got absolutely no interest in pleasing the general public at all,' he told Vermorel. 'I don't want to, because I think that largely they're scum. They make me physically sick, the general public. They are scum. And I hope you print that, 'cos that is my opinion of 99 per cent of the shit that you find out in the street who don't know a fucking thing. I don't wanna please cunts like them.'

Sid spoke like a terrorist – or perhaps that commune-dwelling bogeyman Charles Manson – able to dehumanise the human race that he blamed for his, and the world's ills. At the root of it all, though, was the deep self-loathing that fame (and the cultural power that came with it) had only served to magnify. Many came to punk to exorcise or resolve their problems; Sid was helpless to do anything but disseminate his.

3 November 1977 – News breaks that Russ Meyer has gone back to America and The Sex Pistols film has been put on hold.

Who Killed Bambi? drove an even bigger wedge between the band and Malcolm McLaren than had existed already. McLaren had got them in the papers, and got them record deals, but they were still paid a relative pittance while the manager – leather briefcase under his arm, Savile Row shirts under his mess of red curls – was hot-shotting it round the globe. They'd also begun to question the motives for McLaren's oft-repeated assertion: 'I really like the idea that the band really hate each other.' Was it simple hyperbole, or for reasons rather more sinister?

As an authority figure who deprived him of the money he craved for his instant highs, McLaren was the object of much Vicious abuse. 'I'm gonna beat him up next time when I see him. Cunt,' he'd say. 'That fucking toss-bag. I'd smash his face in quite happily.'

John Tobler quizzed him about McLaren for BBC Radio's *Rock On* that autumn. Sid drew him an amusing character sketch: 'He was a miserable little artist from the East End with pretensions of being middle class. In his closet in Clapham, he's got this really ridiculous picture of this awful load of scribble, it's meant to be a chair . . . He was trying to be all artistic and impress us and we were laughing our heads off thinking, What an idiot!'

So why put up with him, asked Judy Vermorel on another occasion. 'I hate his guts,' said Sid, 'but I like him just enough to be our manager. I can't think of anybody else that I could tolerate.'

But even that fragile tolerance was put under further strain towards the end of 1977, when McLaren threatened to kick Sid out of the band, and hatched several aborted attempts to pack Nancy off to New York on a one-way ticket.

SID VICIOUS: 'They plot against me as well.'
BBC INTERVIEWER: 'Why do they plot against you, Sid?'
SID VICIOUS: 'They say that I can't play nuthin', that I'm stupid.'
JOHNNY ROTTEN: 'That isn't a plot. That's just a fact!'

Never Mind The Bollocks proved a huge, if controversial success, and after a promotional blitz, the band members retreated to their various hideaways while McLaren attempted to reactivate the film project.

All the noise now came from Sid and Nancy's corner. 'Everyone knows that when a bird starts poking her nose into a rock 'n' roll band, it's suicidal,' says Steve Jones in *The Filth And The Fury*. 'That's when he started getting fucked up and not caring about playing.' And Sid hadn't cared for several months.

Matters reached a head one night, late in November, when Sid turned up for a rehearsal only to discover that no one else had. As he always did when faced with any difficulty, large or small, he drank. Then he returned to his room at the Ambassador Hotel in Bayswater, where he was staying until a new flat had been sorted out for him. He abused Steve Jones on the telephone, attempted to throw himself out of a third-floor window, and was saved by a distressed Nancy, who clung desperately to his belt. By now completely out of control, Sid then proceeded to trash the hotel room, and beat Nancy unconscious. They'd fought often, as hurt couples do. But this time, it was more serious. The police arrived, found a variety of pills and slapped drug charges on the pair.

Sid was becoming more vicious than ever, especially when he felt his position in the group was under threat. But he knew that McLaren needed him, that the manager regarded him as the real thing, as he told Nick Kent in *New Musical Express*. 'He just realised that what I was doing was just living out that original idea of the band as four complete nutters going out and doing anything and everything. Just having fun, which I always reckoned was the whole thing about the Pistols from the very beginning.'

It didn't feel like fun to everyone else – all of whom agreed that the 'Sid problem' was exacerbated by Nancy. With short tours of Britain and then Holland lined up, the hierarchy decided that she should go. There are various versions of how Nancy was to be bundled off to Heathrow, all beginning with packing Sid off to the dentist, and all concluding with her howling so loudly that the driver, Sophie Richmond, couldn't go through with it.

Anne Beverley told Alan Parker that the episode 'achieved two things. It made the bond between Sid and Nancy watertight. And Sid's resentment at Malcolm grew so intense that day that he never shook it off. He began to think the man was a fool, a wicked, self-centred manipulator who hated everyone.' A few days later, Sid and Nancy were installed in a cottage at 8 Pindock Mews in a quiet cul-de-sac in Maida Vale. They shared a rare moment of domestic bliss prior to the band's departure for America in the New Year.

AS MISERABLE as the rest of the band had become, Malcolm McLaren – still ostensibly orchestrating the chaos – was having such a good time that he knocked up a T-shirt and a poster to celebrate the band's two Christmas Day concerts in Huddersfield. Over a cartoon image of street kids, he wrote:

'They are Dickensian-like urchins who, with ragged clothes and pockmarked faces, roamed the streets of foggy, gaslit London pillaging . . . setting fire to buildings, beating up old people with gold chains. Fucking the rich up the arse and causing havoc wherever they go. Some of these ragamuffin gangs jump on tables amidst the charred debris and the burning torches and play rock 'n' roll to the screaming delight of the frenzied, pissing, pogoing mob. Shouting and spitting 'Anarchy', one of these gangs call themselves The Sex Pistols. This true and dirty tale has been continuing throughout the 200 years of teenage anarchy and so in 1978 there still remain The Sex Pistols. Their active extremism is all they care about and that's what counts to jump right out of the 20th century as fast as you possibly can in order to create an environment that you can truthfully run wild in.'

It was a wonderful piece of rhetoric, but among the band, only Sid still genuinely embodied the chaos. Rotten was already considering a recording career, with or without The Sex Pistols, while Steve and Paul simply wanted to keep the show on the road. They didn't give a toss about Malcolm's subversive literary excursions, or about belonging to some 200-year-long tradition of teen rebellion. But the havoc that was forever taking place in McLaren's head, and that was now barely concealed in the day-to-day running of the band, was about to run riot on what was – for this most British of rock bands – the unlikeliest stage.

5. 'I WAS THE ONLY GUY WITH ANY BIT OF ANARCHY LEFT'

Q: 'Who you gonna give a good kicking to over there, Sid?'
SID VICIOUS: 'Everyone. Everyone that I meet or see.'
Q: 'There are 300 million people in America.'
SID VICIOUS: 'I'm gonna give them *all* a kicking.'

SID WAS as good as his word. During The Sex Pistols' 12-day tour of America, Sidney Vicious of London Village lived up to his reputation, administering as many kickings as he could muster. Unfortunately, both for him and for the group, each and every blow was directed at the same figure of hate – himself.

The consequences of Sid's punk martyrdom were dire. Within hours of the tour's end, he was turning blue in a Haight-Ashbury heroin den. Across town, in the plush MiYako Hotel, the other three members of the band were about to deliver a lethal blow to The Sex Pistols' future: No Future.

But in bringing the Pistols' brief, explosive career to a premature end, the American tour can in many ways be regarded as a necessarily perfect punk rock moment. The Sex Pistols had, in many ways, done their work. The first issue of *Sounds* in 1978 predicted great things for a trio of Sid-related acts – The Slits, Siouxsie And The Banshees and Glen Matlock's new band, The Rich Kids. From the relatively ordinary Stiff Records stable to a whole host of thrillingly imaginative acts, from Mark Perry's Alternative TV to The Fall and Throbbing Gristle, punk had transformed the domestic rock landscape during the previous twelve months. The Sex Pistols had led the way, but after a year in the headlines – rarely for musical reasons – they were now in danger of being left behind.

America remained in the Dark Ages. Despite the pioneering impact of CBGB's and Max's Kansas City in New York, and pockets of enthusiasm for punk on the West Coast, the country was still dominated by (supposedly) inoffensive AOR: Fleetwood Mac's *Rumours*, not rowdy calls for social disorder and 'the death of rock'. 'It was all disco and hippies,' remembers photographer and McLaren's longtime mate Joe Stevens, 'The Doobie Brothers, The Bee Gees and Olivia Newton-John. Then Sid showed up in his Sex Pistols gear.'

'Rock Is Sick And Living In London' is how *Rolling Stone* introduced The Sex Pistols in an eight-page cover story in October 1977. And when the Pistols touched down at JFK Airport in New York, at 7pm on Tuesday 3 January 1978, Sid especially didn't want to disappoint. Even before the band had left Heathrow, Sid – annoyed that Nancy had been instructed to stay in London – had got himself embroiled in a row with photographers. 'You can fuck off,' he grunted. 'We don't need the press. We don't need nobody.' Passengers about to board the Pam Am flight complained and the police were called. In New York, Sid found a softer target. 'We're better than anyone, ain't we?' he told reporters. 'Except for The Eagles. The Eagles are better than us.'

Sid came through customs dressed in his regulation black jeans, and a green 'God Save The Queen' T-shirt. His hair, now longer than ever, was elevated with the help of heaps of Vaseline and talc. Noel Monk, who headed a team of burly, bearded minders employed by Warner Brothers to keep the band in check, instantly had Sid marked out as the problem Pistol. Monk, who later wrote a warts 'n' all account of the entire American venture, had strict instructions to prevent trouble at any cost. When US Immigration initially rejected the band's visa applications, Warner had to take the matter right to the top in order to rescue the tour. And they were in no mood to gamble with the $1 million surety they'd been obliged to post.

Visa Application: John Simon Beverley
– Assault on 2 policemen (discharge)
– Criminal damage (discharge)
– Taking of Ford Transit (£20)
– Destroying a policeman's handset (£10 with £4 compensation)
– Possession of an offensive weapon (a flick-knife) and assault on a
policeman (£50 with £25 compensation)

Monk's early suspicions soon turned out to be fully justified. Suffering from acute heroin withdrawal, as well as grand delusions of his premier Pistol status, Sid Vicious was every bit as unmanageable as the 'I'M A MESS' badge he wore on his lapel suggested. In many ways, the tour marks the pivotal moment in Sid's life, leaving a legacy of terrifying images and on-the-road horror stories that graphically document his full embrace of the disgust he insisted lay at the core of punk's meaning. From this point on, any complexities or contradictions in his life are erased by the spectacle of Sid Vicious – The Performance. Here was punk rock's clockwork sculpture, wound right up and walking the plank between life and death. 'Sid became like an unleashed animal,' said John Lydon.

Malcolm McLaren, the focus of the band's collective wrath in the weeks leading up to Christmas 1977, was back in London doing business as the tour got underway. Instead of McLaren, the group found themselves answerable to Monk's man-mountains, each one looking every inch like he'd just been bussed in from Altamont. No band member was to venture away from the tour bus without his 6'5", 240-lb chaperone and, Monk insisted, there were to be no hard drugs on the tour.

It wasn't long before Sid felt the physical force of his hellish guardian angels. Having already mauled a stewardess on the flight from New York to Atlanta, he snatched impolitely at a Warner Brothers publicist, prompting a punch in the stomach from Monk that had the London weakling doubled over in pain.

Later that same day, on the eve of the band's first show, Sid tried it on with 'DW', Dwayne Warner, who'd been assigned to him as his personal bodyguard. Swigging from a bottle of peppermint schnapps, his constant companion during the tour in the absence of the harder drugs his body craved, he turned to DW and said, 'Well, if you're so fucking tough, why don't you take me on?' After a mystified silence, the big guy took Sid's head and put it on first terms with the bathroom sink – several times over. Sid was impressed: 'OK, enough! I like you. Now we can be friends.'

He didn't learn his lesson. A little later, Sid started complaining about another guard, Camel, whom he took a dislike to because he refused to fight. Sid promised to blow Camel's brains out at the end of the tour.

On the way to the first show, at the Great South East Music Hall in Atlanta, Sid – now desperate for heroin – got out of the tour bus at a red light. He was hastily retrieved, but it was clear that he was already weak from withdrawal. After the show, during which the band was showered with pigs' noses and feet, Sid downed a pint of vodka then made his escape.

The rest of the group was forced to fly on to Memphis the following morning without him. Another guard, Glen Allison, eventually located the errant Pistol in the city's Piedmont Hospital. Having scored, Sid ended up in a drug shooting gallery, where he promptly carved 'I WANNA FIX' in his chest with a kitchen knife. His host thought he'd be better off in hospital.

According to Monk's account of the tour, the rest of the band ran out of patience with Sid as early as Friday, 6 January, when he finally joined them in Memphis. Rotten welcomed him with a caustic 'Oh, look, here comes Mister Drug', and the others did their best to ignore him. Malcolm McLaren, who'd now joined the tour, admitted to Monk that he was unable to control Sid. 'He'll kill me,' he told him, 'he hates me.' Steve Jones wished they could have Glen back. Sid's withdrawals became so bad that he turned to a concoction of schnapps and Valium to help him sleep. Inevitably, he was unable to keep much food down.

As the group crossed the border into Texas on Saturday, Sid insisted he must have a cowboy hat, then pulled out a knife and sliced a 7' gash into his left arm. 'I'm really happy,' he told Monk, by way of explanation. Rotten was singularly unimpressed. 'Our friend with the drugs has cut himself.' Once settled in adjoining rooms at Austin's Ramada Inn (Monk had taken over the responsibility of looking after Sid), Monk suggested that any repair to the arm would be painful. 'Yeah, Monk. Make it hurt. Make it fucking hurt,' said Sid. After Monk cleaned up his charge, the pair went for a walk. At that moment, Sid was 'a pleasure to be with', remembered the security manager.

Bob Gruen, who had joined the tour in Atlanta, also recalls moments when Sid seemed more subdued than suicidal. 'When they were trying to dry him out and keep him away from dope, he was actually quite talkative and friendly. We'd spend time on the bus talking. He'd say how much he missed Nancy, ask me questions about her New York days.

'Though he wasn't an intellectual, there was a spiritual side to Sid. On stage, he'd go nuts, but on the bus things were often quieter. We'd play these reggae tapes that Don Letts had made, especially this one song by Dr Alimantado called 'Born For A Purpose'. Basically, the message was, 'If you have no reason for living, don't determine my life'. It's kinda upbeat and positive, and it was one of Sid's favourite songs.' It was also, adds Letts, 'famously John's favourite reggae tune'.

Pining for Nancy didn't prevent Sid from satisfying his belatedly awakened sexual appetite elsewhere. On the journey down to San Antonio, on a Sunday, Monk noticed that Sid was constantly itching. It was, Sid explained, 'some bad disease' he'd caught because 'I fucked some bird before I got here.' He then told Monk: 'I gotta get some girls out here.'

By the time of the Baton Rouge show, on Monday, 9 January, Sid was ready to explode. And the fans queued up to help him. Sid called out from the stage for girls; one leapt up, French kissed him, then fell to her knees and yanked Sid's jeans down. Backstage, Sid fucked another admirer on a bar, in full view of everyone, while taking swigs from a bottle of beer.

At the end of the show in Tulsa two nights later, Sid spotted a formidable blonde in the crowd. 'I wanna do that big bird,' he told Monk, who duly sent her up to Sid's hotel room. She turned out to be a transsexual, prompting Sid to tell the minder: 'I wasn't sure if I was supposed to suck her cock or her cunt.' But Sid wasn't finished yet. Around four in the morning, Monk heard Sid call out and walked into his room to find him receiving a blow job. The dutiful girl was also covered from her head to her breasts in diarrhoea. 'Apparently, her boyfriend said he wanted her to have an experience she wouldn't forget,' says Bob Gruen.

Sid was now in the habit of showering all manner of unlikely gifts on his audiences. At Randy's Rodeo in San Antonio, where brawls broke out throughout the show, he responded by swinging his bass into the crowd on a couple of occasions. 'This guy tried to climb up on stage and fucking attack me, so I smashed his fucking brains out with my guitar,' Sid explained. His adversary seemed to think Sid's actions were entirely reasonable in the circumstances. 'He knew that I meant physical harm and I have to say I was ugly about it,' he explained. Rotten, with the wit of the devil, provided a decidedly black commentary: 'Oh dear, Sidney seems to have dropped his guitar.'

Other nights, Sid would spit into the moshpit, insult the crowd, or use the audience's heads as a handkerchief. And then there was his crowning achievement, at the Longhorn Ballroom in Dallas, a performance that more closely resembled a battle scene than a musical concert.

'Cunt, I'm hungry! I want my food and I want it now!' It was lunchtime, and Sid, who had already demolished a six-pack of beers, was ordering a meal in a Texan truckstop as the tour bus made its way towards Dallas. Noel Monk wasn't at all impressed by Sid's address to the bemused waitress, and so admonished him in the only way Sid could understand – with a blow to the stomach. The bassist apologised, took a bite out of Monk's hamburger while he waited for his steak and eggs to arrive, then rushed off to the loo where he threw up all over the walls.

By the time The Sex Pistols were ready to go on, Sid was dangerously delirious. Another bout of all-day drinking had left him dazed and confused, yet continually craving the heroin that would help ease his restlessness. But once in the bear pit, Sid fed off of the prevailing mood of violence, both from the crowd and on stage. Rotten spat out his words with genuine contempt, as he hung on the mike stand, his back arched like a silverback gorilla. One of a handful of truly charismatic rock frontmen, not much could upstage him.

To his right, though, a spectacle was unfolding that reduced Rotten's performance to a sideshow. While flu-ridden Rotten sweated, Vicious, his 'GIMME A FIX' scar now highlighted with a Magic Marker, dripped blood.

'These San Franciscan punkettes were motioning for Sid to come over and as he leaned over, the blonde one [Helen Killer] punched him right in the face,' remembers Bob Gruen. 'Sid reeled back. He had blood pouring out of his nose, and the biggest smile on his face. He thought it was hilarious.'

Gruen couldn't take his eyes off this theatre of cruelty. 'He wiped a little of it off with his hand and spat it back at this girl. Then she took some and spat it back at him. This went on for a few minutes. Then Sid grabbed a beer bottle from the top of his amp, smashed it and scratched it into his chest twice. Noel Monk jumped out, grabbed Sid's hand and held it up, as if to say, Look at what you're doing, Sid. Then Sid started playing but you couldn't hear anything. Eventually, he realised that when he broke the bottle, he'd turned the amp off. He was far more into the show than the actual playing.'

Sid kept up the showmanship. He poured lager on his wounds, and bellowed 'All cowboys are faggots', as if it was the only thought in his head. Once in a while he located the one string that remained on his bass.

'Sid was a tosser tonight,' said Steve Jones angrily after the show. 'He didn't even know the key for 'Pretty Vacant'.' Tosser or not, his antics were creating headlines – which was great news for McLaren, but less welcome to the wary Warner Brothers executives. They'd seen the writing on the wall and were already courting Rotten with a view to a possible solo career. That was made easier when, midway through the tour, Cook, Jones and McLaren chose to fly to the remaining few destinations, leaving Rotten and Vicious to squabble with each other – and their minders – on the tour bus.

As the bus pulled out of Dallas and drove in the direction of Tulsa, photographer Bob Gruen stayed on it too. 'We pulled into a truckstop, so I said to Sid, "Let's go get a burger." He wasn't meant to leave the bus, but everyone was asleep, so we both went in and ordered. Sid was wearing his "I'M A MESS" badge.

'Then some cowboy, who was with his wife and daughter at a table, got talking to Sid and invited him to join them. Then the guy said, "You're Vicious, eh? So how tough are you?" And he stubbed a cigarette out on the back of his hand. So Sid casually reaches across his plate and cuts his hand and lets the blood drip over his eggs and steak. The guy freaked out and left, taking his kid and wife with him.'

Gruen has a second story from this last leg of the American tour, prior to disembarking in San Francisco for the unexpected – though not particularly shocking – denouement. 'I had these classic New York, heavy duty motorcycle boots, like the ones Johnny Thunders wore. And Sid loved these boots. I was asleep on the couch at the front of the bus and the boots were on the floor next to me. According to Joe Stevens, who saw it all, Sid put the boots on, and walked around in them. He then took a knife out, put it to my throat and said to Johnny and Joe, 'If I kill him, I can keep his boots.' The two of them said nothing!' Stevens survived the night. Sid kept the boots.

6. FALL OUT

'I don't think anybody wanted to continue, but no one had the guts to say it. So I phoned John up and told him what I thought of him and where I thought he was at . . . I think I was better than any of the others. John's completely finished.'
– Sid Vicious, in a phone conversation with Roberta Bayley

ACCORDING TO Steve Jones, 'It was Sid who broke the band up . . . on the American tour 'cos of his habits. He thought he could do no wrong, be 'Jack The Lad', while all the time he was fucking up, playing different songs from us.'

Rotten agreed, as he told Caroline Coon in 1978, adding that he 'was bored stiff with Sid's juvenile behaviour. I was very anti-drugs from the start, and I tried to help Sid for a year. But I've had enough of that social work rubbish.'

Asked by Julian Temple about his departure early in 1978, 'Useless' disagreed, his explanation suggesting that open warfare had broken out between him and the newly restyled John Lydon. 'That's a load of cobblers. I was just playing bass and leaping up and down. He thought I was trying to take over his position as the new Johnny Rotten.'

The sub-plots came together in, of all places, hippie central San Francisco. Only Steve Jones and Paul Cook had managed to maintain anything like an amicable relationship among the Pistols' entourage. But, in the face of the open contempt Rotten, McLaren and Vicious had for each other, that wasn't enough to save the band.

A number of specific events conspired to bring the group – minus Sid – together in a room at the MiYako Hotel in San Francisco on Tuesday, 17 January, for one final Sex Pistols meeting. McLaren's insistence that the band fly off to Rio to record with Train Robber Ronnie Biggs; the fact that Lydon had been holed up in a low budget motel in San Jose with the crew, some 25 miles out of the city; the encroaching mood of paranoia that had pursued the tour, made worse by rumours that the CIA were monitoring the entourage; and insecurities all round, which Warners' constant courting of Rotten, did nothing at all to help.

Even Rotten had got his old apocalyptic tongue back, telling DJ Bonnie Simmons before the show at Winterland on Saturday 14 January: 'I don't like rock music. I don't know why I'm in it. I just want to destroy everything.'

Ironically, that same day, Sid was visited with a glimpse of the positive. 'Most of our records are banned 'cos we're telling the truth,' he said. 'The straights, the grown-ups . . . can't take anarchy. They want everything ordered so that life is nice and safe. They're closet cases. They ain't ever been out of their closet since the day they were born.' Mr Freedom probably hadn't read a word of an anarchist text, but he got the gist of its positive – as opposed to the more commonly held nihilist – message. 'Rules are meant to be broken, right. When there's no more rules or categorisations. When there are no more niggers or whites. When there are no more punks, no more dirt. When there are just people. That is when things are gonna be OK.'

Sid continued to express his pathological fear of growing old. 'Grown-ups are people who've become redundant. I'm gonna be dead before I'm anywhere near that age. We're just a bunch of kids, and we always will be kids. We won't change . . . We'll probably be dead in like two years.' He certainly would be, and the group itself had barely hours to go . . .

Shortly after the band's shambolic performance at Winterland, the biggest venue they'd ever played, Sid was in a heroin haze in a grubby part of the city and about to turn blue. The simmering rivalry with Rotten, or 'Rod Stewart', as he was sometimes called by Vicious and McLaren during the tour, had turned into open warfare, which only encouraged Sid to misbehave. 'We hated each other at that point,' Lydon admitted years later, adding that Sid's heroin sojourn in San Francisco 'buggered him up'.

In truth, the damage had been done much earlier, way back in the early chapters. Sid seized on punk's celebration of uselessness because that's how he felt and that's how he felt others ought to feel. But nobody did it better, and that knowledge empowered him, gave him protection. Sid would never have concluded the Winterland show with the words, 'Ever get the feeling you've been cheated?', because however badly he performed, there was honour in the fuck-up.

The Pistols, and especially Rotten, had got above their station. Sid's rebellion was to walk away from the backstage flatter-fest, where Annie Leibovitz had attempted to coax Rotten and Vicious into the frame for one of her famously stylised shots. 'Fuck him,' said Rotten. 'Why should I have to go over there to that bastard? Tell the wanker to come over here!' Vicious volunteered a curt 'Fuck off!' then walked out on the band, a trio of Sid-struck groupies in tow.

A few hours later, a call came through to John 'Boogie' Tiberi in his hotel room. 'These kids were saying, 'Sid's here',' says Tiberi. 'It was literally in a squat on the corner of Haight and Ashbury. And Sid was going blue. I picked him up and started walking him around. I had no experience of that kind of thing. It was just what I heard you did. [A minder] Rory turned up at 2am and Sid was coming round: it worked. He phoned up Bill Graham who arranged for a car.' Graham recommended that Boogie get Sid to an acupuncturist in Marin County. 'I went back the next day and Sid was in the bathroom. He'd no idea of what happened . . . or how he got there.'

When Tiberi informed him of the break-up, Sid was furious and immediately telephoned Rotten. Yes, it was true, it was a fait accompli, and it was something for which he would never forgive his old friend. McLaren picked Sid up and tried to take him to discuss the matter with Rotten in San Jose. Sid told him he'd had enough, then promptly had a fit in the car. Later, he overdosed again.

Rotten flew to New York with Joe Stevens on 18 January. 'Livid? Yes, he'd lost the best job he's ever had,' Stevens says. 'And to this day, regardless of whether he's doing television shows or movies or making records, it was still his best gig and he knew it.'

Nevertheless, Stevens believes that leaving was a decision he had to make. 'I don't think John wanted anything further to do with Sid.'

Joe Stevens was sheltering Rotten from the British media, which had flown en masse to New York. Malcolm, Steve and Paul were flying to Rio. And on 17 January, Sid Vicious left for Los Angeles with Sophie Richmond, who chaperoned him for one day and night, before 'Boogie' Tiberi took over. He hadn't reckoned on finding Sid in free fall – with no band, no McLaren and no Nancy, the drugs were more necessary than ever. After making a dodgy drug deal on Sunset Strip, Sid was taken to a doctor, who prescribed him methadone in a bid to keep him away from heroin.

The idea was for Boogie to take Sid back to London, get him cleaned up, then send him out to join Cook, Jones and McLaren in Rio. Setting out on Thursday, January 19, the pair only got as far as New York. Unwilling, perhaps, to begin to comprehend the events of the past few days, Sid's psyche demanded a knock-out blow, and augmented the effects of the methadone with several Valium tablets. Midway through the flight, he collapsed into a semi-coma. 'We couldn't wake him up,' says Boogie. 'Even the TWA stewardess was trying to put ice cubes down his shirt.' After touching down at JFK, Sid was rushed to Jamaica Hospital in Queens.

It wasn't quite the 'suicide drama' that the headlines suggested. But with Nancy a few thousand miles away, and Sid now estranged from the group that had at least given his life some focus (if not necessarily a lifeline), he was thrust back into a lonely self-reliance from which he never really recovered. And self-reliance, for someone as fractured and as emotionally unsteady as Sid, wasn't a good thing.

A blizzard in New York that weekend meant that Sid – by now a front-page news story – suffered alone in hospital. Neither Boogie, Bob Gruen or Roberta Bayley were able to visit him. Just a few miles away, in Joe Stevens' Greenwich Village flat, was Johnny Rotten. 'I said to John, I know where that hospital is, though it's not gonna be easy with this blizzard. Do you wanna go? And he said, 'I don't care about that son of a bitch.' I asked him again, on the drive out to the airport, and he said, 'Nah, I don't wanna see that cunt.' He had no tolerance for heavy drug use, he felt that McLaren was irresponsible, and he had no intention of getting back with Steve and Paul. John was thinking about getting a reggae band together. We put him on the plane, he went back to London and he formed Public Image.'

Sick, alone and virtually friendless, Sid Vicious had no alternative but to return to London, into the arms of the one person in the world who understood him: Nancy Spungeon.

Sid discharged himself on 21 January. His doctor, Bernard Gussoff, told the press that, 'Mr John Ritchie, a self-admitted prior narcotics addict . . . has responded well to immediate treatment.' Unhappy at Sid's premature departure, he also sounded a note of caution: 'The patient has been strongly urged to have follow-up medical care and long-range control of the narcotic problem.'

In a taped conversation with photographer Roberta Bayley, who called him at the hospital on 20 January, Sid admitted, 'I'm lonely . . . I'm just sitting here on my own.' He pined for the prepubescent security of a pile of Marvel comics, explained that his 'overdose' was an accident ('You know you get pissed a lot quicker in the air'), before she asked him: 'What happened with this group of yours?' 'I left them,' he said, striking a tone of grandness. It was, he claimed, his call to Rotten that started the chain of events, before announcing that Cook and Jones would 'fail' and that Rotten was 'completely finished'.

Rotten was clearly bothering Sid. 'He's finished as a person as well,' he continued. 'He's just not what he used to be.' When Bayley suggested that recent events might 'shake him up a little bit', Sid struck a more conciliatory tone: 'Yeah, that's what I'm hoping. That it'll shake him up and then he'll be able to do something. That'd be good if he could do that, but otherwise if it doesn't shake him up and get him out of it, then as a person, not only will he not do anything, but also nobody will even want to know him. They'll say, "Oh, didn't you used to be Johnny Rotten"?'

After a short inquest into the tour ('I was the only one still putting any real energy into it'), the conversation turned to Sid's health. 'I can't drink,' he admitted. 'The doctor said that if I drank anything like the way I've been drinking for the past . . . however long, that I've got about six months at the absolute outside to live. And the drugs as well.' When she suggested that he ought to hang around New York for a day or two, he declined. 'If I went out anywhere I wouldn't be able to resist the temptation. That'd be the trouble. I'd end up just boozing myself out.'

ROBERTA BAYLEY: 'Well, what're you going to do? If you go back to London, it's just the same thing.'

SID VICIOUS: 'Yeah. I probably will die in six months, actually.'

ROBERTA BAYLEY: 'You have to straighten out for a while.'

SID VICIOUS: 'I can't straighten up. I just can't be straight.'

ROBERTA BAYLEY: 'You could. Just as an experiment.'

SID VICIOUS: 'I suppose I just have to. I haven't figured out yet quite how I'm gonna do it 'cos I haven't been straight in like four years. I had hepatitis and when I got out of hospital I just really fucked myself up as badly as I could. I don't know why, but everybody said you can't do it, so I just went ahead and done it. It's my basic nature.'

ROBERTA BAYLEY: 'Well, your basic nature's gonna get you in a lot of trouble.'

SID VICIOUS: 'My basic nature's gonna kill me in six months.'

7. SID SODS OFF

'PINDOCK MEWS was their only real home,' Anne Beverley told *Sid's Way* author Alan Parker, referring to Sid and Nancy's flat in Maida Vale. 'They made it real, put up their posters, moved in Sid's jukebox and motorbike. I had high hopes when they moved in there, but most of [that] was based on the pair of them cleaning up.'

Sid 'n' Nancy's new love nest was situated down a quiet mews road, a short walk from Warwick Avenue tube station. Deceptively quiet for this part of west London the area also had a particularly good reputation for scoring drugs. And, despite the sobering advice that Sid was given back in New York, drugs – hard drugs – is what he required to celebrate his reunion with Nancy Spungeon, and to avoid thinking about the consequences of The Sex Pistols' split.

Some heroin users can still function to some degree while on the stuff. For Sid, heroin had no other function than as a Grade A assist into fuck-up-land. He didn't write on it, or play. He barely spoke. Most people's memories of heroin Sid is of a shaking and withdrawn wreck – with a similarly smacked out female wreck at his side.

'I really got to know the guy just before he moved into the Maida Vale flat,' says Nick Kent. 'I was going to score some heroin from a Turkish guy who lived in some squat close to Pindock Mews, and I saw Sid standing on the street. It was the dead of winter, and all he had on was his leather jacket, no shirt and a pair of jeans. He had all these marks over his body. I said, "What did you do to yourself, man?" He said, "Oh, I just got bored earlier today." He was shaking; he was withdrawing and having a hard time.

'I took him to this dealer's place, a Turkish prog rock drummer with a long beard who was importing heroin from Persia. It was all very squalid, little bags of heavily cut stuff. And Sid had like £5 on him. McLaren wouldn't give him any money. So I gave him £5. He was eternally grateful, like, 'Wow, you really helped me out, man. No one else will.' He kept saying it over and over again. After that, he was like a dog that wouldn't go away.

'He always had this heroin problem because he was born with it. I think he realised that. And he was addicted to Nancy as much as he was to the fucking drugs. It was sad. He knew that McLaren was pimping him, and Nancy too, but he didn't have enough cerebral faculty to be able to mull over anything.'

Only one piece of advice seemed to stick: both Nancy and McLaren constantly told Sid that he, not Rotten, was the true figurehead of punk rock. And Nancy always carried a bag of cuttings to prove it. 'I saw Nancy once round at Jordan's in Hyde Park Square, and she had carrier bags full of 'Our Clippings',' Marco remembers. 'God, it was pathetic! What sort of rock star cuts out their clippings, puts them in a scrapbook and carries them around? She was a complete rock star wife.'

'I'm so glad I'm out of that group,' Sid told journalist Chris Salewicz, and anyone else who was still listening. Which, as early as spring 1978, was Nancy Spungeon and noticeably few others. The music press avidly reported Rotten's Jamaican sojourn, his name change to Lydon and his formation of Public Image Limited (PiL) later that spring. It also carried stories about Cook and Jones joining forces with Johnny Thunders. And that legendary bassist? 'Sid Vicious' plans are unclear,' deadpanned *Sounds* in April.

Sid fought back in the occasional interview. 'I'm an intellectual,' he raved in one. 'I'm a highly original thinker. Rotten's just jealous because I'm the real brains behind The Sex Pistols. They were so fucking useless they had to come to me because they couldn't think of anything by themselves.'

But Sid had already become – and was always destined to be – punk's short story. Rotten, now plain John Lydon, was its rich, multi-versed poem, crying out for ever closer inspection. Take a keen eye to much of the debut PiL album, issued in autumn 1978, and you'll find plenty of evidence that Sid was still on his mind that spring. On 'Low Life', a phrase Lydon liked to use when referring to junkie/victims, he spits, 'You fell in love with your ego'. The album's laborious, brain-crunching opener, 'Theme', was built around the phrase, 'I wish I could die'. Sid was all over the record.

Sid 'n' Nancy spiralled into a feckless existence. They fought, they fucked, they fell over. When Lech Kowalski's film crew turned up at Pindock Mews to shoot an interview for his DOA punk documentary, Nancy demanded money upfront – as the couple always did – while a knife-wielding Sid nodded out, scalding her with his cigarette. It was left to Nancy to do most of the talking, and when she spoke, a perfect epitaph fell out: 'Sid 'n' Nancy, we were partners in crime, we helped each other out.' Nodding out was normal in the Vicious household. 'I sleep all day,' Nancy once told her mother. 'And I never think about the future.'

When Julian Temple managed to shoot an interview that spring, Sid was a little more animated. Physically, though, he looked wrecked. One cheek was cut and bloody, his right eye was virtually closed, and he was carrying the first hint of a Great British beer belly. Occasionally spitting or pulling wax from his ears, the mess in the red swastika T-shirt virtually confessed to his addiction. 'Nobody wanted to rehearse or do anything,' he explained. 'It's a logical conclusion – boredom. I'm that way inclined. So what do I turn to?

'You can't get comfortable and you sweat,' Sid continued, describing the symptoms of heroin withdrawal. 'You're boiling hot and you pour with sweat and your nose dribbles and all of a sudden you get the colds and the sweat turns to fucking ice on you and you put a jumper on and then you're boiling hot and you take it off and you get cold again. Like, you just can't win. You lie down, you sit up. It drives you insane.' He barely paused to draw breath.

Sadness filled his face, there was a numb pain in his delivery and not a trace of irony as he concluded: 'I don't want to be a junkie for the rest of my life. I don't want to be a junkie at all.' These were the words of a pained young man. But the pull of destiny was stronger still. Sid stayed a junkie for the rest of his life. Sure it hurt but, locked in his immature psyche of perpetual need, and with no faith in any way of life other than the one he'd pursued and perfected into a virtual art form, Sid, like Ziggy Stardust before him, was programmed to 'play it too far'.

'I'll die before I'm very old,' Sid said in April 1978. 'I don't know why, I just have this feeling. There have been many times when I've nearly died.' Nancy Spungeon too had been close to death many times. And like Sid, she was hopelessly drawn to the cult of the living dead, a lure that seemed to move up a notch during spring 1978. That's when the Sid 'n' Nancy story drifts hazily into impending tragedy and degradation, the pair's self-inflicted wounds nevertheless tempered by a sweetness that sometimes bordered on the cheesy.

It's a measure of how much time the pair now had on their hands that Nancy remembered to send a Mother's Day card in March. 'We both love each other very much and take care of each other and we have a very beautiful relationship that you would be proud of,' she cooed. The mood changed as she apologised for her shaky handwriting: 'Sidney is playing bass right next to me and the bed is bouncing like hell.' Finally, and most revealingly of her partner's character, she stated: 'Sid thinks the world of you too. Believe me, that's rare. He rarely takes a liking to anyone.' Ever the '70s schoolboy, he inscribed a childish 'Luv from Sid' to a woman he had yet to meet (though he had asked her for the occasional cash subsidy over the phone).

'Sid was a troubled man,' says Glen Matlock, who lived close by and began to see him more regularly during 1978. 'But he wasn't lonely because he was with Nancy all the time.' And Nancy was more troubled still. 'She was one of those people you'd take one look at and say, bad news. She was always coming round to see my girlfriend Celia to get her jeans let out, because she was becoming a right lard arse. One day, I went into the kitchen and there was Nancy eating an ice cream with her arm over a bowl and blood dripping into it. She'd slashed her wrist but she's eating an ice cream. I said, "Alright Nancy, what you doin'?" She said, "I'm killing myself because Sid doesn't love me any more."'

Another neighbour, Alan Jones, insists that while Sid wasn't exactly a lonely figure, 'he did like to keep himself to himself. He would never let too much of his guard down. We would see each other a lot when he moved to

Pindock Mews. I'd walk past the laundrette and see Sid sat there watching the dryer, then they'd come back to my place for tea and crumpets. I really liked them. They were fantastic when they were round my place. I wouldn't have had them there otherwise. I certainly wouldn't have somebody shooting up and screaming there.

'I didn't notice any change in him. That's what I liked about him. Some of the others, like John, had changed. Sid was always funny, always nice to me. I never saw drugs, and I know what the effects of drugs are. They were both very lucid, very together. I'll always remember Nancy holding on to Sid, cuddling him. I thought, "God, these two!"' One day in May, Sid came round with a card for Jones. It read: 'From The Sex Pistols.'

There wasn't too much scope for a non-playing musician, even in the aftermath of punk, by which time Steve Jones was able to play as well as the records he used to emulate, and Lydon was now working with Wobble, whose bass-playing was as inventive as Can's Holger Czukay.

One night, at the Speakeasy, Sid sat in with Johnny Thunders' latest project, The Living Dead. 'Johnny promised Sid that he could play this one gig,' The Only Ones' Peter Perrett told Nina Antonia. Perrett, also part of the ad-hoc combo, remembered rehearsing a cover of The Monkees' 'Steppin' Stone'. 'Sid was totally hopeless. I said to Sid, 'Just play E'. He didn't know where E was on the bass guitar.' Perrett moved Sid's fingers around the fret. 'After the soundcheck, Johnny said, "He's too useless, I'm not going to let him play."' Perrett argued that Sid would be heartbroken, and so a compromise was reached. Sid could join them on stage, but his amp wouldn't be switched on.

At Thunders' insistence, a topless Nancy introduced the band. 'Johnny probably didn't notice but Sid was really hurt by it,' Perrett remembered. 'That was ironic because half the world had already seen her like that.'

Sid cut an even sadder spectacle. For the first three or four songs, he leaped about and threw out his best clichéd rock 'n' roll poses, before realising that nothing was coming out of his amp. As he called for a roadie to fix it, Thunders rushed to the mike: 'Thanks very much Sid . . .' 'Sid slinked off,' Perrett said. 'He was a very sad character.'

With Sid 'n' Nancy that night were Vic Godard and Clash road manager Johnny Green. 'He was just awful,' says Green, 'but beautifully awful! He was hanging on to the backline and I was watching him and thinking, "Fucking hell, the bass stack's coming down on top of him."'

'It was like he fainted,' adds Vic Godard. 'He fell right back through the drum kit, smashed the whole lot up, and had to be carried off. I was speaking to him about five minutes before. He was out of his head.'

While nowhere near good enough for Thunders' aptly named The Living Dead, Sid was, thought scam-meister McLaren, a perfectly imperfect front for a continuing Sex Pistols project. Despite the acrimony that erupted during the US tour, McLaren promised money, a larger share of the spotlight and an expenses-paid trip to Paris. But, Sid insisted, Nancy had to come too. Sid, rejected by both band and record company just weeks earlier, was a Sex Pistol once more. The Wit had, it seemed, been usurped by The Twit.

McLaren welcomed the chaos that Sid brought to the band's public image, but when it came to his front door – or, in this instance, his hotel room – he couldn't handle it at all. The small entourage of McLaren, filmmaker Julian Temple, Boogie and Sid 'n' Nancy spent much of March and early April in Paris attempting to shoot some short scenes for McLaren's continuing film project. Steve and Paul ('a pair of sheep who do what Malcolm says', according to Sid) were back in London, as was Lydon, who was about to serve a writ on McLaren's management company Glitterbest.

In many ways, McLaren saw Sid as his way of exacting revenge on Lydon. He knew that by promoting the more easily marketable Vicious to the status of frontman, Lydon's standing among the public would be severely diminished. It worked, too, but at some cost to his nerves. The pair argued almost as soon as they arrived in Paris. Sid, acting on Nancy's orders, demanded that Malcolm sign a piece of paper surrendering his management rights before they began shooting. Even Julian Temple agreed that 'Sid was really very, very difficult to work with, largely because of the heroin,' at this stage.

Matters came to a head when, during an internal phone conversation at the Hotel Brighton, in the Rue de Rivoli where the entourage was staying, McLaren told Sid he was 'just a fucked-up junkie' who had 'no future of any kind'. Sid passed the phone to Nancy, ran to McLaren's room wearing only a pair of swastika underpants and Bob Gruen's cherished biker boots, kicked the door open and leapt on his quarry. 'The guy's hatred was very clear,' Temple remembered.

In a postcard Nancy sent to her parents back in Philadelphia, Paris in the spring was idyllic. 'Love Paris,' she wrote. 'It's a really beautiful city with pretty parks and squares. Have been here for three weeks, so we had a chance to really look around. I bought so many things – clothes, French make-up, jewellery, etc.'

She neglected to tell them that they'd intended to film Sid walking around the Jewish Quarter wearing his swastika T-shirt. Or that Sid was to fake an act of matricide for the film. That Sid would beat up waiters if his vodka and tonic turned out to be vodka and orange. That Julian Temple once found the pair of them so sick from methadone and heroin use that they'd jammed both their heads down the toilet bowl. That the couple got banned from their hotel because they'd smashed all the mirrors. Or that Nancy had cut her wrists once again because 'Sid doesn't love me'.

Out of this chaos came Sid's most perfect pop moment, a punk rock assassination of 'My Way', probably the most schmaltzy, self-satisfied song of the 20th century made famous by the king of smooth, Frank Sinatra.

Julian Temple's original idea had been to record the Edith Piaf evergreen, 'Je Ne Regrette Rien', but Sid hated the song. He wasn't that keen when someone from the Pistols' French record label, Barclay Records, recommended 'My Way' until Nancy suggested he rewrite some of the lyrics. Sid personalised it with transparent references to his own life: 'I ducked the blows', 'I shot it up' and 'I killed a cat'. It didn't all go Sid's way, though. Adamant that the song be given The Ramones treatment, Sid eventually succumbed to Temple's suggestion that the first verse be given a queasy orchestral treatment, courtesy of the Penguin Café Orchestra's Simon Jeffes.

Sid's vocal was recorded piecemeal. 'He was so ill that it was actually physically difficult for the guy to do it,' said Julian Temple. By 3 April 1978, and after two nights in the studio, they finally had a finished take, assisted by Steve Jones, who had been flown over to bring some order to the session.

Lydon claims that when he listens to Sid's version of 'My Way', 'it sounds like me.' Possibly, but then didn't every punk singer chew and spit his words out in those days? There is no doubt who the line 'What is a prat who wears hats?' was aimed at, though. 'Silly boy,' Lydon writes in his autobiography, 'he hated my hat collection.'

Sid needed no hat to distract from the majesty of his overall appearance. In black, skin-tight jeans, white tuxedo, and hair punkishly black and not unlike Bowie's Ziggy Stardust look, he appeared every inch 'the first monster child of the hippie generation' that Julian Temple (to Jon Savage) intended him to be. 'There was a cartoon element to him, totally, and that's epitomised by the 'My Way' video,' says Steven Severin. 'That's the Sid I know and remember. That's exactly the humour . . .'

At the film's climax, Sid takes out a gun and fires indiscriminately at the bourgeois audience. Unlike the performance, which was shot at the Paris Olympia, the crowd scenes were filmed in London, at the Screen On The Green cinema. 'Malcolm rang me one night,' Anne Beverley told Alan Parker. 'He told me he wanted Sid to shoot me in the movie. I told him he could go and fuck himself.' A lookalike was hastily found to play the part of Sid's mother.

Back in London, later in the summer, Sid recorded two rock 'n' roll standards, Eddie Cochran's 'C'mon Everybody' and 'Something Else', then filmed a few promotional scenes for the forthcoming film. He regarded this as his final act as a Sex Pistol. McLaren had likely hoped so too. (And maybe even Steve and Paul did too, whose original version of 'Silly Thing', titled 'Stupid Cunt', was inspired by Sid.) Over the summer, McLaren had come up with the idea of the band members each meeting nasty ends in the film. Sid, cast as 'The Gimmick' in what McLaren now dubbed simply *The Swindle*, was to go out in a blaze of glory in a high-speed motorbike crash.

Sid no longer needed The Sex Pistols. With Nancy Spungeon managing him, he was going to New York to carve out a fabulous solo career for himself. But first they needed money to pay for the plane tickets.

THE PREVIOUS summer, The Sex Pistols, their entourage and their fans had been hounded by an ugly constellation of royalists and right-wingers, Teds and tabloids, anyone, in fact, who fancied a post-pub pop so long as they had numbers on their side.

Summer 1978 was marked by a violent incident that helped convince Sid he was so isolated in his home town that he might as well take Nancy's advice and try his luck in New York.

In fact, the year had been marked by Sid getting into many scrapes – with Paul Weller, with Wings guitarist Jimmy McCullough, with well-built R&B singer Frankie Miller, with an unnamed American Marine. Invariably, he came off worse in every incident, and these series of scrapes left him with permanent damage to his right eye, which now drooped, making him look more comatose than usual.

But by far the most psychologically damaging incident took place outside John Lydon's house in Gunther Grove.

There had been some dialogue with Lydon earlier that summer, which had convinced Sid that the two might work together again. Interviewed for a new music magazine, *Flexipop*, Sid was effusive with his praise. 'He was my friend,' he said, 'a really good guy. I liked that guy so much, I really admired him. He was so radical. I don't know whether he regarded me as his best friend, but I regarded him as mine.'

A short while later, one hot August night, Sid 'n' Nancy found themselves outside Lydon's flat. Nancy was shouting at the top of her voice: 'Sid's gotta be the frontman!' Sid resented the fact that Lydon guarded his privacy in his impressive ivory tower, so he attempted to kick the door down. But when no one showed any interest in letting them in, the pair walked off to score some more drugs. They had recently registered themselves at Bowden House, a private hospital in Harrow-on-the-Hill, for another methadone cure. But as always, they were unable to stick to it.

Then the phone started ringing. Among the small group of mates Lydon had round was Wobble. 'I picked it up and Sid was ranting and raving. Fuck knows what I was doing. I'd been on uppers, and now I'm on Tuinol coming down on a couch on the second floor. He phoned again and again, but we ignored it. So he came round and kicked up a fuss. It was completely inappropriate.

'I remember hearing the door being kicked. Sid was a fucking nuisance by that point. I can't remember if I went downstairs or he came upstairs, but I got the blame for hitting him with an axe, which is not true. I think he got threatened with an axe by a third party – neither me or John. I mean, if you hit someone with an axe, you split their fucking head open. What happened was that he got pushed down the stairs and knocked his head on this metal boot-scraper at the bottom. That was the last time I saw Sid.'

The incident was subsequently celebrated on the sleeve of PiL's debut single, 'Public Image', which proudly proclaimed 'I was wild with my chopper . . .' next to a picture of Wobble.

Later that month, on 22 August, a young sound engineer, John Shepcock, was found dead at Pindock Mews after a night with Sid 'n' Nancy. Even they, thick-skinned through a combination of rampant narcissism and the cloak of drug abuse, could now see that London was not the place to continue their habits.

'You get to a point in life where you think, This isn't funny any more,' says Wobble. 'And that's what I told Sid. You know what you're doing. I firmly believe that even the most disturbed people at some level are making a choice about where and how you wanna be. And if you decide to close down, maybe it's gonna be difficult to get it back. You're like a computer that has lost half of its memory capability. You need a powerful realisation to overcome that, and most people do not get to that point.' And certainly not Sid 'n' Nancy, for whom close-down (chemically induced or otherwise) had always been the soft, alluring option.

'A few years ago, I went to have lunch with [UK music industry supremo and Warner Brothers boss] Rob Dickens,' says Glen Matlock by way of an aside. 'And he said, "You know the best band you were ever in?" I said, "Yeah, the Pistols." He said, "No, you're wrong . . . The Vicious White Cats." I said, "Why didn't you offer us a deal then?" He said, "You were all too out of it."'

The Vicious White Cats were hastily put together by Sid and Matlock after a meeting in their Maida Vale local, the Warrington. 'I sometimes stayed at

Celia's place round the corner, so I'd often bump into them. One day, Sid said, "What's all this about us being enemies? Let's do something about it." And about five days later we did that show.'

Inevitably, it was left to Matlock to put a band together. He called up ex-Damned drummer Rat Scabies, then fronting his own group, The White Cats, and guitarist Steve New from Matlock's own combo, The Rich Kids. Matlock was down to play bass, while Sid, buoyed by his starring role in 'My Way', which had recently outsold all the other Sex Pistols singles, was the ticket-shifting frontman.

The makeshift band spent a couple of days rehearsing at John Henry's in Islington, where they worked up Pistols-era covers such as The Monkees' '(I'm Not Your) Steppin' Stone' and Dave Berry's 'Don't Give Me No Lip', Sid's own 'Belsen Was A Gas' and versions of 'C'mon Everybody', 'My Way' and The Stooges' 'I Wanna Be Your Dog'.

Inspired by Matlock's dexterity ('Glen, I can't believe it, you can play the bass all the way through a song without stopping!'), and perhaps a vague idea that Nancy ought to have her own instrument, Sid helped himself to a brand new Fender Mustang bass that was leaning against a wall in the rehearsal studio. 'I said, "Sid, if you take it, it's really obvious who's had it.' But he simply walked past the Portakabin offices and put it in my car.

'After the second day's rehearsal, we started to pack up our equipment, and one of the guys said, 'That's not going anywhere until we get the bass back'. Sid totally denied he had anything to do with it. I told him that if we don't get our equipment, we can't do the show, and if we don't do the show you don't get any money. He called up Nancy, who wrapped the bass in a plastic bin liner and gave it to the cab driver. But she'd already painted it emulsion black, so as I handed it over, I said, "Let's go." We all saw the look on his face as he took it out and saw it was still dripping wet!'

Johnny Green stage-managed the show, popularly dubbed 'Sid Sods Off', which took place at the Electric Ballroom on 15 August. 'I thought it was fucking great, at least at the soundcheck,' Green says. 'Sid really attacked each song. At soundchecks the people hanging around usually stare at their fingernails. But Sid gave a complete performance, with all the dynamics, movements, eye contact, everything. He was wonderful.'

A few days earlier, Paul Cook and Steve Jones had played there as The Greedy Bastards. 'Theirs was the cocaine night,' says Matlock, who admits to being 'pissed out of my head' for the show. 'Ours was the booze and smack night.' That explains why, as Green remembers it, 'Sid was fucking useless by the time of the show, stoned out of his head. He didn't move, apart from grabbing his balls a couple of times and lifting his arm in the air. He was dozy; there was no attack in his voice, and no movement. It was his big occasion, and he got it arse about face.'

The crowd didn't notice. 'We'd sold the place out,' says Matlock, 'and it wasn't exactly the Hope and Anchor or the Wankers Arms. We went down so well that we did the set nearly three times because we kept getting called back.'

Matlock reckons Sid was more than passable as a singer. 'He didn't have the gift of the gab lyrically, like John had, but he was a rock 'n' roll singer.' No one had a chance to assess Nancy's talents as a backing singer because her mike was turned off throughout.

Captain Sensible, who earlier that day had led a march in Fleet Street in protest at DC Thompson's decision to drop the 'Melody Lee' character from *Bunty* magazine, arrived in time to catch the show. 'Sid was sensational in the "My Way" video, but he was pretty ropey on stage,' he admits. 'But I'd rather have seen Sid shambolic and embarrassing himself than see any of that technically perfect rock that was on the go at that time. It was bloody entertaining! You never knew whether they'd get to the end of a song together, or if Sid was gonna launch himself into the audience, and pick on some really big bloke.'

He saved that for the party afterwards, which took place on a boathouse in Chelsea Reach where Joan Jett was staying. 'We were all pretty smashed by the end, and me and Sid ended up there with all these people from Thin Lizzy,' Sensible remembers. 'There was a big fight and Sid got a pasting.'

A few days later, Matlock met Sid for one last beer in their local before he headed off to the States. 'He said, "You'll never see me again. I won't make it past 21." He was going to find a new life, but it wasn't about getting clean. It was about money. They were fed up with Malcolm mucking them around. I'm sure he was keeping them short of money because he didn't want them to go and stick it up their arms. But I'm sure they didn't see it like that.'

This
Intolerable
Void

'There's never been a more self-destructive person on the face of this earth. That was impressive but in a shocking and disturbing way. The thing that was truly shocking was the way that he would neglect basic junkie rituals. If you're gonna shoot up, you gotta cook the heroin and clean it up, you gotta use clean works. He was continually giving himself dirty shots, "bone crushers". They literally feel like every bone in your body is being ravaged. He'd have 13 or even 30 in six months. Those things can kill you, but he was too stupid to learn.

'The last time I ever saw him he was wearing an eye patch. I said, "What are you wearing that for?" He said, "I had another dirty fix last night and I've lost the use of this eye." It's like having an epileptic fit for several hours; you start shaking uncontrollably and lose control over your whole body. You get very hot, then very cold. It's worse than the worst flu bug you can imagine. The guy was having seizures from his drug use, and it was causing him to lose the use of his limbs. He couldn't even use his arm to play bass because he had shot it and fucked it up and it was useless. And he was losing his eyesight. He was burning the candle at both ends, and bringing another few matches to singe the middle. He was aware where he was going. He wanted to go. He didn't care. He didn't think about living a long life at all. He never talked in those terms.

'It became impossible for him to live without heroin because of this intolerable void. If you wanna stop, you've got to find some spiritual agenda to cling on to, whatever it is. It's gonna be larger than you. If you're a hopelessly absorbed person, whose idea of nirvana is sitting on the toilet for an hour while listening to The Ramones and reading about yourself in the New Musical Express, you're never gonna have a very fulfilling life.'

Nick Kent

Thursday, 24 August 1978:

Waved off from Heathrow by a small gathering of friends, including The Clash's Mick Jones, Sid and Nancy flew first class to New York. Among their hand luggage was a bottle of Fairy Liquid soap. Inside it was methadone. From the outset, this new venture was a risky enterprise.

As soon as they arrived, the pair took a cab to the Chelsea Hotel, where the ghosts of Dylan Thomas, Janis Joplin and an old Leonard Cohen song stalked its late 19th-century corridors. As they walked through the doors, and into the lobby, it was as if Sid 'n' Nancy had entered some crazy detective story with a cast of hundreds and more than one sticky ending.

EILEEN POLK (friend): 'I always avoided the Chelsea. All these midtown hotels were full of pimps and prostitutes and junkies and drug dealers.'

JIMMY ZERO (Dead Boys guitarist): 'It was kind of deathly in the Chelsea at that time. There was a feeling something very bad was going to happen if everybody kept going on the way they did. The place attracted a bunch of weaklings acting like tough guys, people who weren't strong enough to face who they were. There was almost a death worship. It was hip to hate, hip to be aloof, hip to be cruel, hip to be rude. It's scary that it had such an impact that it killed people.'

EILEEN POLK: 'Everyone on the scene was attracted to each other. There was something that drew us to each other and that factor was damage.'

JIMMY ZERO: We were living at the Chelsea Hotel at the time Sid and Nancy came over. There was a lot of anticipation among that Lower East Side underground scene there that they were coming, and a lot of fear. We had heard terrible things about him, some true, some exaggerated and most false. Unpredictable violence was the vibe.'

CHEETAH CHROME (Dead Boys guitarist): 'I was there the night he got into town. I met him at Max's, upstairs in Peter Crowley's office, while I was booking some shows. Sid said he wanted to do some gigs, so we came up with this idea of going out as The Music Industry Casualties. He seemed nice enough, but he was very whipped. He couldn't get a word in because Nancy kept talking. He was tired, maybe a little dope sick, so he wasn't really communicative. We had a few beers, then we went back to my place. I remember him waking up Jeff Magnum [Dead Boys bass player], and saying, 'You reckon you can beat me up?' '

BOB GRUEN: 'I saw him in Max's too. Malcolm had given him about £10,000 to leave England, and he literally had one thousand £10 notes, all in English pounds. And he says, 'Bobby, could you lend us $10 to get home?' He didn't have any cab fare. Sid was already really out of it. He stood there with his arm crooked holding this glass, sucking his drink with a straw, and as soon as he finished, Nancy took the glass and put a new one in his hand.'

JIMMY ZERO: 'I was rooming at the Chelsea with [Dead Boys singer] Stiv [Bators], who nudged me and said, "I want you to meet Sid." I looked up and Sid Vicious was standing over my bed. His closed eye scared me most. I didn't know whether it was from an infection, or if he'd been hit or had some sort of congenital problem. There was something wrong.'

EILEEN POLK: 'Nancy had been considered a lower level groupie when she was living in New York in '76. When she came back with Sid Vicious, she wouldn't let anybody near him if they'd been mean to her when she was first in town. She came to Revenge, the clothes shop where I worked, and introduced me to Sid. When they left, I remember going out on the corner to watch them, and everyone parted like the Red Sea as they walked by.'

HOWIE PYRO (musician): 'Johnny Rotten had come and he was a total asshole. But Sid was totally cool. He was just into his thing – copping drugs, talking to people. He was pretty wasted. A junkie's a junkie. You're either high or you're sick. If you're sick you wanna get high. That's how it is.'

JIMMY ZERO: 'He had no direction. The Sex Pistols briefly provided him with one, but when he was cut loose, he was a boat without a rudder. He had no idea where to take it. I never felt that Stiv was doomed. He wanted to live to see another day. I didn't sense that with Sid. Sid seemed so lost and confused. He didn't know what he wanted.'

KATE SIMON: 'I took these pictures of Stiv with this big knife wound up his chest, but he was a charming guy with wit and personality. There was no parallel between him and Sid.'

JIMMY ZERO: 'He was a self abuser. That was not uncommon. Stiv did that all the time, but with Stiv, there was a calculation to it. With Sid, you got the impression that it ran deeper, that he was trying to hurt himself for real. There was something really deep and troubling about him. He wanted to hurt himself and show the world his wounds.'

CHEETAH CHROME: 'It was obvious that Sid was a junkie from the start, 'cos he kept whining about how sick he was. He'd say, "I've gotta get some dope or else I'm gonna kill myself." He'd say that repeatedly.'

JIMMY ZERO: 'Sid was a full-maintenance guy. He was constantly getting beaten up. He told me that the black guys would beat him up every day when he went to the methadone clinic. He was a victim. I knew a lot of the guys I'd see coming in and out of Sid and Nancy's room, just bad looking guys. I think of that William Burroughs quote about heroin being the ultimate merchandise. You'll crawl through a gutter of filth to get the goods if you have that habit. Keith Richards once said that you had to be a registered drug dealer to be a bellman at the Chelsea. And that wasn't much of an exaggeration.'

CHEETAH CHROME: 'Sid didn't seem a happy person, perhaps because he couldn't get what he wanted, or what he thought he deserved. In England, everybody would be doing things for him. Coming to New York, you had to be a grown-up and be able to handle yourself, and he wasn't used to that. He'd been hanging out with The Sex Pistols for two years. He was a kid.

'One time, he came to see us play at CBGB's, and of course he hated us. I heard he threw a glass at me, a proper pint glass, one of those big mugs. But we used to get that all the time.'

BOB GRUEN: 'Nancy used to say, 'We're in the Chelsea, why don't you come by and take pictures of us?' I'd say, 'Nancy, you look terrible, get some sleep for a couple of days and then I'll come over.' I wouldn't take pictures of friends of mine looking like that.'

JIMMY ZERO: 'We would walk through the front entrance of the Chelsea, and he and Nancy would be coming out. We could sense the vibe, and then make informal bets: 'I'll bet you a beer that he will knock her down before they get to the corner of the street.' And more often than not, he would swing and hit her. She was a small person, and Sid was skinny and tall for a rock 'n' roller, but he would lay right into her and down she would go. It was a very dysfunctional relationship that was based as much on self-hatred and hatred and resentment of the other person as it was on love.

'You'd go up to greet Sid, and before your hands could meet, Nancy would be there with her hand out, glaring up at you. It was like, You have to shake my hand first, then I might allow you to shake Sid's hand. It was kinda sick. Having the rock star boyfriend fuelled her, but it wasn't as fulfilling a life as she thought it would be. She wasn't stupid, just mentally ill. The pair of them felt like a nightmare ticket.'

HOWIE PYRO: 'Nancy was just this annoying creepy person. She lived in a delusion, like she was the queen of the fucking world. She was sucking the glory out of him.'

ARTHUR KANE: 'Sid was living in the Chelsea, and having this high-profile decadent lifestyle. He'd met The Dead Boys and was gonna do a gig with them. Then he found our downtown studio space, Sunset Sound. He came down with Nancy, who was slightly overprotective of Sid. But it was the blind leading the blind. That's what the problem was. Two young people too strung out on heavy drugs. I could see they were pretty wasted.'

CHEETAH CHROME: 'We tried to rehearse a couple of times but it was a disaster. The original line-up was me, Sid, Jeff Magnum and Jerry Nolan. One time, we met at Max's for dinner before going down the rehearsal studio. Somebody had gotten Sid some Tuinols, so he had four of those because he was having trouble getting his dope. He fell asleep with his face in the steak, so that was the end of that. We didn't get to rehearse.'

JIMMY ZERO: 'We were fired by Nancy. She fired us because she said we played too well, and there was a taboo against that back then. One time, Nancy refused to speak to us and passed out in the salad at Max's. We received word next day that we were out of the picture. She wanted people to back up Sid who were either English, or in The Heartbreakers, because she thought those were the coolest people of all. Sid seemed like a fart in a windstorm. He'd do anything she told him.'

EILEEN POLK: 'I went to the first gigs that Sid played at Max's and they were packed. You could hardly move for people. People came in from all over the place. There was a fascination about somebody who would self-destruct publicly on stage. He had a good band – Mick Jones, Steve Dior, Arthur Kane, Jerry Nolan – but he seemed to be out of it. Sometimes, he would come out of his stupor and crack a joke, but he wasn't trying to entertain. He read the lyrics to 'My Way' off a piece of paper.'

HOWIE PYRO: 'It was very exciting to see a Sex Pistol on stage. It didn't matter that it was pretty awful. I don't think anyone expected them to have written songs. Everyone knew it wasn't a band.'

ARTHUR KANE: 'Rehearse? We rehearsed a bit! The New York Dolls were never interested in exact time measures. It's all about human emotions, not whether it's perfect or not. We revelled in sounding imperfect and a bit screwed up. We played either two or three shows at Max's Kansas City, and by the third show, there were 4,000 people outside trying to get into a hall that held 600. This never even happened with The New York Dolls. The band had to go through the back window and down the fire escape to get out of there.'

JOE STEVENS: 'Sid was awful. He didn't hold it together, he didn't talk to the audience, he had nothing to say. He just was like a very inarticulate Johnny Thunders.'

JIMMY ZERO: 'It seemed to prove what I felt in my heart – that rock 'n' roll was dead. You'd finally reached a point where the art form was so decadent that the poster boy for it doesn't know how to play. I thought, "This is actually perfect".'

MICK JONES: 'We just about managed the five songs. It was a nightmare between shows . . . a serious drug thing. I didn't want to but Joe [Strummer] made me do it. The rest of the guys were as out of it as you can be without being dead.'

BOB GRUEN: 'The show at Max's was really kind of pathetic because he didn't finish any songs. Some people thought it was funny, this guy who was so out of it that he couldn't do a show, but most people said, 'What's the point of that?' Nancy was saying, "It's OK Sid, just do the next one!" He didn't have much awareness of where he was.'

CHEETAH CHROME: 'When The Dead Boys first played New York, Dee Dee Ramone had this 007 knife and threw it on stage as a present for Stiv. When Stiv told Sid the story, Sid wanted the 007. It was very common in New York, a standard knife. I remember him playing with it. Sid thought he was tough with it, but my girlfriend could have taken it off him!'

JIMMY ZERO: 'We all had these knives, and we were dumb enough to carry them around. Why? The short explanation is that we were assholes. They were large switch knives with a five-inch blade, which was a lot for a knife that you carry in your pocket. Sid thought this knife was amazing, and so Stiv said, "I'll take you up to this place on Times Square." And that was the murder weapon. They bought it long before the murder. I saw Sid constantly flicking that knife, back at the Chelsea, even in the street.'

JOE STEVENS: 'I got this call from McLaren in London. He said, "Bit of a problem up at the Chelsea." He said would I go up there, find out what's going on, and give me a call right away. So I grabbed a taxi and went up there. The morgue truck was still outside. I bullshitted my way in past the cops in the lobby. Sid and Nancy's room was on the first floor. The door was open and I looked on the floor and there was a body bag with Nancy inside.

'I went back down to the lobby and out comes Sid, handcuffed, dressed in black and looking scared to death. He sees me and gives me a shove with his shoulder. I go flying across the lobby. Someone said, "Why did he do that to you?" I said, "I'm not sure but I think they were scaring the hell outta him, so he decided to become Sid again." Mr Tough Guy. It was his last Sid moment. He didn't wanna look like chicken shit coming through the lobby.'

GLEN MATLOCK: 'Stiv Bators told me that some guy had come round selling gear, and then realised he didn't have any for himself. So he went back knowing that Sid and Nancy had bought loads and might have some left over. But by the time he'd got back to their room, Sid was sparko. A fight ensued and Nancy was stabbed with a knife that had been lying around. When he woke up the next morning, he found his knife in Nancy's stomach. He didn't have a clue what went on.'

EILEEN POLK: 'Victor Collichio, who went on to direct *Summer Of Sam*, claimed to have been in the room the night Nancy was killed, but earlier in the evening. [Spungeon was killed in the early hours of 12 October 1979.] He told me that she had invited some people over, but when he showed up to this so-called party, there was Nancy really out of it and Sid passed out on the bed. Victor left. He thinks Sid was far too out of it to even lift a knife that night. And, apparently, Nancy had a lot of money, but when they arrested Sid, they didn't find a lot of money in the room. Yet he'd just played several gigs at Max's.'

CHEETAH CHROME: 'They had a real bad habit of flashing their cash. One time I was in Times Square with them the day he supposedly bought the knife, and Nancy was dropping rolls of $100 bills on the ground. People would be following us.'

BOB GRUEN: 'When you're surrounded by junkies you don't really wanna tell everybody you've got $2,000 in cash in a paper bag. But then, if someone was robbing her and stabbed her, they wouldn't leave her walking around. I don't think she was murdered.'

ARTHUR KANE: 'A lot of people ask me if I think Sid killed Nancy. The answer is no. He was in love with her, you know. Like many rock deaths, it happened in the middle of the night, when everyone else is asleep. That's when those crimes take place.'

CHEETAH CHROME: 'I have to say first that The Dead Boys were all out of town when it happened! I asked Sid about it a little later when I saw him at Max's. And he said, "I dunno." I've always thought that she couldn't wake him up and wanted attention, like, "Sid, if you don't get out of bed now, I'm gonna kill myself." I always thought she stabbed herself, 'cos the knife was in her stomach. I can see her all downered out, hoping Sid would save her, this big drama. But it ended up with Sid never waking up and her bleeding to death.'

EILEEN POLK: 'Rockets Redglare was a drug dealer who was trying to be an actor, and he was always trying to get near Sid. People like that were always available when Sid and Nancy wanted drugs. They latched on to him for the money or for associating with somebody famous.'

CHEETAH CHROME: 'Rockets Redglare was an idiot, a big overweight guy with a lot of medical problems. He used to get Dilaudads that he used to sell or give away in order to get to hang out with people like Sid or me.'

JOE STEVENS: 'I saw Rockets Redglare years later, getting drunk in a bar shortly before he died. He was a taxi driver in *Desperately Seeking Susan* with Madonna, and appeared in a couple of [Jim] Jarmusch films. He could deliver dialogue. He was dealing and those dealers are always very suspect. I'd heard that Nancy had cashed a cheque from Virgin two days earlier. There's no way they could have disposed of all that cash.'

HOWIE PYRO: 'There's a theory that Rockets Redglare did it? That's bullshit. I'd known him since I was a little kid. He ran this store on 8th Street where they sold futons. He was just some junkie who told everyone everywhere that he killed her. And if he had killed her, someone somewhere would have listened. He couldn't possible have. He was just a hog for hype.'

KATE SIMON: 'I met Rockets a few times. All I remember is that he needed teeth. There would be concerts held to raise money for Rockets' teeth.'

BOB GRUEN: 'I thought the way they did it in the movie was really well done because Nancy was kind of a whiner. He'd say, "OK Nancy, you want the knife here's the knife." Just to shut her up. But I can't imagine Sid stabbing Nancy on purpose. Or anybody. She was cut badly and staggered to the bathroom and bled to death. If someone was there to kill her, you'd stab a couple of times. Killing isn't like a deep cut and then you leave. If they stagger to the bathroom, they're still alive. I see it more as a one of several accidental scenarios and not as murder.'

EILEEN POLK: 'The police thought that couples killed each other all the time in New York. And here's two people, stumbling around stoned out of their minds, playing with knives. It wasn't unlikely that one of them would end up dead.'

VIC GODARD: 'I can't imagine anyone out of their heads on heroin doing anything to anyone. Unless you mixed it with something totally the opposite, like cocaine or drink. Methadone? No way. I just couldn't believe it. It's really difficult to see someone as a killer, someone like that.'

ARTHUR KANE: 'Like all these crimes the police have to pin it on someone. There's a lot of injustice over here.'

JOE STEVENS: 'The next time I see Sid was at one of his court appearances. I figured that whatever happened, he was gonna get convicted. Having a name like Sid Vicious was definitely not going to help in a court of law, an English guy coming over and killing a girl from Pennsylvania.'

JONH INGHAM: 'I was in LA and suddenly I see Sid Vicious is on Rikers Island for killing Nancy. I mean, Sid Vicious on television, in America, in the news! This is weird. I thought, poor Sid. It really felt like somebody chucking their life away.'

NICK KENT: 'There's a shot of him coming out of court after one of his trials. And someone puts a microphone in his face for a comment, and he just bashes it away and has a look in his eyes. And I'd spent enough time with him to see that all the innocence, all the boyishness, was gone. I saw that in those few seconds. He had changed. He was absolutely aware of where he was going. He did not want to live. A lot of people don't want to live. But there's no reason to build that into an art form, or to build statues for those people. The image is a veneration of a lot of what's bad in the human spirit.'

ALAN JONES: 'I do like the description of "*Romeo And Juliet* in Hell", though. I think it's quite sweet. I don't believe he killed her. I will never believe that. It just wasn't in his nature to do that. Yeah, ok, he put on all the bravado ... he genuinely, genuinely loved her. I just hope she loved him back as much as he loved her. It would be awful if that wasn't the case.'

STEVEN SEVERIN: 'Back in England, everybody was so busy doing what we were doing. It was all just postcards from hell.'

BOB GRUEN: 'I was surprised when they put him on the cover of the *New York Post*. "Punk Rocker Kills Girlfriend" or whatever. The band had broken up, and there wasn't a lot of interest in them. They put out one record that got played on underground level. They weren't The Sex Pistols as you know them today, iconic classic band of the punk era. It was over and they were gone.'

JOE STEVENS: 'The *NME* called me and said, "See if you can find anyone who has anything to say about Nancy." I stuck my micro-cassette recorder in front of a whole lotta punk rock faces, and I couldn't get anyone to say anything nice about her. To be hated so much at only 20 years old . . .'

HOWIE PYRO: 'We went to Rikers Island prison with his mum. She was staying with Eileen [Polk] at her house. We were hanging out with her, she was really cool, trying to take care of things. She seemed pretty mellow. She certainly wasn't hysterical. We went out every night, to Max's Kansas City, usually. I don't think she got off on it. She wasn't meeting and greeting.'

JOE STEVENS: 'Malcolm and I visited Sid in Rikers. McLaren told him, "We're gonna get you out." He was starting to cook up things for the film. All he had to do was get him out of jail. Malcolm was working on all these things, the Rockets Redglare theory, other theories, and repeating all this stuff to F Lee Bailey's team. They would have cooked up something. I mean, they got him out on bail, which was amazing.

'It was really shocking to see him in jail. They'd taken all his clothes away. He had no leathers, no belts no chains, no lockets. He wanted things, a copy of *PUNK* magazine, yogurt, milk, and some other mags from England. He was in T-shirt and shorts, and he actually looked pretty good. They'd cleaned him up. Some of the scars on his arms were even starting to go away.'

HOWIE PYRO: 'Everyone loved him. After he was sent to prison, he became more than simply a guy who'd been in The Sex Pistols. I don't mean that in a morbid way. I mean in a more magical way, like, 'Can he be real?' '

JOE STEVENS: 'The next time I see Sid, he's brought into Central Criminal Court, Manhattan, and we've got F Lee Bailey in his defence and I'm not allowed in the courtroom. I'm waiting outside and Sid comes out and he's free. They got him out on $50,000 bail. I was amazed. I'm not sure what happened there; that was very fishy.'

CHEETAH CHROME: 'When he came out of Rikers, and he was straight, you'd run into him then and he was much nicer. He'd grown up a little bit.'

JOE STEVENS: 'His mother had arrived by then. She showed up with a packet of Woodbines and a box of tea. She was just a real drag and had this horrible, dirty Afghan-style coat. But she was a mother of a kid accused of murder. The two were told to live together somewhere in Manhattan, and report the location to the courts. And he's gotta do methadone every day, and a urine test at the discretion of the court once a week. He's under a heavy hammer, and he hates his mum. We find this shitty hotel and he's staying there, a really horrible place, living in separate beds.'

EILEEN POLK: 'Why didn't they put Sid and his mum up in a decent hotel, where they had a telephone and a television and a comfortable bed and a kitchen, instead of letting him stay in some dump in midtown where every junkie in town knew where he was? They were so broke. They had no food, they had no phone. I had to pay their hotel bill. It was ridiculous. Anne had spent her life savings just to come over to New York to help her son. And she was demonised in the press and I don't think she deserved it.'

NICK KENT: 'She'd phoned me up at the *New Musical Express* after he got arrested, and asked to come over and talk to me. She asked if I could help or if the *NME* could help and do a benefit for Sid. It just so happened that The Clash were three or four streets away having a reception for something, so I took her round to see The Clash. And they ended up doing a benefit.'

JOE STEVENS: 'One night, when McLaren was still in town, we got a call from Ma Vicious in the middle of the night. She said, "Sid's tried to kill himself," so we get in a taxi and go to their room and there he is on the bed. It turns out he cut his wrists the wrong way, but he was bleeding good. His mum was flipping out, and McLaren didn't know what the hell to do. I think Sid thought he was going to die, so I said, "Sid, you're gonna be meeting your maker real soon. What happened with you and Nancy?" He said, "Joe Stevens, let me tell you something. I'd never kill her. I love that woman. I want to be with her now, and I'll be with her soon."

'I asked him what happened that night at the Chelsea. He said, "We were just having a bit of a fight and were poking each other." It's probably quite true, because when you're a junkie, you're a haemophiliac, your blood doesn't coagulate. That's part of being a junkie. He probably poked her a little bit and they thought nothing more of it. He crashed out. She crashed out, and bled to death. Then the stretcher came and the ambulance took Sid away to Bellevue Hospital's psycho ward.

'We're at Max's upstairs one night, waiting for some band to come on, and the place is pretty empty. I was talking to this girl Michelle Robinson. She was a customer or a cocktail waitress. I started hitting on her. It looks like I'm gonna do pretty well. I bought her a drink and she knows I'm a photographer. Then Sid walks in. She says, "Oh my God, is that Sid Vicious?" I said, "Yeah, I know him." She said, "Will you introduce me?" I said, "Yeah, but there's a problem." She said, "What?" I said, "Well, he may kill you . . ." They left together.'

HOWIE PYRO: 'We all knew Michelle. She was another obnoxious girl, not a real punk rock girl, who'd hang out on the scene. No one knew what she did.'

JOE STEVENS: 'She was a nice girl, an aspiring actress who had an apartment in the West Village, Bank Street. She was in contact with her parents, and not into drugs as far as I knew. Sid was supposed to be staying with his mom, but he moved in with her.'

EILEEN POLK: 'Michelle was a little emotionally fragile. For some reason, she was drawn to rockers, people who were exciting and dangerous. Sid spent time with Michelle when he wanted to be quiet, left alone and have a nice place to stay.'

ARTHUR KANE: 'There is a girl who'd be a perfect suspect but she's dead too. She was a girlfriend of mine and Dee Dee Ramone's for a while called Miss Connie. One night, after Nancy had been killed, Sid was out on parole, and he'd met Connie. They went to several people's houses, and every place they went to they broke all the glasses in the house. I don't know what that was about. Connie was an ageing groupie and a severe heroin addict, truly a desperate character. If she wanted to be with Sid, the only person in her way would have been Nancy.'

EILEEN POLK: 'Connie was a junkie and a prostitute and we had a couple of fist-fights. I later heard she died. Her life was even more desperate than Nancy's.

'Then Sid got into that fight with Patti Smith's brother Todd at Hurrah. Everyone said that Sid hit Todd Smith with a Heineken bottle. Sid's version is that he was drinking some kind of alcohol out of a glass cup and Todd Smith had a Heineken bottle and they had gotten in a scuffle and Sid's glass and Todd's bottle had collided and shattered. And that's how Todd got injured. Todd's version was that Sid had pinched his girlfriend, that he was coming to the rescue, and that Sid was drunk and abusive. They arrested him because of the fight, and his bail was revoked.'

JOE STEVENS: 'He bottled Todd and he blinded him in one eye. He lost a lot of points on that one.'

CHEETAH CHROME: 'Who knows what happened there. I'd met Patti and Todd [Smith] and I'd wanted to hit 'em both myself.'

EILEEN POLK: 'Sid probably used drugs when he was back in jail, but I don't think he had anything strong. Anne [Beverley] told me she snuck some heroin in for him once. She said she did that because he was really sick and going through withdrawals, though I wasn't even sure I believed her. Maybe she was also doing it to protect him from some of the predators in the jail. Rikers Island was a really nasty prison.

'I went to the courthouse with Anne at around eight in the morning [1 February 1979], and the judge gave him bail. We were surprised. Michelle, Anne, Sid and I got to Michelle's apartment around noon. Then Jerry Nolan arrived with his girlfriend Esther. No one was really expecting Jerry. Jerry and Sid started going at Anne asking for money. I saw Anne give him a $100 bill. I said, "Anne, what are you doing?" She said, "If I don't give Sid money, he's gonna go out and find drugs and find money anyway." Her motivation for giving him that money was that he promised he'd come back.

'Sid goes out with Jerry Nolan and I'm thinking, "We're never gonna see them again." And then they come back within an hour, and they're not high! Sid didn't seem to be on anything. I thought, "This is weird!" So I went out to buy some spaghetti for dinner, and when I got back, we had a normal party. It wasn't even a heavy drinking party. We had some beer, Anne cooked us spaghetti, it was kinda nice. Anne had integrity. She may have been an enabler for Sid, but she wasn't a bad person. She had specifically invited people over to Michelle's the night that Sid died because they weren't junkies. She wanted people to show Sid a good time, and none of us did any drugs that night.

'Sid was in a good mood. He was talking about how he had made friends in jail, how he thought his lawyer was going to get him acquitted. He had a positive attitude about the trial. He didn't seem to be as depresed as he had been with Nancy when he was doing a lot of drinking and heroin and methadone. That's why I don't believe it was a suicide. Somebody who's about to commit suicide doesn't talk that positively about his future.'

HOWIE PYRO: 'In the early evening, he was totally excited and hopping around to The New York Dolls album, dancing and playing air guitar. I felt really lucky to have seen this side of him. I don't think it was a side that he showed that often. It wasn't like this dreary dark scene. It was very happy, goofy. Sid was wearing this Seditionaries button-down shirt with nudie playing cards and pictures of Johnny Thunders in the pockets.'

EILEEN POLK: 'What happened was that with the $100, Sid had arranged for the drugs to be delivered, and the people who delivered them showed up around midnight. They were British. Sid introduced one of the guys to his mother as somebody who would be helping photograph his album cover. So that's another remark that makes me think he wasn't about to commit suicide, because he was talking about his next record. Nobody had any heroin that night until these people arrived. As soon as they showed up, Howie [Pyro] and [The Misfits'] Jerry Onie and I agreed that this is not what we came for. I said, "Let's get out of here. I don't wanna be part of this."'

HOWIE PYRO: 'It was for him. It was his party. Dope isn't a sharing drug like pot or something! He went off in the bedroom, got high and OD'd right away. It was really scary and everyone freaked out.'

JOE STEVENS: 'The dealer told Sid that the whole scene had changed, that the stuff was really powerful now, and not to get too crazy with the first hit. Sid figured it was some kinda hustle by the dealer, so he did a mighty load and turned green.'

EILEEN POLK: 'We were just about to leave when Sid passed out, so we had to revive him. He'd come out of the bathroom, then staggered and fallen on the bed in Michelle's room and he'd gone out. It was instant. I didn't see him shoot any heroin. It took, like, two hours for us to revive him. We shook him, wrapped him up in blankets. Finally, he came around and the first thing he said was, 'Sorry I scared you all.' Now that doesn't sound like a person who intended to kill himself. That sounds like somebody who accidentally OD'd.

'He got up to walk, and I said to Anne, "St Vincent's Hospital is only a couple of blocks away, don't you think we ought to take him there?" She said, "No, the press will make a circus of it, he'll go back to jail." And Anne said, "He's not gonna go anyway. There's nothing I can do to make him go." That's when I and Howie and Jerry left.'

JOE STEVENS: 'Ma Vicious crashed on the couch, and apparently had her load in a pocket. Michelle had set the alarm for 8:30 so they could get over to the methadone check, then went to sleep. Sid apparently got up in the middle of the night, went into his mother's purse, did the load, went back to bed and died.'

EILEEN POLK: 'We had gone to Hurrah, which was the only place we knew would be open. We were kinda nervous and wanted to relax. Then I went home at three in the morning, and I got this call at around 7am. It's Michelle and she says, "Sid's dead." I thought he probably just passed out, so I ran over there. But as soon as I saw the crowd of press in front of her apartment, I knew it was true.'

JOE STEVENS: On the day of Sid's death, I'm in my favourite coffee shop in Greenwich Village and they've got the FM radio on. "Sid Vicious is found dead in his girlfriend's apartment in the West Village." It was nearby, and I had a good idea where Number 15 Bank was. Her flat was on the first landing. I made it up the stairs, then the cop stops me. Michelle sees me from the window, comes down and let's me in. The place is all in darkness with cops walking around and Sid's mum is freaking out. I took Ma Vicious aside and said, "You know how all these rock 'n' roll stories get out of hand. This one'll get embellished in an hour. You trust me right?" I never shafted them on anything. I said, "Why don't you give me the true story and we'll get it out through the *NME*." That's what happened.

'We went into the back bedroom. There's a cloth over the lamp. I sat on the edge of the bed, she sat in a chair and I kept slipping off the corner of the bed. When my eyes became acclimatised to the bad light, I realised that Sid was lying in the fucking bed. He had a piece of tape across the top of his mouth, and a plastic tube going under the tape to his nostrils. He wasn't covered; he was naked.'

EILEEN POLK: 'Anne and Michelle were crying, the police were taking photos, Sid's body was in the bedroom, and Joe Stevens showed up at some point. Michelle and Anne were taken down to the police station for questioning, and I'm in the apartment alone sitting on the bed with a dead body answering the phone, with all these people trying to find out what's going on. It was very upsetting.

'Sid's body was covered with a blanket. He didn't even look dead. I touched him. He was cold so I knew he was dead. I tried to avoid looking at him. There was major denial. When Michelle called me to say that he was dead, I didn't believe it. Then when I got there, and I saw the body I still couldn't believe it until I put my hand on his hand. It was cold. He was lying on his back, and he looked like he was sleeping.

'Anne stayed at my house after Sid died. She called up Mrs Spungeon, and said that Sid had requested that he be buried next to Nancy. Mrs Spungeon said no, and that's when Anne decided she'd have Sid cremated. The funeral was on 7 February 1979, and it was in New Jersey, in a quiet place where Anne knew she could have some privacy. Jerry Nolan was there. Michelle came with her girlfriend.

'Then Anne decided that she was going to put the ashes on Nancy's grave, to honour Sid's request. Jerry Onie drove us to Philadelphia. We went to Nancy's grave. We thought it was going to be some quiet cemetery in the countryside, but it was this big gated community place, where you go through security and have people accompanying you to the graveside. It started to snow, so we said some prayers, put some flowers on Nancy's grave and then left. Anne said, "I couldn't take the ashes out in front of these people."

'We wanted to look at the ashes because none of us had seen ashes before. So we went into a bathroom in a mall and prised the can open with nail clippers. It was bizarre! Then Anne said, "I'm gonna do this anyway, I have to do it for Sid." So Jerry pulled up round the back of the cemetery, and Anne took the ashes, jumped over the wall and shook them over Nancy's grave. It was snowing and cold and horrible.'

Acknowledgements

Thanks to everyone who agreed to be interviewed for this book (and to one or two past interviewees whose quotes I thought relevant again here): Joe Andoe, Mike Baess, Jeremy Colebrooke, Cheetah Chrome, Caroline Coon, Rikki Ercoli, Vic Godard, Johnny Green, Bob Gruen, Debbie Harry, Ed Helmore, Jonh Ingham, Alan Jones, Arthur Kane, Nick Kent, Robbie Krieger, Don Letts, Richard Lloyd, Mandy Pete, Glen Matlock, Michael Moorcock, Kenny Morris, Mark Perry, Marco Pirroni, Barry Plummer, Eileen Polk, Howie Pyro, Henry Sabini, Captain Sensible, Steven Severin, TV Smith, Rob Simmons, Kate Simon, Siouxsie Sioux, Simone Stenfors, Poly Styrene, Nikki Sudden, Joe Stevens, Ray Stevenson, Julian Temple, Jah Wobble, Jimmy Zero.

And to Pat Gilbert, for providing the Mick Jones and John Tiberi quotes, and Simon Price for the Chrissie Hynde material.

Special mention must be made of "SEX: Too Fast To Live Too Young To Die" (Only Lovers Left Alive, 2003), the Marco Pirroni-complied collection of songs originally found on the jukebox at SEX, 430 King's Road in Chelsea during the mid-'70s. Mastered at high volume, it's a perfect accompaniment to the early chapters in this book.

Various people kindly opened doors and other avenues of research during the making of this book: Nina Antonia, Mark Blake, Dave Brolan, Penny Brignell, Paul Burgess, Chris Charlesworth, Joseph Wilford-Cole, Andy Davis, Peter Doggett, Daryl Easlea, Pat Gilbert, Clinton Heylin, Matt Higham, Barney Hoskyns, Trevor King, Jacqueline McKillion, Andy Neill, Alan Parker, Margaret Saadi and Paul Trynka.

Others provided inspiration in less obvious ways: Alan from the Hill, Andrew, Margaret, Alejandra, Laura and the Tide Tables crew, Elizabeth Benjamin, Fiona Bleach, Hannah Cohen, Diana Duran, Yvette Elkington-Cole, Lora Findlay, 'Flamenco' Jackie, Julie-Anne Fraser, Sarah Hinsley, Erika Lewis, Martha and Tara, Norman Paytress, Reia, Sarah Smith, Carine Seon, 'Polish' Tomas and his amazing customised tea, Lois Wilson.

Special thanks to Albert Depetrillo at Sanctuary, who showed extraordinary patience with my demands for more time, and to Iain MacGregor for commissioning the original book.

Bibliography

And I Don't Want To Live This Life - Deborah Spungeon (Corgi, 1984)

Bob Harris: The Whispering Years - Bob Harris (BBC, 2002)

Chaos! The Sex Pistols - Bob Gruen (Omnibus Press, 1990)

The Dark Stuff: Selected Writings On Rock Music 1972-1993 - Nick Kent (Penguin, 1994)

England's Dreaming: Sex Pistols And Punk Rock - Jon Savage (Faber, 1991)

I Was A Teenage Sex Pistol - Glen Matlock with Pete Silverton (Omnibus Press, 1990)

1988: The New Wave Punk Rock Explosion - Caroline Coon (Omnibus, 1982)

No One Waved Goodbye: A Casualty Report On Rock'n'Roll (ed Robert Somma) (Charisma Books, 1973)

The One And Only Peter Perrett: Homme Fatale - Nina Antonia (SAF, 1996)
Rotten: No Irish No Blacks No Dogs - John Lydon with Keith and Kent Zimmerman (Hodder & Stoughton, 1994)

Satellite: A Book Of Memorabilia, Locations, Photography & Fashion - Paul Burgess & Alan Parker (Abstract Sounds Publishing, 1999)

Sex Pistols Day By Day: The Sex Pistols Diary - Lee Wood (Omnibus, 1988)

Sex Pistols File (ed Ray Stevenson) (1978, Omnibus Press)

Sex Pistols: The Inside Story - Fred & Judy Vermorel (Omnibus Press, 1987 updated edition)

Sid's Way: The Life And Death Of Sid Vicious - Keith Bateson & Alan Parker (Omnibus Press, 1991)

Siouxsie And The Banshees: The Authorised Biography - Mark Paytress (Sanctuary, 2003)

Sniffin' Glue: The Essential Punk Accessory - Mark P (Sanctuary, 2000)

Vacant: A Diary Of The Punk Years 1976-79 - Nils & Ray Stevenson, Thames & Hudson, 1999)

Vicious: Too Fast To Live - Alan Parker (Creation Books, London, 2004)

Vivienne Westwood: An Unfashionable Life – Jane Mulvagh (Harper Collins, 1998)

The Wicked Ways Of Malcolm McLaren - Craig Bromberg (Harper & Row, NY, 1989)

Other useful research tools included the Julian Temple-directed *The Filth And The Fury*, "The Heyday" cassette (Factory Records, 1980), Nina Antonia's sleevenotes for The Heartbreakers' *LAMF* reissue (Jungle) and www.thefilthandthefury.co.uk

Index

About the Author

MARK PAYTRESS is a rock journalist and author of several books, including the definitive biographies on Siouxsie And The Banshees (also published by Sanctuary) and Marc Bolan. He contributes regularly to *MOJO* magazine. He lives in London.